Unicode in SAP® Systems

 PRESS

SAP PRESS is a joint initiative of SAP and Galileo Press. The know-how offered by SAP specialists combined with the expertise of the publishing house Galileo Press offers the reader expert books in the field. SAP PRESS features first-hand information and expert advice, and provides useful skills for professional decision-making.

SAP PRESS offers a variety of books on technical and business related topics for the SAP user. For further information, please visit our website: *www.sap-press.com*.

Horst Keller, Sascha Krüger
ABAP Objects
ABAP Programming in SAP NetWeaver
2., completely new edition 2007, 1059 pp., with DVD
ISBN 978-1-59229-079-6

SAP NetWeaver Master Data Management
Loren Heilig, Steffen Karch
2007, 331 pp.
ISBN 978-1-59229-131-1

Marc O. Schäfer, Matthias Melich
SAP Solution Manager
2007, 490 pp.
ISBN 978-1-59229-091-8

Markus Helfen, Michael Lauer, Hans Martin Trauthwein
Testing SAP Solutions
2007, 367 pp.
ISBN 978-1-59229-127-4

Armin Kösegi, Rainer Nerding
SAP Change and Transport Management
2., revised and extended edition 2006, 725 pp.
ISBN 978-1-59229-059-8

Nils Bürckel, Alexander Davidenkoff, Detlef Werner

Unicode in SAP® Systems

Galileo Press

Bonn • Boston

ISBN   978-1-59229-135-9

1st edition 2007

Translation Lemoine International, Inc., Salt Lake City, UT
Editor Stefan Proksch
Copy Editor John Parker, UCG, Inc., Boston, MA
Cover Design Nadine Kohl
Layout Design Vera Brauner
Production Steffi Ehrentraut
Typesetting Typographie & Computer, Krefeld
Printed and bound in Germany

© 2007 by Galileo Press
SAP PRESS is an imprint of Galileo Press,
Boston (MA), USA
Bonn, Germany

German Edition first published 2007 by Galileo Press.

Contents at a Glance

Contents

Preface

The only constant is change. Not only are there a daunting number of languages, divided into language families, but every language inevitably changes over even a relatively short time. Continuous communication is the reason.

A significant challenge during the fast-paced development of information technology and computers was therefore the attempt to encode language and the characters associated with it into a form suitable for machines, so as to be able to store and exchange data. Data exchange was, and still is, particularly challenging, since one must define certain standards in order to ensure the smoothest possible data exchange between different computers and programs. Over time, it became clear that the variety of different formats introduced—particularly with increasing globalization—were still unable to represent languages sufficiently well, and that there were even errors during data exchange between heterogeneous IT platforms.

The solution to this omnipresent problem was the introduction of Unicode. For the first time, a globally accepted, uniform standard had been created that, thanks to the fixed assignment of *one* number to every character, guarantees that texts in any language can be displayed and transmitted without error, both today and in the future.

"When the world wants to talk, it speaks Unicode."[1] Besides the basic   Contents
principles of Unicode, this book also describes how Unicode is supported by SAP as the future technological basis for all its software products. This book is intended for a broad audience: from the top manager or CIO who needs to decide how the enterprise's ERP system can best be converted to use Unicode, to the project manager who introduces new Unicode-based software, to the IT specialist who needs to know the steps to make in-house software Unicode-capable or how an existing ERP system can be converted.

---

1 This was the motto of the 20th International Unicode Conference in 2002.

Structure After a general introduction in **Chapter 1**, you will read in **Chapter 2** how languages are generally supported in SAP systems. **Chapter 3** then covers Unicode-based installations and shows how existing solutions can be converted. It first describes the basic architecture of an SAP Unicode system (Section 3.1). Based on that foundation, there is a detailed description of a Unicode conversion of an MDMP system (Section 3.2). In Section 3.3, we will discuss combining an upgrade with a Unicode conversion. ABAP enabling and the handling of interfaces form a very large part of a Unicode conversion, so Sections 3.4 and 3.5 are devoted to these topics separately. To conclude the chapter, we will describe the options for expansion into countries for which Unicode is a requirement (see Section 3.6). How you can effectively manage these projects is the topic of **Chapter 4**, after which **Chapter 5** discusses the topic of translation. **Chapter 6** summarizes the key points of the first five chapters with respect to Unicode installation and conversion.

The book is structured so that you can read selected chapters or sections independently. For instance, a programmer with basic Unicode knowledge could simply read the information in Section 3.4 regarding "ABAP and Unicode" to discover how programs can be verified for execution in a Unicode system and, if necessary, how they must be changed.

In all explanations, great value is placed on specific practical examples that we, the team of authors (from SAP Globalization Services), can guarantee. We all have years of experience with the introduction of Unicode into SAP software, whether in internal SAP projects like the *Unicode Enabling* of SAP R/3 Enterprise or the global support of SAP customers, as with Unicode conversions.

Acknowledgements   The authors would like to take this opportunity to thank all the SAP customers, partners, and colleagues who helped with the creation of this book, particularly for all the valuable discussions. Our particular thanks go to the management of SAP Globalization Services for the opportunity to write this book.

Nils Bürckel, Dr. Alexander Davidenkoff, Dr. Detlef Werner
Walldorf, St. Leon-Rot, February 2007

Globalization has become extremely important for most enterprises. The different aspects of globalization are briefly outlined in this chapter, after which we will go into detail regarding languages and Unicode.

1 Introduction

1.1 Globalization and Localization

Rapid changes in international markets, accompanied by the need to reduce costs and improve quality, make it necessary to run core business process on a global level while keeping those processes as simple as possible for local employees to use. Moreover, reorganizations, company mergers, and spin-offs are continually changing enterprise structures around the world, requiring speedy action.

Global business processes

To meet today's requirements for a truly global IT solution, software must handle global and local processes at the same time and still be flexible enough to accept changes. For instance, English may be used as the companywide language, while a local language is used in many countries in which marketing or production occur. The concept of *globalization* is therefore the idea of developing software that handles all the business requirements of companies operating globally, and thus consists of a "neutral" core (*internationalization*), but which can easily be adapted to the requirements of individual countries (*localization*).

Globalization, localization, and internationalization

Some functional elements, like time zones, thus fall into the area of internationalization, while others belong to localization (country-specific reporting requirements, for example) or belong properly in both areas, as do currencies or languages. The support of global processes represents another example. Figure 1.1 illustrates these requirements of global software solutions.

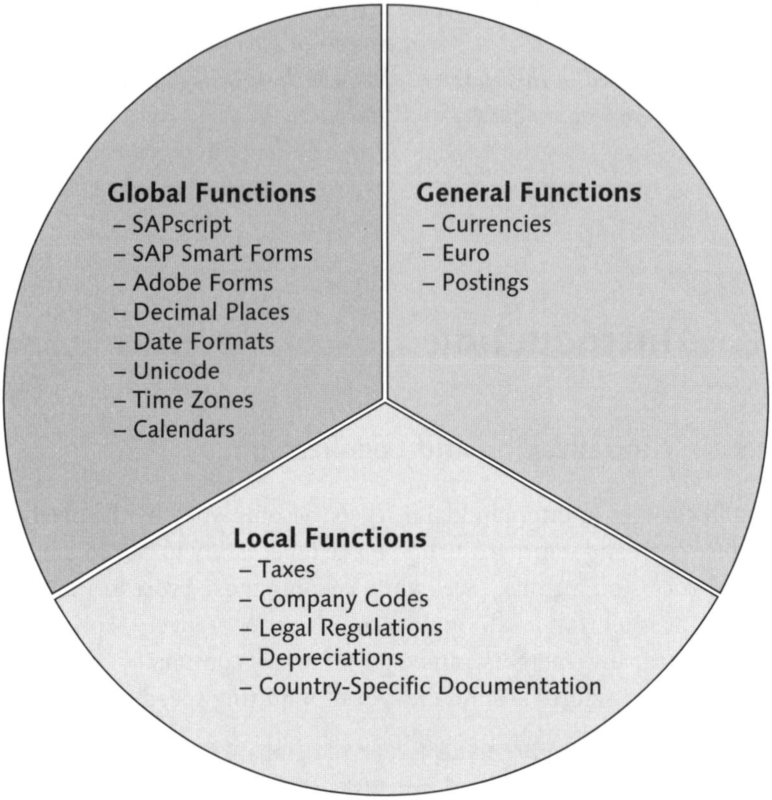

Figure 1.1 Global and Local Software Functions

SAP Country Versions

When an enterprise commences activity in a new country, the locally applicable legal requirements must be complied with, date or decimal formats taken into consideration, and local details business processes must be noted. For this purpose, SAP offers the *SAP Country Versions*, which have been developed with exact knowledge of the requirements in individual countries. These versions are continually improved by SAP Globalization Services in order to take the latest changes into account, and all standard country versions can be combined as needed in a single installation. Some examples of the local functionality covered by SAP Country Versions are as follows:

- Charts of accounts
- Depreciation rules
- Tax calculations
- Payment processes

- Reporting
- Sales processes
- Payroll

This versatility of SAP software is also complemented by the support of industry-specific requirements, such as the particular business processes of the automotive industry or the chemical industry.

Every global company must certainly work with more than one currency in its various business processes, so the software used must support different means of payment. For this reason, there is no "primary" currency, but rather all possible currencies are handled at the same time, and companies can add new currencies at any time. A U.S. company could thus conduct invoicing in U.S. dollars, while its subsidiary in France would use euros, and the production facility in Thailand could work with baht. At the same time, company groups can be consolidated into different, freely selectable currencies. Another option is the simultaneous tracking of payment transactions in more than one currency, and it is also no problem to use the different currency conversion rates.

Currencies

Typically, users think and act in their local times, and expect that the business processes modeled by software can be used in local time. A global company, however, has processes that involve different time zones or systems and users who work in different time zones. This can lead to problems when postings are delayed or batch jobs don't start on time. Therefore, it is important for applications to store times and dates correctly and convert them if necessary. Note that the manner of technical implementation can differ depending on the specific requirements. The system primarily differentiates between system time, user time, and object time, and can, for example, correctly display a stored production time in the time zone of the production plant.

Time zones

Every globally active company is faced with the challenge of having to handle different languages. The software used must therefore have the following functionality:

Languages

- Support for different languages in the user interface
- Translation into different languages

▶ Display and printing of characters of different languages

▶ Simultaneous operation of all the requirements listed above

These requirements for language support have different causes. First, there are the users who log into the system and want to see as much of the user interface or error messages in their own language as possible, or need to enter texts and data in that language. Business partners—like customers—expect invoices and business letters in the local language. In this context, it is especially important that every country imposes legal requirements for reporting or the availability of individual documents in the national languages. In SAP ERP 2005, for instance, SAP therefore supports more than 30 languages. The software also includes different options for performing translations.

By the far the most important aspect of these different requirements (and unfortunately one of the most overlooked) is the technical support for languages in the system. This is a prerequisite for custom translations and for the use of the language versions provided by SAP.

1.2   Language Support in IT Systems

Languages, characters, and code pages

Every language consists of a series of individual characters, like the letter "O" for instance, which are stored by the computer in a binary format. To be able to store the characters for one or more languages in the most uniform way possible, it has long been the practice to define *code pages* that represent a map of assignments between characters and their representation as one or more bytes.

Based on the number of characters in a language, a distinction is drawn between *Single-Byte code pages* (one byte for the encoding of one character, as for European languages) or *Double-Byte code pages* (as for Asian languages).

As an example, Figure 1.2 shows the most frequently used code page for Western European languages, "ISO Latin-1." In this code page, you can see two areas: The characters in the upper area are called *7-bit ASCII* or the *common character set*, because they appear in every code page and are always encoded uniformly. The lower area shows the special characters, which are used in this particular character set table to encode the French, German, and Finnish languages.

	0	1	2	3	4	5	6	7	8	9	A	B	C	D	E	F
0																
1																
2	SP	!	"	#	$	%	&	'	(	)	*	+	,	-	.	/
3	0	1	2	3	4	5	6	7	8	9	:	;	<	=	>	?
4	@	A	B	C	D	E	F	G	H	I	J	K	L	M	N	O
5	P	Q	R	S	T	U	V	W	X	Y	Z	[	\	]	^	_
6	`	a	b	c	d	e	f	g	h	i	j	k	l	m	n	o
7	p	q	r	s	t	u	v	w	x	y	z	{	|	}	~	
8																
9																
A	NBSP	¡	¢	£	¤	¥	¦	§	¨	©	ª	«	¬		®	¯
B	°	±	²	³	´	µ	¶	·	¸	¹	º	»	¼	½	¾	¿
C	À	Á	Â	Ã	Ä	Å	Æ	Ç	È	É	Ê	Ë	Ì	Í	Î	Ï
D	Ð	Ñ	Ò	Ó	Ô	Õ	Ö	×	Ø	Ù	Ú	Û	Ü	Ý	Þ	ß
E	à	á	â	ã	ä	å	æ	ç	è	é	ê	ë	ì	í	î	ï
F	ð	ñ	ò	ó	ô	õ	ö	÷	ø	ù	ú	û	ü	ý	þ	ÿ

Figure 1.2 Code Page ISO Latin-1

While the Latin-1 or Latin-2 code pages (Eastern Europe) can support several languages at once with their special characters, this is not possible with the Asian Double-Byte code pages, as illustrated in Figure 1.3. Every ellipse in the figure shows the languages handled by a code page. English is always possible, since it is included in the common character set and is therefore present in every code page.

Language support with code pages

If an ERP system is installed with the Latin-1 code page (a *single code-page system*), the users can use not only English but also Danish, Dutch, Finnish, French, Italian, Norwegian, Portuguese, Spanish, or Swedish.

Single code-page system

For an installation with the Japanese Double-Byte code page, however, this variety is reduced to just English and Japanese. This situation conflicts with the need for global usability and thus has been one of the great challenges in the past few years in the design and implementation of globally usable software.

The core question has been as been: "How can I come closest to supporting all the languages in the world in one system?" In the last few years, there have been primarily two ways of approaching this goal:

Language combinations in one system

▶ Definition and creation of new code pages which support a (limited) number of languages and contain all the characters needed for that combination

▶ Using a combination of existing code pages in one system

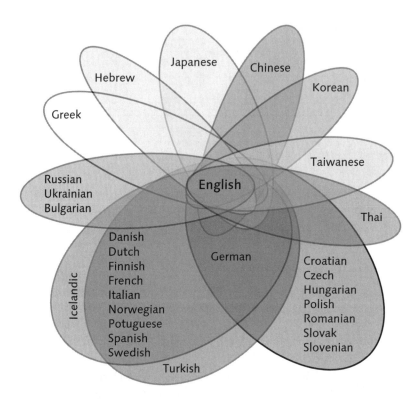

Figure 1.3 Languages and Code Pages

SAP actually followed both approaches, both of them plagued by different limitations and potential sources of error, from incorrect display of characters to actual data loss. The technical prerequisites for
the full support of all languages in the world simply did not exist
before Unicode.

Put another way: All these earlier solutions, some of which are still in
use today, should be regarded as obsolete since the introduction of
Unicode, and should be replaced *as quickly as possible* with the modern technology of the Unicode-based system.[1] As the globally recognized standard, Unicode now represents the ideal solution for international customers. That's why we will describe this technology in
great detail in the chapters to come.

---

1 Section 2.2 summarizes these different pre-Unicode concepts for (technical) language support, because knowledge of them is necessary to understand Unicode
   conversion.

1.3   Unicode

The Unicode standard and ISO/IEC 10646 assign numbers to the characters of all important languages in a consistent and uniform manner, regardless of the system, the program, and the language. In a Unicode-based system there is only *one* character set: the "Unicode code page," so to speak. Different formats for the encoding of these characters provide the capability of defining millions of characters, so that historical scripts, symbols, and arrows can be used in addition to languages. Moreover, the Unicode standard also reserves number ranges for "private" use, so that companies have the option of defining their own characters and symbols and using the latter with uniform fonts, for example.

Unicode standard and ISO/IEC 10646

The fact that the Unicode standard is a "real" standard that encodes characters completely regardless of hardware or software gives it two great advantages over all other attempts to combine languages.

Unicode standard is a "real" standard

First, Unicode data can be exchanged between IT systems without worrying about conversion algorithms or even data loss. Second, characters from different languages can be combined as needed, for example on the screen or when printing (see Figure 1.4).

What is Unicode?

ما هي الشفرة الموحدة "اليونيكود"؟   in Arabic

什麼是Unicode(統一碼/標準萬國碼)?   in Chinese (traditional)

What is Unicode?   in English

რა არის უნიკოდი?   in Georgian

Τι είναι το Unicode?   in Greek

यूनिकोड क्या है?   in Hindi

Cos'è Unicode?   in Italian

ユニコードとは何か？   in Japanese

유니코드에 대해?   in Korean

Что такое Unicode?   in Russian

Figure 1.4 Character Combinations with Unicode

1.3.1 Character Encoding

The Unicode standard doesn't just determine the uniform number of every character, but also defines different standards for the representation of those numbers in bits (*Unicode encoding forms/schemes*).

Basically, a distinction is made between representation in bytes, words, or double words, corresponding to 8, 16, or 32 bits per character. Each format, UTF-8, UTF-16, and UTF-32 (*Unicode Transformation Format*) has its advantages and its disadvantages, and thus each can be used to leverage its particular strengths, as described in the following bullet points. Conversion between the formats is easy.

Variable length ▶ **UTF-8**
UTF-8 is a variable-length encoding; that is, a character can be represented with one or more bytes. The advantage is more efficient use of memory resources because the characters needed for English, (the common character set), for instance, need only one byte for representation, just as in the non-Unicode code pages. Therefore, this encoding is used for data transmission, such as with the *Hypertext Transfer Protocol* (HTTP) or in *remote function calls* (RFCs) in the SAP system. Many database manufacturers also use this space-saving format.

Use of byte pairs ▶ **UTF-16**
UTF-16 uses byte pairs for the representation of characters, because these words can be handled very quickly at the CPU level and can be used, for example, on the application server of a Unicode-based SAP solution. Most languages used in daily business on a global basis can be represented by byte pairs (2 bytes can represent about 65,000 characters, enough characters is enough for the majority of the languages of the world). The rest can be represented with a corresponding multiple of byte pairs (e.g., 2 × 2 bytes).

In UTF-16, moreover, there is independence from hardware, as either the little-endian or big-endian format may be used, depending on the manufacturer (see Chapter 2). Some database providers also use UTF-16.

High memory requirements ▶ **UTF-32**
UTF-32 is used less often, because it results in greater memory consumption: Every character is represented by a 32-bit code. This means, for instance, that even a "normal" character from the

Latin alphabet (such as "A") will take up 4 bytes. Only one of those 4 bytes carries actual information, but 4 bytes are still taken up in memory.

The advantage of this format is that every character really does take 4 bytes. Unlike the other formats, the logic in UTF-32 need not determine the amount of memory actually needed based on the first byte. However, this advantage is cancelled out in most applications by the high memory requirements.

At this point, we already can see that the number of bytes needed for the representation of a character is larger than in a non-Unicode system. In the Western European area, for example, every character in non-Unicode requires just one byte, while in the case of Unicode special characters require at least two bytes. This can result in higher requirements either for memory or processing speed, depending on the encoding and characters used, and this must be considered when planning a Unicode installation. We will explain this in more detail in the chapters to come.

Memory require-
ments and pro-
cessing speed

1.3.2 Java and Unicode

We have explained why Unicode is the technically ideal solution for the display, storage, and transfer of data. But there is another important technical aspect: Java.

The object-oriented programming language Java is enjoying ever greater popularity and—as a modern standard—is itself Unicode-capable. For this reason, it makes little sense to use Java programs in a non-Unicode-capable environment. When writing characters defined in a Java program into a non-Unicode file, for instance, errors will occur because the target system is not able to interpret these characters correctly and thus may cause data loss.

For this reason, there are also limitations on the functionality of Java-based applications in the enterprise resource planning (ERP) environment. For example, modern self-service applications with a non-Unicode back end using multiple code pages may only be written in English.

1.3.3 Unicode Development

Unicode Consortium

Since its founding more than 10 years ago, the Unicode Consortium (*http://www.unicode .org*), a non-profit organization, has continued to work on the development and extension of the Unicode standard and support its use in software applications. The consortium is exclusively financed by the contributions of its members, who come from a variety of companies and institutions in IT. Moreover, it is an open consortium; that is, all institutions and private persons who want to support the Unicode standard and work on its extension can join.

Unicode versions

For the last few years, more and more characters have been defined in the Unicode standard (currently there are more than 100,000), and this has been documented by a corresponding change in version number, from Unicode 1.0.0 in 1991 to the version current today, Unicode 4.1.0. The entire content of the Unicode standard and information about the various versions are available on the Internet. For instance, for Version 4.1.0 the relevant page is at *http://www.unicode.org/versions/Unicode4.1.0.*

The standard versions published by the Unicode Consortium over the years are summarized in Table 1.1 (see also the details at *http://www.unicode.org/unicode/standard/versions/enumeratedversions.html*). SAP continually supports and updates its products with the newest Unicode version.

Year	Version	Comments
1991	1.0.0	First version
1996	2.0.0	Rework of Korean characters
1998	2.1.0	Additional Euro character (€)
1999	3.0.0	Addition of 11,000 different characters
2001	3.1.0	Another 40,000 Asian and other characters
2002	3.2.0	Additional Filipino scripts and mathematical symbols
2003	4.0.0	More additional characters
2005	4.1.0	More additional characters

Table 1.1 Standard Unicode Versions

No characters defined in the Unicode standard will ever be removed later, so that this standard is the first in history that can be regarded as extremely future-proof. Data stored with Unicode thus comes equipped with the attribute "long-lived." In the improbable situation that a standardized character must be corrected later, there can only be a recommendation against its use, since by definition it cannot be deleted. This explains why every character is subjected to a strict, critical verification before being accepted, a process that may last months or even years.

1.3.4 Modern Business Processes and New Markets

Thanks to these requirements, Unicode is not just *the* technically perfect solution for the representation of all the languages in the world, but in fact is required for modern business processes and development platforms. If you look at your own company first, there are immediately two areas where multiple languages are absolutely necessary: employees and master data Many companies employ personnel from countries other than the one where they are based, and need to store the names of all employees in the correct language and with the corresponding characters. This is a requirement that can only be met by using Unicode.

Entering new markets with Unicode

In the area of master data for many other types of enterprise data that must be available globally, Unicode plays an important role. For instance, in a globally used ERP system you can be sure that all fields can always be displayed correctly in any language on the input devices (even those locally installed) and can also be edited without errors.

Global master data

Another reason for the rapid spread of Unicode installations is the increasing importance of the expansion of traditional sales and distribution channels onto the Internet. If a smaller company with comparatively low costs opens a Web shop, the products or services offered are automatically visible for Internet users around the world. Once a customer orders something through that Internet page, the back end must be able to store customer data such as address and name, an ability that can only be guaranteed using Unicode. If, for example, a company operates a thoroughly interesting and well-presented Web store with the Western European code page, orders from Asia will never arrive, given that the addresses will be stored incorrectly and cannot be interpreted. Failing to use Unicode in this case would lead directly to lost sales both because of the loss of

Sales expansion on the Internet

orders already placed by customers and the lack of orders from new customers.

"€" and Unicode

> **Note**
>
> Not only in global scenarios, but even in small or local installations, it can be very sensible to choose to use Unicode: For instance, the correct € symbol can be stored and printed instead of "EUR."

Data exchange between business partners

Unicode isn't only the optimum technical basis when selling products or services, many other scenarios are also simplified by the introduction of Unicode. Between business partners such as suppliers, wholesalers, and retailers, there is an ongoing need to exchange different sorts of data, whether directly through network connections or using storage media. When implementing these processes before the introduction of Unicode, many questions had to be considered in great detail in order to implement data transfer without errors and with as few technically mandated limitations as possible. These included the following:

▶ Are code pages available for source and target?

▶ Do the code pages for the source and target use the same codes for all special characters?

▶ Does the medium support the code page correctly?

▶ Do I need any conversion programs?

▶ In the worst case, do business processes need to be changed (for instance limiting them to English for data)?

Unicode simplifies the implementation of business processes

Today, if both source and target use Unicode, all these questions are moot. No matter what hardware and software is used by the communication partners, all data is always correctly and completely transmitted, regardless of the language. Previously it was not unusual for optimized processes in the company to be adapted to an insufficient IT environment and therefore run less than optimally. Today, however, the implementation of the data transfer scenario with Unicode is oriented exclusively to the required business processes. This is how it should be!

> **Sample scenario**
>
> Another example should demonstrate that Unicode also offers advantages even if only one system in the connection supports this standard.

In a globally involved enterprise, SAP NetWeaver Business Intelligence (BI) is operated as a system for data reporting, and receives data from local SAP ERP systems installed in different countries. If SAP NetWeaver BI is the only installation running under Unicode, all the data from the non-Unicode systems can be converted and then made available correctly for reporting in all languages and with all the characters needed.

1.4 Summary

Besides the topics of localization (SAP Country Versions), currencies, time zones, and translation, technical language support is a very important component of business software used on an international basis. In non-Unicode implementations, a relatively large number of code pages support only a small number of countries. The ongoing progress of globalization is increasingly hindered by the incompatibility of the different code pages. This was already the case before Unicode was available as a global standard.

In summary, it can be said that Unicode is an essential part of a modern IT landscape today, at least in some areas. In Chapter 2, we will continue this argument in detail, based on SAP's own history.

From the single code page system in one country to the multi-national, central installation with integration of different external systems: In this chapter you will get an overview of the different concepts of technical language support, from its beginnings in SAP R/3 to the SAP Business Suite with Unicode.

2 Language Support in SAP Systems

2.1 From Single Code Page Systems to Unicode

The need for suitable language and text processing in computer systems already existed in the early years of commercial use. The options were very limited, particularly due to the limitation of the character length to 7 bits, with which only the ASCII character set (127 characters) can be represented. Other 7-bit code pages (such as EBCDIC) will not be considered further here for simplicity's sake. With the later 8-bit technology, it was possible to display another 128 characters, which set the stage for the processing of a complete character set or alphabet of a simple language[1]. Thus different code pages were defined by multiple manufacturers and institutions, all of which provided a binary encoding for every character in a certain group of languages.

Desire for language processing in the early years of the computer industry

However, there were no uniform standards, so that a certain character in a language could have different binary codes depending on the code page. For instance, the two code pages for Cyrillic, Microsoft MS 1251 and ISO 8859-5, use different encodings for the Cyrillic characters, while the ASCII characters had identical encodings. These gaps in uniformity often still make it difficult and costly today to exchange texts in these languages between different systems with different code pages.

---

[1] The character set (alphabet) of a simple language technically can be fully covered with 1 byte per character. Examples are all the Western and Eastern European languages.

For the rest of the discussion, however, we first must define what we actually mean by a character, a character set, a code page, and other terms.

2.1.1 Characters, Character Sets, and Code Pages

Character as abstract object

A *character* is an abstract object with a certain informational content, which is usually present in written form. Characters can be letters, character elements or printed characters of a language, but also numbers, punctuation marks, or symbols from mathematics, chemistry, music, etc. Examples are letters from different languages (A, B, C, ה, ع, й), symbols (⇨, ₡, ♯, ♭) or ideographical characters (众, 偹, 哗), used in the Asian languages.

Character set as coherent unit

The *character set* contains all the characters of a particular coherent unit, such as in a language. That set of all characters can be displayed uniquely on a computer system without knowing the exact encoding. The character set Latin-1, for instance, contains all the characters of the Western European languages, or—more simply—the alphabets of the languages. But so that we can also talk about the non-alphabetic languages, particularly the Asian languages with many thousands of characters or composed characters, we need a term other than "alphabet." The term *language group* describes all the languages which use the same character set.

Code page

On a computer system, a character is stored in binary or hexadecimal format as a sequence of bytes which is called an *encoding (code point)*. The *code page* contains every concrete code point for every character in a certain character set. For a code point in the following, we will use the usual hexadecimal notation from the literature, `0x<hex code>`. For instance, the letter A has the code point `0x41` in the ASCII code page. For the code point of a character in the Unicode code page, we use the notation `U+<Code>`, so the letter A has the *Unicode code point* or *Unicode scalar value* `U+0041`.

The code page is the concrete binary or hexadecimal encoding of each character of a character set in the computer system. While the character set for a language is unique, in general there are multiple code pages per language; that is, the same character may have different encodings. For example, the code pages ISO 8859-2 and

Microsoft MS 1250 both describe the Latin-2 character set for Eastern European languages but in some cases have different encodings.

In SAP systems, multiple code pages are necessary for the different system components:

▶ A system code page for the application server

▶ A front-end code page for the PC on which the user is working

▶ Peripheral code pages for printers and communication with other systems (e. g. via remote function call, or RFC)

▶ The database is technically configured by default in single code-page systems using an ASCII-based Latin-1 database code page (for instance, WE8DEC for Oracle databases). This not relevant for languages in the applications, however.

In the following sections of this chapter, we will primarily be looking at the system code page, which plays the central role. A basic prerequisite is that a unique conversion be possible between the system code page and the front end and peripheral code pages, so that special characters can always be displayed correctly in all possible cases.

2.1.2 Historical Development of Language Processing at SAP

At SAP, the topic of languages was already important in the days of SAP R/2. After the break-up of the Soviet Union, Eastern Europe and Russia became popular as a new market, so there was a demand for languages with new character sets. SAP R/2 applications were translated into Russian and Czech, and the EBCDIC code pages were used in that effort. The Asian countries, and Japan in particular, were interesting for SAP. However, in SAP R/2 there was no clear and uniform concept yet of how languages and their different character sets should be supported from a technical standpoint.

In the development of SAP R/3, right from the start internationalization was taken into account as an important concept. In order to gain an early presence in the important Japanese market, both the Japanese code page and also a translation into Japanese had to be implemented. Even in the first release of SAP R/3 in 1992, the technically

Internationalization in SAP R/3

extremely complicated Double-Byte technology[2] was available for Japanese, as well as a translation of the most important SAP R/3 applications.

In the following years, more and more languages were added with more character sets. Table 2.1 provides an historical overview of translated languages. Western European languages were supported right from the start with SAP R/2 and SAP R/3.

Year	Release	Languages
1990	SAP R/2	Russian
1992	SAP R/2	Czech
1992	SAP R/3	Japanese
1993	SAP R/3	Japanese as standard in SAP R/3
1994	SAP R/3	Chinese (simplified, Mandarin)
1995	SAP R/3	Korean, Thai, Greek, Turkish
1996	SAP R/3	Chinese (traditional, Taiwanese)
1998	SAP R/3	Hebrew
2000	SAP R/3	Other Eastern European languages
2005	SAP R/3	Arabic (Unicode only)

Table 2.1 Historical Overview of Translated Languages

In the current release, SAP ERP 2005, more than 30 translated languages are offered, including 13 different character sets in the standard, of which 12 are also available as SAP single code pages. Arabic, due to its very complicated right-to-left writing (*BIDI technology*[3]) is a unique case and is only available in Unicode. It should be noted at this point that future new languages with new character sets will only be supported in Unicode.

---

2 Double-Byte languages consume two bytes of memory for each character (ideograph). SAP supports the Double-Byte languages Japanese, Korean, simplified and traditional Chinese, and, with some limitations, Hong Kong Chinese. For double-byte processing, the SAP kernel switches into a special Double-Byte mode.

3 BIDI (bi-directional) means the ability to change the writing direction dynamically, which is particularly necessary for the languages of the Middle East (e.g., Arabic, Farsi).

You will quickly comprehend that the use of a language with a complicated character set is not simple. Even the layman can see the basic problems in simple languages. If you log onto a German PC on the Internet, for instance, and happen to call up a Russian Internet page, or you receive a Russian email, characters will often be displayed that are completely unrecognizable, even if you know the Russian language.

That is because the PC is set for German, a language with the Western European character set. You can change your browser settings so that you can see the Russian correctly (see Figure 2.1). But if you return to your previous German Internet page, you will be surprised to see that the German umlauts (ö, ü, ä, ß) will suddenly be gibberish; you first need to set your browser settings back to Western European.

The reason for these problems is the language itself. Because German and Russian use different character sets and code pages, you have to set up your Web browser accordingly. In Microsoft Internet Explorer, for instance, that is done using the menu entries **View • Encoding • Western European (Windows)** or **Cyrillic (Windows)**. The Internet page itself—that is, the URL—often says nothing about the language used. Thus, in some cases you really need to experiment before finding the right encoding in your browser.

Figure 2.1 Russian Internet Page with Western European Browser

This simple example demonstrates the general problems involved in multilingual applications, which in the commercial use of SAP products in a global enterprise have an even stronger effect. The code page of the language used is a technical property that is not directly visible in the application itself. The end user, after all, wants to use the application directly without needing to worry about technical details.

2.1.3 Single Code Page Systems

As long as an SAP system is only operated with one character set and one code page—in this case we speak of a *single code page system*—these problems don't exist. On the other hand, that means that a multinational enterprise would have to limit itself to languages with that character set for each system in order to avoid all the problems described.

Global character set

Let's take a closer look at the code page ISO 8859-1 for the Western European Latin-1 character set, which you already got to know in Chapter 1. In the lower half of Table 2.2 (character range 0–127, shown in hexadecimal with 0x00 - 0x7F), all the 7-bit ASCII characters are specified, including the English alphabet, the numerals, and some special characters, while the range 0x00 - 0x19 is reserved for internal control characters. This 7-bit ASCII character set is generally also called the *global character set* and is identical in all ASCII and ISO code pages.

	0	1	2	3	4	5	6	7	8	9	A	B	C	D	E	F
0																
1																
2	SP[4]	!	"	#	$	%	&	'	(	)	*	+	,	-	.	/
3	0	1	2	3	4	5	6	7	8	9	:	;	<	=	>	?
4	@	A	B	C	D	E	F	G	H	I	J	K	L	M	N	O
5	P	Q	R	S	T	U	V	W	X	Y	Z	[	\	]	^	_
6	'	a	b	c	d	e	f	g	h	i	j	k	L	m	n	o
7	p	q	r	s	t	u	v	w	x	y	z	{			}	~	

Table 2.2 Global Character Set of Code Page ISO 8859-1 (Lower Half)

---

4 SP (0x20) represents the space character.

In the upper half of Latin-1 shown in Table 2.3 (character range 128–255; hexadecimal `0x8A-0xFF`, of which `0x8A-0x9F` undefined), there are all the national special characters, like the German umlauts, the French ê, and the Spanish ñ. As you can also see, the lower-case and upper-case letters have different encodings. The alphabet of a Western European language therefore uses a certain part of the global character set and some special characters from the upper range.

If you examine the alphabet of an Eastern European language with its special characters (including upper- and lower-case letters)—e. g. Polish (Ą ą Ć ć Ę ę Ł ł Ń ń Ó ó Ś ś Ź ź Ż ż) or Czech (Á á Č č Ď ď É é Ě ě Í í Ň ň Ó ó Ř ř Š š Ť ť Ú ú Ů ů Ž ž Ý ý)—you will see that these are not present in Latin-1. For the Eastern European languages, therefore, another character set Latin-2 with code pages ISO 8859-2, Microsoft MS 1250, and others were developed.

European languages with non-Latin-1 character sets

	0	1	2	3	4	5	6	7	8	9	A	B	C	D	E	F
8																
9																
A	NBSP5	¡	¢	£	¤	¥	¦	§	¨	©	ª	«	¬	-	®	¯
B	°	±	²	³	´	µ	¶	·	¸	¹	º	»	¼	½	¾	¿
C	À	Á	Â	Ã	Ä	Å	Æ	Ç	È	É	Ê	Ë	Ì	Í	Î	Ï
D	Ð	Ñ	Ò	Ó	Ô	Õ	Ö	×	Ø	Ù	Ú	Û	Ü	Ý	Þ	ß
E	à	á	â	ã	ä	å	æ	ç	è	é	ê	ë	ì	í	î	ï
F	ð	ñ	ò	ó	ô	õ	ö	÷	ø	ù	ú	û	ü	ý	þ	ÿ

Table 2.3 Character Set of Code Page ISO 8859-1 (Upper Half)

The languages Russian and Greek don't use Roman letters at all, but rather have their own characters and therefore need their own character sets. The Russian alphabet, for instance, uses letters from the Russian character set (а б в г д е ё ж з и й к л м н о п р с т у ф х ч ш щ ъ ы ь э ю я) here, just the lower-case letters. Even though one can usually "guess" the special characters with Latin-2 languages, since the Roman letters are similar except for the accents, with Russian and other Slavic languages like Ukrainian or Bulgarian you have a completely different alphabet.

---

5 `NBSP` (`0xA0`) represents the non-breaking space.

For all European languages, the five character sets Latin-1, Latin-2, Latin-4 (the Baltic languages), Cyrillic, and Greek are needed. But since a single code page system can only display and encode a maximum of 256 different characters uniquely, more code pages are necessary.

Double-Byte languages

Asian languages have several thousand characters or combined characters. The languages supported by SAP[6], Japanese, Korean, simplified and traditional Chinese, therefore need two bytes per character. So we use the term *Double-Byte languages*. With two bytes, a maximum of 65,535 characters can be displayed uniquely, so that all the Double-Byte languages listed could be uniquely definable. But this is unfortunately not the case; instead, each of these languages has its own code page, and the code pages overlap in large ranges. Only the global character set is identical for all these languages.

Multibyte languages

The Thai language is an exception: Its character set contains 87 character (elements) with consonants, vowels, and tone marks, from which about 2,000 combinations can be composed. A linguistically complete character is thus combined from multiple individual characters in the character set. Thus a complete character may occupy between 1 and 3 bytes and in special cases even 4 bytes; here, we use the term *multibyte language*.

In Figure 2.2 you can see the Thai code page, which in the range 0x00-0x7F is also identical with the 7-bit ASCII character set (not shown) and in the upper range 0xA1-0xFB only describes the individual character elements. The linguistically correct character compositions must be performed by the software, such as when displayed in Microsoft Windows or when printing.

We could name a few more languages which use other character sets and code pages. But the limits of a single code page system are now already clear: Only languages in a single language group can coexist in a system with no technical problems, if they all use the same character set and one code page.

---

6 More precisely, we should speak of language character sets, as there are many Asian dialects which use the same character set.

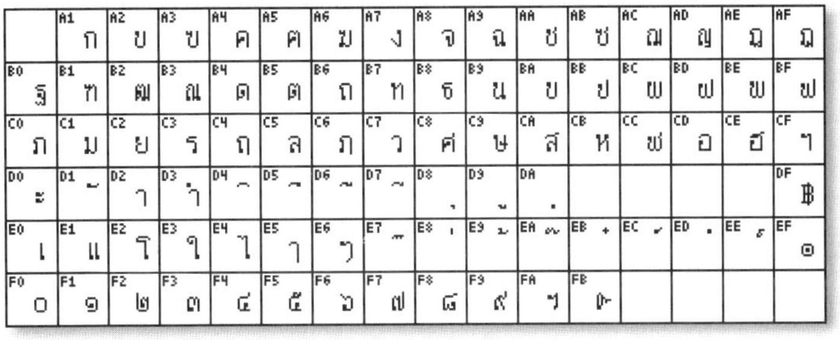

Figure 2.2 Thai Code Page

There are multiple single code pages from different manufacturers for the same character set. To be as standards-compliant as possible and support a number of platforms, SAP uses only the ISO-8859 code pages and uniform Asian code pages for the system code page of the application server.

Table 2.4 shows the list of single code pages and assigned languages[7] in SAP systems[8] (see also Figure 1.3 in Chapter 1 and the code page tables in Appendix A).[9]

Code page	SAP code page	Languages supported
ISO 8859-1	1100	Danish, Dutch, English, Finnish, French, German, Italian, Icelandic, Norwegian, Portuguese, Spanish, Swedish
ISO 8859-2	1401	Croatian, Czech, English, German, Hungarian, Polish, Romanian, Slovakian, Slovenian
ISO 8859-4	1900	Lithuanian, Latvian, Estonian, English
ISO 8859-5	1500	English, Russian
ISO 8859-7	1700	English, Greek
ISO 8859-8	1800	English, Hebrew
ISO 8859-9	1610	Danish, Dutch, English, Finnish, French, German, Italian, Norwegian, Portuguese, Spanish, Swedish, Turkish

Table 2.4 Single Code Pages and Languages in SAP Systems

---

7   The languages are technically useable even if there is no SAP translation available (for instance, Estonian).

8   For simplicity's sake, we will use the term ISO code pages for all languages.

9   Baltic languages with some limitations (see SAP Note 198489).

Code page	SAP code page	Languages supported
Shift JIS (SJIS)	8000	English, Japanese
GB2312-80	8400	Chinese (simplified), English
Big 5	8300	Chinese (traditional), English
KSC5601	8500	English, Korean
TIS620	8600	English, Thai

Table 2.4 Single Code Pages and Languages in SAP Systems (cont.)

The uniquely defined characters in a code page place clear technical limitations on which language combinations are possible in a single code page system.

2.2 Combination of Languages in a System

Combination of languages in a system

In the early days of SAP R/3, many multinational enterprises took the approach of installing a separate SAP system for each country or business area, and operating only one or a few languages with one character set or one code page. But even by the middle of the 1990s, several global customers were asking the critical question of how multiple countries in a region or even multiple continents could operate together on a single SAP system. That immediately made it clear that the approach of operating an SAP system for each country or language group would not last. The customers had quickly recognized that a global system with multiple countries is significantly more efficient and cost-effective for IT operations than one system for each country's language or language group.

Single instance system approach

Numerous analyses and studies show that for a global enterprise the *single instance system approach*[10] offers significant advantages over a decentralized architecture, and so a solution for a global system had to be found. Not only are the business and commercial aspects important here, but there is also an interesting political aspect. In May of 2005, 10 new countries joined the European Union (EU), and they were Eastern European and Baltic countries. While previously only

---

10 The single instance approach means a central IT architecture with one global system and one database, on which all the countries and languages of a globally active enterprise are implemented.

Greece was the only EU member nation with a non-Latin-1 language, now countries with languages from the Latin-2 and Latin-4 character sets had joined. This event was motivation for many European and even international enterprises to expand into these countries, so existing SAP systems would need to integrate these countries as well.

Even in the middle of the 1990s, it was clear to the entire IT industry that a technically optimum solution for the character-set and code-page problem required a uniform character set that could uniquely cover all languages with a single code page in all IT systems. Not by coincidence, the Unicode standard was created in the early 1990s, which fulfilled exactly that requirement.

It had been clear for a long time that for uniform text and language processing on a computer system, a standard was needed that ideally would define all characters uniquely, without confusion, and in a platform-independent manner. But Unicode was still not commercially usable; there were neither operating systems nor databases which enabled Unicode for industrial use at that time. So SAP had to limit itself to the statement that Unicode might well be the perfect solution, but that it would take many years before it was ready for commercial use.

To be able to offer global customers a solution, the technologies described below were developed, although they were all designed as temporary solutions from the start, to last only until Unicode was available. Unfortunately, an incorrect "tricky" approach known as "fooling the system" also gained some widespread use, and it will also be briefly presented.

Technologies for language support

Table 2.5 shows the different release-dependent technologies for language support in SAP R/3 before the introduction of Unicode.

Technology	Release
MNLS (*Multinational Language Support*)	SAP R/2
"Fool the System"	At the start of SAP R/3
Blended code page systems	SAP R/3 (Release 3.0D to 4.6D)
MDSP (*Multiple Display Single Processing*)	SAP R/3 (Release 3.0D to 4.6D)
MDMP (*Multiple Display Multiple Processing*)	SAP R/3 (Release 3.1I to SAP ERP 2004)

Table 2.5 Release-Dependent Language Support in SAP R/3 Before Unicode

Below, we will focus on the description of MDMP. Because most global SAP customers without Unicode are currently running MDMP, the most important aspects of converting an MDMP system to Unicode should be explained.

2.2.1 "Fool the System"

Unsupported procedure

The "fool the system" approach is an unsupported procedure in non-Unicode systems to "smuggle in" non-configured languages or to use an incorrect character set, which cannot be prevented from a technical standpoint, or at least only to a limited extent.

The end user logs into the SAP system in a configured language, and then simply switches the keyboard to the desired language, without worrying about whether this is allowed. The data is often correctly displayed, but the SAP system interprets it incorrectly. For instance, if the user logs on in English on a Chinese PC and then switches the keyboard to Chinese, a Chinese character entered will be interpreted as two Western European special characters, which can lead to all sorts of problems, even including data inconsistency and corruption. This is often practiced with single code page systems or with MDMP with the wrong log-on language.

During a Unicode conversion, "fool the system" can be treated as an MDMP system (see Chapter 3), but the unsupported languages must be known, and texts already corrupted can only be repaired manually.

2.2.2 MNLS System

Initial approach for multilingual language support

As you have already seen with single code page systems, the database in a non-Unicode SAP system only processes the data as binary, and does not perform any code-page-specific operations.[11] So the database doesn't know which code page the data belongs to which it stores; the code page is interpreted on the SAP application server and front-end level.

Thus, even in early releases of SAP R/3, the approach developed of determining one code page per application server and implementing

---

11 The SAP database of a non-Unicode system is configured by default with a Latin-1 code page.

a multilingual system that way. The users of a certain code page—e. g., Russian—would log onto a dedicated application server configured for that code page, and would run their transactions there. As long as all the relevant data from a user was only exchanged between that server and the database, the data was processed correctly. SAP called this procedure *Multinational Language Support*, with the acronym MNLS.

Unfortunately, precisely that important prerequisite could not be implemented, given that the entire client/server architecture of SAP R/3 with distributed processes and services worked against the concept. For instance, the data from the Russian user might be sent not only to the Russian application server but also to another server with another code page during a posting process. With MNLS, there was also no reasonable way to do load distribution between the application servers. For these and other reasons, the MNLS approach soon had to be abandoned.

2.2.3 Blended Code Page System

For the combination of certain languages with different code pages, the encodings are still unique despite the combination—there are no overlaps—or it can even happen that the special characters of a language are defined in more than one code page. For instance, the German special characters are identically defined in the Latin-2 character set and code page ISO8859-2, so it is possible to operate Eastern European Latin-2 languages and German in a single code page system, which can in fact be configured in SAP systems. However, in that case no other Western European languages with other Latin-1 special characters, such as French, can be used at the same time.

For more language combinations

If one takes this approach further, there are other combinations of languages without code-point overlaps in different code pages. The code points in the Japanese Double-Byte SJIS code page behave particularly well: The relevant first byte is almost always in the range 0x8A-0x9F, which is unused in the ISO 8859-1 code page. That means it is possible to "construct" a new single code page which permits the combination of Latin-1 languages and Japanese (with some limitations). SAP took advantage of this fact to develop the code page "Eurojapan" from release SAP R/3 3.0D on, and other so-called *unambiguous blended code pages* (a unique combination of ISO code pages created by SAP, whereby Eurojapan is composed of the two code pages ISO 8859-1 and SJIS).

Language combinations extended in this way, however, were very specialized and often not good enough for a truly global system, leading SAP to look for more options. Most SAP applications by default don't include purely linguistic and cultural functions like alphabetical sorting. The conversion of lower-case to upper-case letters, which is controlled by a call to *locale components* in the operating system (technically by calling the function setlocale( )), is often used for search assistants, for instance, and that it is sufficient to ensure that this conversion is correct for every character. The locale component is an operating system component used by SAP that must exist for every language and country/code page combination.

If you look at the different code pages, you will see that the conversion algorithm and some other technical attributes are identical for many ISO code pages. So we naturally might ask whether multiple character sets with identical technical characteristics can be used at the same time despite the ambiguity without causing problems. As of Release 3.0D, SAP developed non-unique *ambiguous blended code pages* and operating system locales with these properties, which allowed still more language combinations than in single code page and unambiguous blended code pages systems, but had the disadvantage of ambiguity.

A great disadvantage of blended code pages is also that SAP had to create and maintain the operating-system-specific locales, which was not always possible and in the end was abandoned. Other disadvantageous were exclusions of certain characters in a language and incompatibility when exchanging data with other systems.[12]

2.2.4   MDSP System

Another solution to extend language combinations started with the approach of separating statically unchangeable from changeable texts. Since the static texts never change, many languages can be combined for them, as long as they can be displayed correctly, while for changeable texts the single code page rule still applied.

---

12 We won't go into any detail on these points, instead referring you to SAP Note 73606.

This was the origin of the MDSP solution (*Multiple Display Single Processing*), which made it possible to import multiple SAP languages that formed the static part. For changeable texts, which included all business data, only one code page was used for data entry. Using a special additional program, the input was check and either invalidated or converted into ASCII characters using transliteration. Here, transliteration means the conversion of special character into a phonetically similar combination of ASCII characters, for instance the German letter "ü" can be written as "ue."

This made it possible to see the user interface in the local language after language import, but the input had to be limited to one character set or converted into replacement characters by transliteration. Despite the transliteration technology, which was possible only for direct input using the SAP GUI application, it was unavoidable that invalid characters might enter the system through other input programs or interfaces.

2.2.5 MDMP System

The most advanced technology before Unicode is the *Multiple Display Multiple Processing solution* (MDMP). It is still in use today in many global SAP systems without Unicode and is supported from R/3 release 3.1I to SAP ERP 2004/SAP ECC 5.0/SAP NetWeaver 2004 (the last only as an upgrade).

Solution for global SAP systems before Unicode

MDMP takes the following approach: Every user and system process is assigned an ISO code page as an attribute, which is either switched to or inherited, by giving a language during log-in or when switching contexts between processes. Multiple ISO code pages can be active in parallel. For instance, if a user logs on in Russian and another in Japanese, each system process switches to the code page of the user currently using it. The same dialog process can thus switch between different code pages; e. g., between Russian and Japanese. An MDMP system is therefore also called a *mixed code page system* or a *dynamic code page switch system*.

In Figure 2.3, you can see the starting menu in an MDMP scenario for the creation of customer orders (Transaction VA01) in different logon languages for the current user in SAP R/3. For the correct display and input on the keyboard, the front end must be appropriately configured for the language. Depending on the language in which the user logs on from a suitable PC, Transaction VA01 is displayed in the user's local language and data can be entered in the appropriate code page.

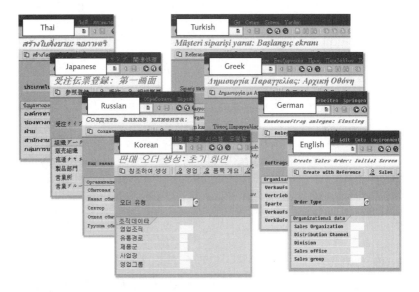

Figure 2.3 Transaction VA01 in an MDMP System with Multiple Languages

MDMP Concepts   What does this concept mean for the operation of an MDMP system?

▶ Just like a single code page system, the database still processes all data as binary, and thus doesn't "know" the language the data belongs to.

▶ The interpretation of the code page takes place on the application server and the front end, not in the database.

▶ The code page is derived from the logon language of the dialog or system user.

▶ The user logs on only in a language matching the code page of a character set. If the user logs on with the wrong language, or changes the character set during the session by switching the keyboard language (which can't be detected by the SAP system), there is a high risk of inconsistency and data corruption.

▶ Applications with linguistically relevant text processing (like the conversion of lower-case to upper-case letters in search screens) must support code-page switching.

▸ Applications with multilingual menus (dynpros) can display unreadable characters which must be ignored and may not be changed.

The MDMP architecture is shown in Figure 2.4. The system is global and the database stores all languages without knowing them. It is, so to speak, a "purely binary storage medium," which simply exchanges byte data with the application servers. Interpretation of the code page and the language of the text data takes place only between the application server and the local PC front end from which the user logs on in the local language to the R/3 system.

MDMP architecture

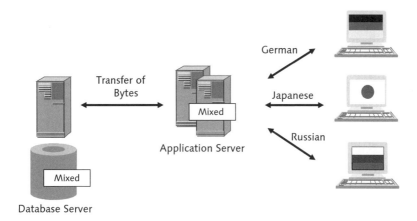

Figure 2.4 Architecture of MDMP

The individual user must log on to SAP R/3 on a PC configured for the local language (e. g., Russian) with a log-in language corresponding to the local language to be able to edit texts exclusively in the local language (Russian) and in English, which uses the global character set and can therefore always be used. If the Russian user were to try to display text data with German umlauts or Japanese characters, he would only see illegible characters (see also Figure 2.5). If he or she were actually to try to change them, this would often result in the loss of these texts. So the user can only correctly see and edit the languages corresponding to the code page derived from the logon language.

MDMP works best when multilingual texts can be uniquely identified using a language key. This is possible, for instance, when the table with the texts has a language key field. Such tables are classified

Tables with and without language keys

as *language-dependent tables*, while tables without such a language key field are *language-independent*. An SAP system contains many thousands of tables, with and without language keys.

One example installation of SAP R/3 Enterprise included 36,703 tables, of which—besides system tables—29,273 were without and 7,223 with language keys[13], thus creating roughly a ratio of about 80 % language-independent to 20 % language-dependent tables. For multilingual use, that's not a good result. There are, in fact, many system tables with pure ASCII characters that play no role, but many language-independent tables contain text fields that can be used multilingually in many applications. For instance, table BKPF has no language key, but it does have a field BKTXT for the document header, in which invoice texts can be entered. These texts are generally multilingual in a global enterprise with multiple countries.

This subdivision into language-dependent and language-independent tables plays a large role in Unicode conversion, as you will see later. The more multilingual texts are stored in language-independent tables, the more difficult a conversion to Unicode will be.

For a clean operating procedure in an MDMP system, multilingual texts should, as far as possible, only be stored in language-dependent tables. In this way, it can always be determined from the language key what language or code page the text belongs to, even if it is displayed incorrectly.

Language key SPRAS

Figure 2.5 makes this clearer: Here, you see a table with a language key **SPRAS** and the color texts in the field **NAME** in different languages. Because of the significant MDMP characteristic that only languages in one code page can be correctly displayed, the user on a German PC only see the German (DE) and English (EN) color texts correctly, while the others for Japanese (JA) and Korean (KO) are illegible. People often refer to these illegible characters as "garbage" or "hieroglyphics." The Japanese and Korean users all see their own languages and English correctly, but the others incorrectly.

---

13 This data was taken from a test system.

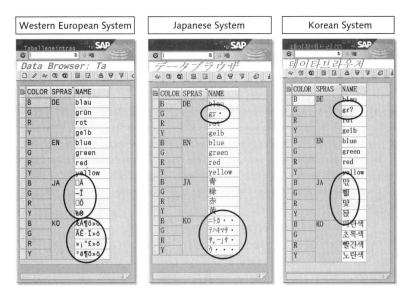

Figure 2.5 Language-Dependent Tables in the MDMP System

Thus English is always legible and can therefore be used in combination with all languages with no problems. Using the language key, it is always possible whenever in doubt to determine the actual language when something is illegible. Without a language key, on the other hand, it is impossible or at least requires a lot of effort.

Golden MDMP Rules

The MDMP characteristics described have led to the so-called *golden MDMP rules* described in SAP Note 73606 and other documents. The most important of those rules are the following:

▶ The logon language is the same as the maintenance language (all languages in a language group with one code page are technically allowed). For instance, to edit Russian texts, you have to log on in Russian. If English is the logon language, only the Western European languages can be edited, but not Russian.

▶ The fields in the primary table key are only allowed to contain characters in the global character set. These fields are used by the database for indexing, for instance, and therefore must be unique.

▶ Multilingual application texts should only be used in language-dependent tables; for language-independent tables the global character set should be used.

The logon language is controlled by different mechanisms, of which the following are most frequently used:

► Direct input of the language key by the user in the logon screen

During logon, the R/3 basis system determines the code page assigned to the logon language and switches the process occupied by the user to the text environment of that code page, so that it can be edited correctly in the user's local language. If the user switches to a different process previously occupied by a user with a different code page, the new process undergoes a code-page switch. This dynamic code-page switching takes place for all process types (dialog, update, batch, enqueue, and spool) by "inheriting" the code page between the processes.

► Configured standard language in the user's master record

For indirect logon methods, for instance Single Sign-On (SSO) with the security product SNC (Secure Network Communication), the language stored in the user master record is the logon language.

► Logon languages of system users

For the users of a different type needed for different system tasks (system, service, communication), internal logon languages are also determined in each one's logon configuration. In an MDMP system, the rule about the correct logon language matching the code page with the data to be processed also applies to these user types.

A globally active enterprise must strictly obey the golden rules of MDMP use, since otherwise there may be problems, even data corruption. But this has turned out to be practically impossible to implement. While the correct logon language is still easy to get under control, the rule for the language-dependent and language-independent tables is very difficult to achieve, and sometimes even impossible for legal reasons. It is legally required in all countries that reports prepared for the financial authorities (such as sales tax) must be prepared in the local language. So it is often necessary to maintain text fields in language-independent tables in the local language, such as the document header text in the table field BKPF-BUTXT.

But even the logon language often presents problems for the global enterprise when it comes to business practice. There is often a need to log on to the system in both the enterprisewide communication language (usually English) and also in the local language; for example to edit Chinese addresses, something which is forbidden in an MDMP system. Because of the increasing trend towards outsourcing, offshoring, and shared service centers in the IT industry, these and similar needs will only continue to grow.

Another very important aspect is that MDMP technology is a proprietary SAP solution and is only designed for ABAP applications under SAP R/3 with a SAP GUI under Microsoft Windows. The SAP GUI has the special feature that it will not interpret and manipulate illegible text fields—that is, fields with texts from the wrong code page—unless they cannot be changed any other way. Other user interfaces, like a Web browser, don't support this kind of "tricky" behavior. From that fact, it can easily be intuited that applications with Web-based user interfaces work with MDMP only on a limited basis, if at all. As we have already discussed here and as we will look at in more detail later, MDMP is not supported in Java-based applications such as SAP NetWeaver Portal.

MDMP technology as a proprietary SAP solution

Let's summarize the important facts about MDMP with a few details:

Summary

▶ MDMP is the only solution so far until R/3 release 4.6C that allows a global system to operate with multiple code pages.

▶ The technical configuration of MDMP is simple.

▶ There is a risk of data corruption.

▶ It results in a high adaptation effort for interfaces to external systems (see also Section 3.5).

▶ MDMP is supported for SAP R/3 as of Release 3.1I and its successor products, up to and including SAP ERP 2004 and SAP ECC 5.0 (for the latter only as an upgrade). In SAP ERP 2005, only Unicode and single code page systems (with limitations) are supported.

As of 2007, new installations based on SAP NetWeaver will only be available in Unicode. Details can be found in SAP Note 79991, other reference and the documentation (see Appendix C). For all other products in the SAP Business Suite based on SAP Web Application Server 6.20 (SAP Web AS) and higher, MDMP is not supported. We will not go into the details of isolated solutions such as SAP CRM and SRM; for more information, you should contact SAP as needed.

Strict compliance with the golden MDMP rules is necessary for multilingual operation with multiple code pages, particularly use of the correct logon language and only the global character set in text fields of language-independent tables. There are only limited possibilities, if any, to control compliance from a technical stand-point, so this must take place at the organizational level.

▶ MDMP is designed exclusively for ABAP applications with the SAP GUI, and there is no support in Java-based applications.

2.3 Unicode in the SAP System

If you look at all critically at the SAP solutions for global multilingual systems described so far, then you will see that none of them are really satisfactory. Even if the golden rules are obeyed in an MDMP system, limits are quickly reached that can be gotten around only with great difficulty or not at all. The reason is simply the unchangeable fact that with the language and code page technology to date, there is no unambiguous representation of all languages and characters in a uniform format. It is simply unavoidable that there will always be problems with this approach.

Even if an SAP system only had language-dependent tables for text fields, that still would not be enough, because the requirements of a multilingual system continually grow. This is particularly true of the need for open and unlimited multilingual exchange of data between various external systems and other software system and platforms.

2.3.1 Multilingual Data Exchange

Without Unicode, different encoding systems are necessary for multilingual data processing

Recall the basic problem that even SAP can't avoid: At the lowest level, computers work with numbers. Letters and other characters are therefore assigned to numbers in order to store them. Before the invention of Unicode, there were hundreds of different encoding systems. None of those encoding systems ever included enough characters. For instance, the EU alone required several encoding system in order to satisfy the need for the languages of all its member nations. Not even for one single language like English or German was there an encoding system which truly included all the letters, punctuation marks, and commonly used technical characters.

These encoding systems are incompatible with one another, because different encodings can either use *the same* number for *different* characters, or *different* characters for *the same* character. Every computer (and especially servers) must support many different encoding systems, and if text is exchanged between different encoding systems or computer systems, this text runs the risk of being mangled.

Unicode assigns each and every character, unambiguously and uniquely, its own number: platform-independent, software-independent, and language-independent. The Unicode standard is used by industry giants like Apple, HP, IBM, Microsoft, Oracle, SAP, Sun, Sybase, Unisys, and many others. Unicode is a prerequisite for modern IT standards and programming languages like Java, XML, ECMA-Script (JavaScript), LDAP, CORBA 3.0, WML, and so on, and is the recognized implementation of the international ISO/IEC 10646 standard. It is supported in many operating systems, all modern browsers, and many other products. The growing acceptance of the Unicode standard and the availability of supporting programs is among the most important global trends in today's software technology.

Unicode as fully recognized standard in the IT industry

The use of Unicode in client/server or many-layered applications and on Web pages enables significant cost savings in comparison with conventional character sets. Application programs and Web sites can be used directly for many systems, languages, and countries, without the need for special, costly adaptations. Text can be exchanged globally with Unicode, without loss of information. With Unicode it is possible to display a variety of characters in all possible combinations, even in different writing directions—such as in Arabic from right to left—together on a single medium.

Global application with Unicode without information losses

2.3.2 Unicode Basics

SAP introduced Unicode with SAP Web AS 6.20 and the applications of the SAP Business Suite based on it, after the different operating system and database manufacturers on whose platform SAP relies had brought Unicode-capable products to the market. The first generally available Unicode-capable SAP product is SAP R/3 Enterprise Extension Set 2.00 (Extension Set 1.10 is also available upon request from SAP). All other products in the SAP Business Suite are available in Unicode and will be described in more detail in Chapter 3.

SAP R/3 Enterprise as the first generally available Unicode product

Unicode defines a single encoding scheme for all characters in the world, exactly and unambiguously. The character sets of particular language or symbol groups are grouped into particular ranges (see Figure 2.6).

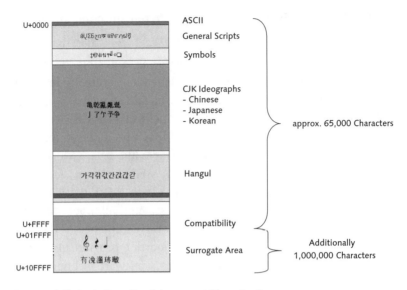

U+0000		ASCII
		General Scripts
		Symbols
		CJK Ideographs - Chinese - Japanese - Korean
		Hangul
U+FFFF		Compatibility
U+01FFFF		Surrogate Area
U+10FFFF		

approx. 65,000 Characters

Additionally 1,000,000 Characters

Figure 2.6 Unicode Encoding Scheme and Character Range

Unicode encoding scheme and character range

While the Unicode standard range encodes two bytes per character and thus 65,535 characters are possible, there are other ranges, including the special *surrogate area*, which makes a huge number of additional characters possible using additional bytes per character. In the following sections, however, we will only look at the standard range relevant for SAP.

Unicode determines an unambiguous encoding for every character (see Section 2.1.1), and the code is written in hexadecimal. That means it is possible at any time to identify a certain character using that *logical* code. Thus the character need not even be displayed to know the language it belongs to; the code alone suffices.

Due to the many heterogeneous hardware technologies and CPU architectures found today in the IT world, however, the Unicode characters are not always processed and stored with the identical code in the database or persistence layer. Rather there are several technical Unicode formats that use a particular algorithm to map a character onto a different code than the one shown above, this mapping being exact and very fast. This has different technical causes and ultimately depends on the manufacturer, which wants to implement the optimum format for Unicode.

2.3.3 Unicode Formats in SAP Systems

The two important formats UTF-8 and UTF-16 are used in the SAP system (see Section 1.3.1). UTF-16 is used on the application server, and every character always occupies exactly two bytes, while the Unicode database uses either UTF-16 or UTF-8 depending on the manufacturer (or special derivatives of the latter). UTF-8 uses a dynamic number of bytes per character, so if an alphanumeric character occupies one byte, the special characters in the languages with simple writing systems occupy two bytes, and the Asian characters generally occupy three bytes.

UTF-8 and UTF-16

For the UTF-16 format, there are also two different sequences in which bytes are processed—*Big Endian* and *Little Endian*—whose selection generally depends on the CPU architecture. For instance Unix operating systems generally use Big Endian with the SAP Unicode code page 4102, and Microsoft Windows servers use Little Endian with the SAP Unicode code page 4103. The two formats differ only in the sequence of values, depending on whether the higher-value byte comes first (Big Endian) or last (Little Endian).

Big Endian and Little Endian

Both UTF formats include the same Unicode character set and are therefore equivalent. The transformations between UTF-16 and UTF-8 are algorithmic, so that no conversion tables are necessary and performance is high. To achieve the best efficiency from storage requirements, performance, and compatibility with non-Unicode systems for data exchange, SAP introduced the formats UTF-8 and UTF-16 with the following properties.

▶ **UTF-16: Unicode transformation format, 16-bit encoding**

  ▷ SAP Unicode format for the application server and UTF-16-based databases

  ▷ Fixed length, one character = two bytes (surrogate pairs = 2 + 2 bytes)

  ▷ Platform-dependent byte sequence (Big/Little Endian)

  ▷ Two-byte alignment restriction

  ▷ Suitable for Unicode enabling of ABAP programs

  ▷ Best compromise between storage usage and algorithmic complexity

  ▷ Full integration with Java and Microsoft environments

▶ **UTF-8: Unicode transformation format, 8-bit encoding**

▶ SAP Unicode format for communication (file, SAP GUI, RFC, XML, etc.) and UTF-8-based databases

▶ Variable length, one character = 1 to 4 bytes

▶ Platform-independent

▶ No alignment restrictions

▶ 7-bit US-ASCII compatible

▶ Standard format for XML processing

For SAP Unicode conversion, therefore, one needs to know the platform and *endianness* is involved, so that the right Unicode code page can be selected. Table 2.6 shows the two Unicode formats used by SAP, UTF-16 (Big Endian and Little Endian) and UTF-8, with an example. For each linguistic character in the left column, the hexadecimal encodings in the different Unicode formats are shown in the right column. First, the Unicode scalar value is determined, from which the other encodings are uniquely algorithmically derived. Unicode encoding tables can be found at *http://www.unicode.org*.

Character	Unicode encoding (scalar value)	UTF-16 (Big Endian)	UTF-16 (Little Endian)	UTF-8
a	U+0061	00 61	61 00	61
ä	U+00E4	00 E4	E4 00	C3 A4
α	U+03B1	03 B1	B1 03	CE B1
會	U+3479	34 79	79 34	E3 91 B9

Table 2.6 Examples of Unicode Formats

2.4 Transition to SAP NetWeaver and Enterprise SOA with Unicode

Multilingual Internet and Enterprise SOA

The widespread acceptance and general "triumph" of the Internet in the past has resulted in new opportunities for industry and the business world to extend traditional business relationships and processes radically and expand them to new business partners around the world. At the same time, the IT industry has in the past few years experienced dramatic changes and a shift in IT technology and system architecture toward efficient modeling and integration of business processes across system boundaries.

This has resulted in a new service-oriented architecture which makes it possible to implement complex global processes through efficient utilization of individual services. This *enterprise service-oriented architecture* (enterprise SOA)—previously also called the *enterprise services architecture* (ESA)—opens up new dimensions for a global enterprise to act successfully everywhere in the world.

The immediate result is a need to be able to process multilingual business processes efficiently across country, language, and system boundaries, with no limitations. It is obvious that this can only be achieved from a language-technology standpoint by the use of Unicode.

Even in the 1990s, SAP realized that a technically perfect, multilingual, global solution could only be based on Unicode. But it took several years for the different operating system and database manufacturers on whose platforms SAP relies to bring Unicode-capable products to market. For the introduction of Internet-capable SAP applications, new technologies and standards had to be introduced. These had a significant influence on the language architecture used to that point.

SAP's path towards Unicode

With the introduction of the *SAP Internet Transaction Server* (ITS) in Release 3.1G, it was possible for the first time to equip SAP applications with Web technology. As a first step, an HTML-based Web browser from Microsoft or Netscape could be used in place of the SAP GUI front end. The advantages are clear: The SAP GUI didn't even need to be installed, the use of a web browser is easy to learn (or already familiar), and there are more technical options. The ITS formed the basis for the SAP Workplace, which can be seen as the predecessor of the SAP NetWeaver Portal (formerly SAP Enterprise Portal).

SAP Internet Transaction Server (ITS)

A significant goal of the SAP Workplace was to provide all users in an enterprise with a uniform, and personalization-, and Internet-capable user interface with transparent access to all systems (e. g., SAP R/3, SAP BW, and external Internet applications). However, SAP Workplace was not really designed for multilingual use in a global enterprise, and it turned out that traditional MDMP technology was unsuitable because it only used a very special configuration and reqired rather complicated user rules.

New technologies for new user interfaces With time, more technologies were developed which all had the same goal: to provide the simplest, most modern, most ergonomic, and most personalized user interface possible, such as like Business Server Pages (BSPs), the PC UI, or Web Dynpro iViews.

If a global enterprises use such new technologies, they naturally will need to use multilingual applications with the new user interfaces with no limitations. This isn't possible without Unicode. For example, Web-Dynpro-based applications are written in Java, which is only available in Unicode.

Enterprise SOA With enterprise SOA, SAP is consistently following a path of service-oriented architectures, allowing the design, development, identification, and use of standardized services for the entire enterprise, which particularly rely on their reusability. Enterprise SOA opens entire new dimensions for exchanging information and performing complete business processes across system boundaries, perhaps with the participation of business partners from many different countries.

While today the entire process chain of a business case is only seldom fully automated, that is a significant feature within enterprise SOA. The focus is no longer the individual system on which a part of the process chain is implemented in the form of one or more Web services, but rather the integration and collaboration of all the systems and services across broad boundaries. That means that every system involved must be able to exchange arbitrary data in arbitrary form without limitations.

For an enterprise with a global system, that means that data and processes are exchanged across national and continental borders between all the business partners involved, from the customer to the different suppliers. It is clear that different hardware and software products must be supported in the systems involved, which must play together as perfectly as possible, like the musicians in a symphony orchestra. A technologically basic prerequisite is an open integration design.

For a global business process with several countries involved, this obviously means that all the languages must be supported in any arbitrary combination. If the different solutions for language support in SAP are compared, it is easy to see that only Unicode is in question as an efficient and cost-effective solution for such a scenario.

Global business process with Unicode

> **Practical scenario**
>
> Imagine an example from the automotive industry: A customer in the U.S. orders a German car. It is assembled in a European country, and the individual parts are fabricated in Asia, for instance in China and Thailand.
>
> In order for the entire process from order entry to the delivery of the car to the customer in the U.S. and the complete and correct billing of all partners to take place quickly and efficiently, many IT systems must communicate and collaborate with one another. It might very well be necessary for the Asian suppliers involved to exchange data in Chinese and Thai, for instance, between an SAP system and one based on Java.
>
> Any attempt to perform such a process in English only or with a single code page would very probably be illegal because of the requirements of accounting in the countries involved. The notion of MDMP would run into trouble during the data exchange between an SAP and any Java-based system of an Asian supplier, or management would feel the pain of the high costs of adapting the interface. MDMP is only known in SAP systems and Java applications work only in Unicode.
>
> Please refer to Section 3.5 for more information on interfaces.

2.5 Summary

SAP supports languages with different character sets and code pages. The architecture of an SAP system is designed by default for character processing in one code page. To enable multilingual global systems before the availability of Unicode, limited specialized solutions were produced—finally MDMP—which made it possible to operate languages with more than one code page in parallel in a system.

With the availability of Unicode as the only technically correct solution in all SAP products, MDMP is no longer recommended and will no longer be supported as of SAP ERP 2005. Single code page systems will still be supported, but may have limitations when using Java-based applications. Here too, Unicode is recommended. New SAP products and all new installations as of 2007 will only be available in Unicode.

Technical lan-
guage support Table 2.7 shows an overview of technical SAP language support and
the resulting recommendations, which we will examine in more
detail in Chapter 3.

Code page technology / Release	Unicode	Single code page system	MDMP*	Blended code page system*
SAP R/3 4.6C	Not possible	Supported	Supported, but not recommended	Limited support (no new installation)
SAP R/3 Enterprise**	Supported and recommended	Supported (for limitations see SAP Note 838402)	Supported, but not recommended	Very limited support (no new installation)
SAP ERP 2004**	Supported and recommended	Supported (for limitations see SAP Note 838402)	Limited support (SAP Note 79991) (no new installation)	Very limited support (no new installation)
SAP ERP 2005	Supported and recommended	Supported (for limitations see SAP Note 838402)	Not supported (SAP Note 79991)	Not supported (SAP Note 79991)

* MDMP or blended code page are no longer recommended; there are general
limitations ("golden rules") for MDMP

** Preferred Unicode conversion release

Table 2.7 SAP Technical Language Support

In this chapter, you will get to know SAP-standard methods of implementing Unicode in your existing system or for new installations. You will find details here on the Unicode conversion of an MDMP system, on combining upgrades and Unicode conversions, on the adaptation of customer programs to the ABAP Unicode syntax, and on communications between Unicode and non-Unicode systems.

3   Implementing Unicode in SAP Applications

3.1   Unicode Architecture

Imagine you have an application that has to be made Unicode capable. To start with, you need to determine certain rules as to how this Unicode version will behave in an IT environment. This is the task that faced SAP when it started development of SAP R/3 Enterprise, the first Unicode-capable ERP release.

Requirements of a Unicode system

The following main criteria are the basis of Unicode introduction at SAP:

► **Compatibility between non-Unicode and Unicode systems must be guaranteed**

Compatibility of systems

This requires that in the ABAP environment (that is, the SAP standard) there is source code which can run on both non-Unicode and Unicode systems (see Figure 3.1). The logical consequence of this is that no explicit Unicode DDIC type may exist that could only be used in the Unicode system. Rather, all ABAP CHAR types (C, N, D, T, STRING) must be stored in the Unicode system by definition as Unicode data. This in turn affects the ABAP syntax rules in Unicode systems.

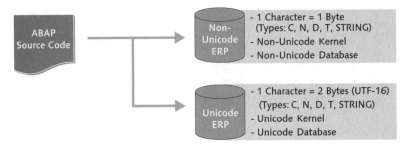

Figure 3.1 Single-Source in the ABAP Environment for SAP Standard Objects

In non-Unicode systems, the difference between character-type data and hex-byte-type data is not particularly great, since both units generally use the length of one byte. An offset can be used, for instance, in mixed structures of both data types.

In a Unicode system, there must be a strong distinction between hex-byte-type and character-type data types, given that the units of the character types are generally no longer one byte. As a result, there is a rule that only an offset to character-type fields may be used in a Unicode system. A series of analogous Unicode-compliant syntax rules can also be derived. Customer programs must be appropriately adapted in a conversion project (see Section 3.4).

Minimum effort ▶ **Unicode conversion of a non-Unicode system must be possible with the least possible effort and cost**

To fulfill this requirement, the Unicode syntax rules were designed in such a way that in most cases only the smallest possible part of the existing source code must be adapted.

Mixed landscapes ▶ **Mixed landscapes—those consisting of non-Unicode and Unicode systems—must be supported.**

This criterion means that in a data exchange between a non-Unicode and a Unicode system the data is subject to automatic conversion if possible. For instance, this applies to transports in mixed landscapes, but also to remote-function-call (RFC) techniques. Restrictions apply in the case of a data exchange between Unicode and MDMP systems (see Section 3.5).

In a mixed landscape, parallel access with different user interfaces to non-Unicode and Unicode systems should be possible, however. This is particularly true of the SAP GUI for Windows. This requirement can only be implemented because the SAP GUI for Windows has a non-Unicode mode and a Unicode mode.

If you consider the consequences of these criteria, you will see the amount of effort that would be involved in a Unicode conversion without any tool support. That gives you some idea of what Unicode enabling of a custom-written software application might mean.

SAP provides numerous tools for the support of Unicode conversion of a complex system landscape by default. For the adaptation of customer programs, there are Transaction UCCHECK, RFC, and the transport system to provide automatic conversion between Unicode and non-Unicode systems, and the SAP GUI provides parallel access to Unicode and non-Unicode systems. Naturally, in this context the R3load conversion tool and Transaction SPUMG should also be considered; these enable the conversion of an MDMP system to Unicode.

Thus, the topic of Unicode is quite comparable to topics such as the Y2K problem or the Euro conversion, for which SAP also provided corresponding tools, although the actual effort of a Unicode conversion is generally greater than for those projects.

As shown in Chapter 1, there exist different techniques (encoding schemes) for the storage of Unicode data. Depending on requirements, different encoding schemes are used. SAP has decided to use UTF16 (Big Endian or Little Endian, depending on the CPU used by the server) in the SAP Web Application Server. The Unicode mode of the SAP GUI for Windows, on the other hand, uses the UTF-8 format (see Table 3.1).

Unicode formats with SAP

Encoding scheme / Attribute	UTF-16 (Big Endian)	UTF-16 (Little Endian)	UTF-8/CESU-8
SAP number	4102	4103	4110
Use in IT environment	Unix	Microsoft Windows applications	e.g. Oracle database (CESU-8)
Use in SAP environment	SAP Web Application Server	SAP Web Application Server	SAP GUI for Windows

Table 3.1 Unicode Encoding Schemes Used in the SAP Environment

The encoding scheme used in the database in the SAP environment varies according to the database type (see Table 3.2). However, like the other formats, this is determined by SAP and *cannot* be selected by the customer. That is, the schemes used are uniquely determined by the combination of database type and server type.

Database	Encoding	Additional space requirements for Unicode
IBM DB2 for Linux, Unix, or Windows	UTF-8	about 10%
Oracle	CESU-8	about 10%
MaxDB	UCS-2	40 to 60%
MS SQL Server	UCS-2	40 to 60%
IBM DB2 for AS/400	UTF-16	10 to 20%*
IBM DB2 for z/OS**	UTF-16	20 to 60%**

* Only very little growth, because the greater part of the ASCII-based database is already on Unicode.

** Large range of variation, because the added requirements are greatly dependent on the compression of tables.

Table 3.2 Encoding Schemes Used on the Databases Supported

As a result, in an SAP Unicode system there are a series of different encoding schemes and thus different hex codes used. However, the conversion from one Unicode scheme into the other is an unambiguous and also not very performance-intensive operation, so that the use of different schemes in the SAP environment is no problem.

3.2   Unicode Conversion

Principle of Unicode conversion

In this section, we will answer the question of how a non-Unicode system can be "turned into" a Unicode system. The goal of a Unicode conversion in the SAP environment is to make all character-type data (fields of data type CHAR) available in Unicode format after the transformation process, while all other data types (example: data type INT or HEX) are stored unchanged.

System copy

To achieve this goal, SAP uses the principle of the *system copy*, in which all table definitions and content are exported into a database-independent format. After the export and subsequent conversion of all data, a new Unicode database instance is built and the data is imported.

Originally, this process was developed for OS/DB migrations as well (that is, a switch of database platforms). For this reason, combined Unicode conversion and OS/DB migration is supported.

> **Note**
>
> In the case of a switch of operating system or database platform, SAP uses the term "OS/DB migration." When switching from a non-Unicode to a Unicode system, on the other hand, the term "Unicode conversion" is used.

3.2.1 Generally Necessary Conversion Steps in a System

Here are the three most important prerequisites that must be fulfilled in order to start with a Unicode conversion.

Unicode Capability of the Release Used

The prerequisite for the use of the system copy method as a basis for the Unicode conversion is the Unicode capability of the release used. On the basis side, Unicode capability is provided as of SAP Web AS release 6.10 (with the exception of z/OS, where Unicode is available only as of SAP Web AS 6.40). However, this doesn't mean that all SAP applications based on these or later releases are automatically Unicode capable. For instance, SAP CRM 3.1 is based on SAP Web AS 6.20, but has not been released for Unicode on the application side by SAP CRM. Only the next release, SAP CRM 4.0, is Unicode capable.

What SAP applications are Unicode-capable at what release?

A current overview of Unicode capability in SAP applications is shown in Figure 3.2. The most current information can be found in SAP Note 79991.

In the case of release SAP R/3 4.6C, which is not Unicode capable, there must first be an upgrade to a Unicode-capable release. Then the preparation steps can be taken in the non-Unicode system for Unicode conversion, such as the adaptation of customer objects to the stricter Unicode syntax rules. This is clarified in Figure 3.3 for an Upgrade to SAP R/3 Enterprise.

If a release is released for Unicode, then all successor releases are automatically also released.

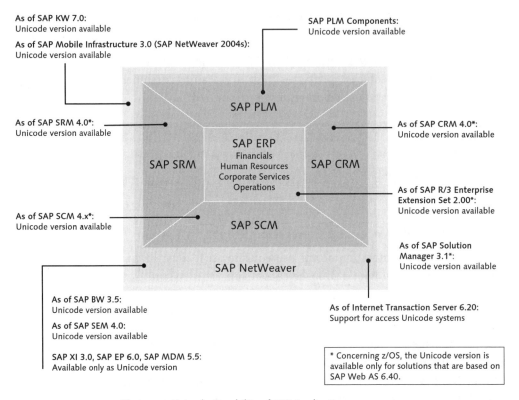

As of SAP KW 7.0:
Unicode version available

As of SAP Mobile Infrastructure 3.0 (SAP NetWeaver 2004s):
Unicode version available

SAP PLM Components:
Unicode version available

As of SAP SRM 4.0*:
Unicode version available

As of SAP CRM 4.0*:
Unicode version available

As of SAP R/3 Enterprise
Extension Set 2.00*:
Unicode version available

As of SAP SCM 4.x*:
Unicode version available

As of SAP Solution
Manager 3.1*:
Unicode version available

As of SAP BW 3.5:
Unicode version available

As of SAP SEM 4.0:
Unicode version available

SAP XI 3.0, SAP EP 6.0, SAP MDM 5.5:
Available only as Unicode version

As of Internet Transaction Server 6.20:
Support for access Unicode systems

* Concerning z/OS, the Unicode version is
available only for solutions that are based on
SAP Web AS 6.40.

Figure 3.2 Unicode Capability of SAP Applications

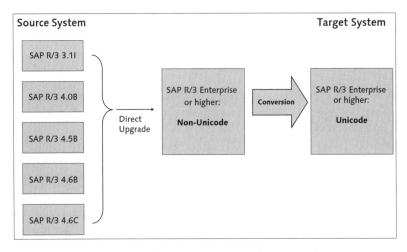

Figure 3.3 Procedure in Case of a Non-Unicode-Capable Source Release

Current Support Package Level

An important prerequisite for a successful Unicode conversion is the latest possible support-package level. This applies in principle for all components in the SAP system, but can also be true for other non-SAP applications that communicate with the SAP system.

Current support package simplifies Unicode conversion

For the actual conversion, a "sufficient" basis support package level is absolutely necessary. This is particularly true for the conversion of an MDMP system, as there still need to be improvements made in this area. At the moment, therefore, there is a separate conversion guideline for each support package level. You can find the current guidelines and some previous versions at the SAP Service Marketplace (*http://service.sap.com/unicode@sap*).

SAP strongly recommends performing the conversion with a basis support package available within this spectrum, ideally with the most current. If the project runs for about half a year, then it can be assumed that the conversion guidelines will still be available at the SAP Service Marketplace and any changes will have been integrated into it.

Basis support package

In the application area, in the case of an obsolete support package level, additional restrictions can be expected. But it may well be that these restrictions are not relevant for the conversion project.

Additional Hardware Requirements Caused by Unicode

Another very important prerequisite is the availability of sufficient hardware. The average additional hardware requirements for a Unicode conversion can be found in Table 3.3.

Hardware requirements must be taken into consideration

CPU	Main memory	Database size	Network (SAP GUI for Windows)
▶ + 30% ▶ Depends on Unicode scenario (MDMP, Double-Byte)	▶ + 50% ▶ Use application server (UTF-16)	▶ UTF-8*: up to + 10% ▶ UTF-16: + 30% to + 60%	▶ UTF-8 ▶ No additional hardware requirements
* + 35% is the maximum for small systems (database size < 200 GB), + 10% is the maximum for larger systems (database size > 200 GB)			

Table 3.3 Additional Hardware Requirements for Unicode Conversion

Additional storage
space needed on
the hard drive

▶ The additional hard-drive storage needed is primarily dependent on the Unicode format used in the database. The languages used under non-Unicode also influence the resources needed. In practice, Unicode conversion of UTF-8-type databases leads to a reduction in database size for most customers. This results from the combination of Unicode enlargement and a reduction due to reorganization effects. Because of the complex influence of many different factors, an exact forecast of added requirements for drive space is impossible. On average, customer systems with UTF-8-based databases (e.g., Oracle and IBM DB2 for Linux, Unix, or Windows) shrink by about 10% after Unicode conversion. For smaller systems, (with a database size of less than 200 GB) there may be an increase in size by up to 35%. This is because some SAP standard tables are no longer compressed under Unicode. This increase, however, is only noticeable in smaller systems.

Main storage
requirements

▶ In the main storage, an average additional requirement of about 50% has been measured at the SAP application-server level. The cause is the use of the UTF-16 format, which occupies (at least) 2 bytes for each character.

CPU requirements

▶ In the CPU area, an average increased requirement of 30% has been measured. Here, there are two possibilities to achieve the specified values: Either 30% faster CPUs can be used, or the number of CPUs can be increased by 30%. Generally the use of faster CPUs is preferred, as this actually compensates for the increased requirements, so that response times remain roughly constant. If only the number of CPUs is increased, then despite the hardware improvement there can be increased response times, given that a process may require more CPU capacity but can only run on a "slow" CPU. Normally, however, the response times are dependent on the average number of work processes per CPU as well. That metric falls as the number of CPUs increases with optimum load distribution, so response times should improve.

Requirements in
the network area

▶ With regard to the network, we need to distinguish between the back end and the front end. In the communication between the SAP GUI for Windows and the SAP system, there are no differences worth mentioning regarding bandwidth needs. The SAP GUI protocol compresses the data sent, and because the information content between Unicode and non-Unicode doesn't differ, there is no increase in resource requirements under Unicode. On the back end, there is generally a significantly higher network load from communication between the different application servers, because that communication is based on UTF-16. In the communication between database servers and application servers, the increased load again depends on the database used. For UTF-8-type databases (Oracle and IBM DB2 for Linux, Unix, or Windows) there is only a slight increase, because UTF-8 is used for communications.

Keep in mind that these numbers represent average values. Depending on the solution used, transaction, and load profile, the numbers may vary upwards or downwards for any given customer. Ultimately, only a conversion test and a direct comparison of the Unicode system with the non-Unicode system can provide final answers regarding the actual difference (in main memory, CPU, and drive storage).

Moreover, you should note that the values in Table 3.3 are based on the SAP application server. The values for increased resource requirements for the database can only be provided by each database manufacturer, and SAP makes no official statements in that regard.

Two Example Preparation Steps

The complex process of a Unicode conversion requires many individual preparation steps, which cannot all be described here. For that reason, we'll limit our discussion to two examples which should illustrate the type of preparations. In Section 3.2.2 we'll go into great detail on MDMP-specific preparation, as that is by far the most difficult and longest task in export preparation.

► **Generating the Unicode Nametab**
The nametabs (tables DDNTT and DDNTF) are tables on the database level. They contain entries with all significant table definitions. The database structure is ultimately reflected by the nametabs.

Adaptation of the nametab as a preparatory step in Unicode conversion

For every table, certain attributes are specified in the nametabs. One attribute is the length (in bytes) of each table field. Here, there is naturally a difference between a Unicode and a non-Unicode system, because in the UTF-16 format the length of a character-type field is twice as large as in non-Unicode. As a result, in the

Unicode system the length for character-type fields must be adjusted in the nametabs.

This task is performed by the report RADCUCNT. It fills the Unicode nametabs DDNTT_CONV_UC and DDNTF_CONV_UC—the shadow tables in the non-Unicode system—with the correct data in the right length for a Unicode system. In the Unicode system, the content of these shadow tables is then copied into the standard nametabs. As a result, in a conversion project, after the RADCUCNT report is completed there can be no new tables added to the system (and no changes to the table structure of existing tables), because these will not automatically be entered into the Unicode nametabs.

Using the UMG_SHOW_UCTABS report, it can be determined whether there are still inconsistencies between the non-Unicode nametabs and the Unicode nametabs. For the Unicode conversion, all DDNT* tables must be exported and imported in an R3load process[1].

The nametab entries can be displayed in the SAP system using the function modules DD_SHOW_NAMETAB and DD_SHOW_UC_NAMETAB. SAP Note 932779 describes in great detail the handling of nametabs during a Unicode conversion.

Special handling of Transaction SE63

▶ **Handling of the Translation Workbench**
Certain tables in the Translation Workbench—the central tool for translation of SAP texts (see Section 5.4.1)—cannot be converted using the standard tools, so they must be handled with their own tool. These are the tables of the proposal pool, which is also explained in more detail in Section 5.4.1.

Moreover, the Translation Workbench has also been completely reworked in basis Support Package 25—for Unicode compatibility as well as for other features—and the proposal pool is now stored in new tables. As a result, there are two different migration programs: one for the "new" tables and one for the tables using Transaction SE63 prior to basis Support Package 25, which was already available in June 2003.

Thus it will generally suffice to convert the new tables. However, in that case it should be noted that—if no conversion was per-

---

1 An R3load process is started during the export. For a more exact description, see Sections 3.2.2 and 3.2.3.

formed — all proposal values generated by transaction before basis Support Package 25 will not be taken into consideration. You can find more information on this in SAP Note 585116.

3.2.2   MDMP and Blended Code Page-Specific Steps

> **Note**
>
> In this section, we will generally be discussing MDMP systems. All the points addressed are also valid for ambiguous blended code pages (see Section 2.2.3). If there are additional restrictions, they will be listed.
>
> A few of the steps listed here, primarily the consistency check, must also be performed for a single code page system.

In an MDMP system (see also Chapter 2), there are the following basic problems: Several code pages are used in one database instance, and the code page in which the data is stored is generally *not* known at the database level. If, for instance, the table in which the entries are stored does not include a unique language key, then the code page used for storage cannot be reconstructed afterwards. For a conversion, however, the source and target code pages must be known for every database entry.

MDMP problems in Unicode conversion

When converting an MDMP system, therefore, in general the entire database (but at least the language-independent part of the database) must be scanned and all records containing no language keys for identification must be assigned a language using other means. That information can then be used during export to determine the source code page.

Such a scan of the entire database is time-consuming and generally cannot be performed during downtime (e. g., on the weekend). The SAP tool used for this purpose is the so-called *code page scanner* (Transaction SPUMG), which is available by default as of SAP Web AS 6.20[2]

Code page scanner

Because the code page scanner is run during production operation, in addition to Transaction SPUMG a repair of any incorrectly converted data in the Unicode system is also necessary. That task is performed by Transaction SUMG, which is run after successful conversion in the Unicode system.

---

2 For SAP R/3 release 4.6C, you can find more information on the code page scanner in Section 3.3.

Transactions SPUMG and SUMG are also undergoing continual improvements and extensions. Thus, new or changed functionality may be provided at the current support package level. The areas described here apply to basis Support Package 59 (in SAP Web AS 6.20). The greater part of the functionality should also be valid for later basis support packages and releases.

> **Tip**
>
> The latest information can always be found in the current Unicode Conversion Guide. Should there be contradictions between this description and the Guide, then the Guide should always be taken as more accurate, as it is continually updated.
>
> The Unicode Conversion Guide and many other Unicode notes are only available in English. Thus it is a good idea for the logon language to be EN when actions are taken in SPUMG or SUMG.

The conversion of an MDMP system is always released from a particular basis support package level specified in the Unicode Conversion Guide, and it can be performed without direct SAP support. For systems with very many or complex code pages, however, SAP recommends the assistance of SAP experts from Globalization Consulting.

General Process of Transaction SPUMG

Overview of the steps in SPUMG

Before looking at the individual steps in Transactions SPUMG and SUMG, you should get to know the general process involved.

▶ First, Transaction SPUMG (see Figure 3.4) is used to specify general settings for the scan. These involve, for instance, the definition of the language keys to be considered in the assignment, or certain vocabulary properties.

▶ Next is the consistency check, in which all tables are divided into various categories.

▶ Then, all areas with data are scanned whose source code pages cannot be unambiguously determined using a language key. This includes a scan of the language-independent tables, scan of the tables with ambiguous language information, and analysis of INDX-type tables. These scans fill the system vocabulary with words containing special characters.

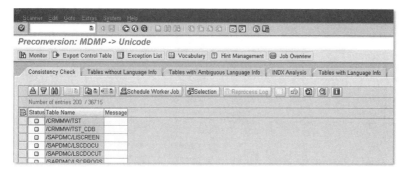

Figure 3.4 Transaction SPUMG

In the SAP system, you will occasionally see other terms, such as "glossary", used to refer to the system vocabulary. In this book, we consistently use the term "system vocabulary" or "vocabulary."

▸ After the scan is complete, there are numerous automatic or semi-automatic methods to maintain the system vocabulary; that is, to attach a language key to the words in use. This is also the scan of language-dependent tables, for instance. One of the methods for system vocabulary processing is manual assignment by users. Depending on the scope and number of languages, this phase can be extremely difficult.

System vocabulary

▸ After the system vocabulary is completely processed, a repair scan for INDX-type tables and a reprocessing scan for database entries not yet uniquely specified (e.g., those with very short word lengths) follow.

▸ In the last phase of Transaction SPUMG, the log from the reprocessing scan (the reprocessing log) must be edited.

▸ Now comes the export using R3load and the subsequent import into the Unicode system.

Figure 3.5 shows a schematic overview of the steps needed in Transaction SPUMG in the order they occur. The size or length of the boxes is not to scale regarding the duration of each step.

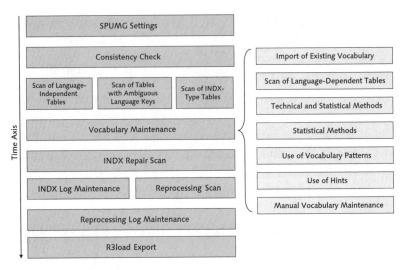

Figure 3.5 Overview of the Functions and Steps of Transaction SPUMG

In Transaction SUMG, the automatic repairs must be made based on the reprocessing log. There may also be a need to perform manual repairs in Transaction SUMG, for instance if the reprocessing log was not completely processed.

Preparations in Transaction SPUMG

Specification of SPUMG settings

Let's take it step by step. In the *language list*, all the languages used in the system and their code pages must be entered. Here, we make a distinction between active and inactive languages: Active languages can be used in the system vocabulary, inactive aren't. Inactive languages, however, are correctly converted in language-dependent tables by R3load, if a corresponding language key is detected.

Previously, the specification of *ambiguous languages* must be performed. Ambiguous languages in this context are those that cannot be uniquely assigned a code page based on the corresponding language key. This is the case, for instance, if the language key field only contains a blank. In the case of an ambiguous blended code page, however, the use of the English language key is possible with multiple code pages, so that in this special case English (EN) should also be specified as an ambiguous language.

Besides the *fallback code page*, which is used as a source code page in case of doubt, vocabulary properties must also be specified at the beginning of the SPUMG actions. These include the *minimum word length*, which defines the length (number of bytes) above which a word is written to the system vocabulary, as well as the specification of *word separator characters*.

To ensure that the database scans produce usable results, we must distinguish clearly between language-dependent and language-independent tables. In an initial, simplified approach, one could assume that all tables containing a language key are language-dependent, while all the rest are language-independent. But if you take a closer look, the following issues arise.

DDIC attribute "text language"

▶ What does it mean when a table has multiple language fields (see standard table T002T)?

▶ Under some circumstances, there are tables that may have a language key that says nothing about the code page of the data stored.

To address these problems, SAP Web AS 6.20 introduced a new DDIC attribute *text language* (**Text Lang.**), used by all fields of data type LANG. This flag serves as an indicator whether the language key contained should be used for conversion of the content of the line involved. For each table, there may be only one active flag.

In the standard table T002T (language names), for instance, there are two fields of type LANG: T002T-SPRAS and T002T-SPRSL. For T002T-SPRAS, the text language flag is set, but for T002T-SPRSL it is not activated. Correspondingly, in Unicode conversion the language key in field T002T-SPRAS is used to determine the source-code page.

In Figure 3.6, the table is shown using Transaction SE11. By double-clicking on the corresponding table field, you can also view the properties of this field in another window. There, the flag can be found in the lower left area. In the case of the SPRAS field it is set, and for the SPRSL field it isn't.

Depending on the release, it also may be necessary prior to the conversion to use the RADNTLANG report to set the flag for SAP standard tables. Here, the report is started and the results at least spot checked for the customer tables. Problems in this area can generally be detected at least during vocabulary maintenance in Transaction SPUMG.

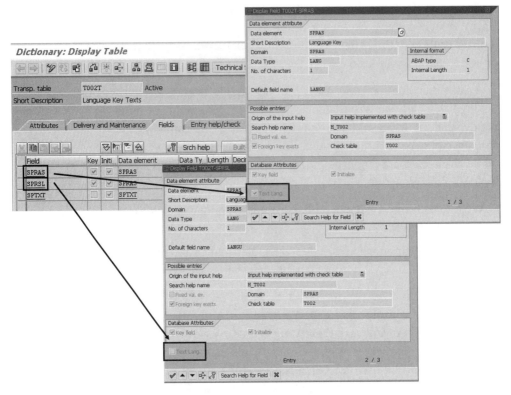

Figure 3.6 Text Language Flag in Table T002T

Besides its use in Transaction SPUMG, the text language flag also plays a role in RFC communications between Unicode and MDMP systems (see Section 3.5).

General information on SPUMG scans

Because the results of the SPUMG scan comprise a large amount of data, filtering options are essential. Thus every view of a scan result can be filtered using selection options (using the **Selection** button). For instance, the view can be restricted to display only erroneous tables or tables with warnings.

Figure 3.7 shows an example scan of language-dependent tables. In the selection window called up with the button, different selections are entered. A limitation to **200** lines is currently the default setting. In this example, the display has been limited to tables with warnings (**Warning Type = 5**), so that only those tables are displayed from which text with special characters has actually entered the system vocabulary.

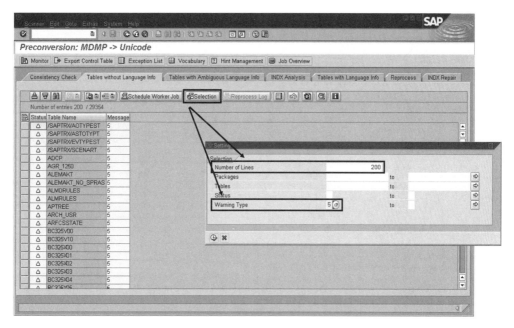

Figure 3.7 Example of the Use of the Selection Button

During the scan it is important that you know how many tables have already been processed. This can be read off very easily using the *scan monitor*'s **Monitor** button. This gives you a good overview of the momentary status of all relevant SPUMG scans. In particular, you can see how many tables if any created problems on each scan.

Figure 3.8 shows the scan monitor. In the **Worklist Overview** area, all the scan areas are listed. Here, you can see how many tables are being processed (in the **In Process** column), how many have not yet been processed (**Initial** column), and how many have already been completely scanned (**Completed** column). In the lower area, you can also see directly which SPUMG-specific batch jobs are still running. In this example, all scans except the INDEX repair scan were executed successfully.

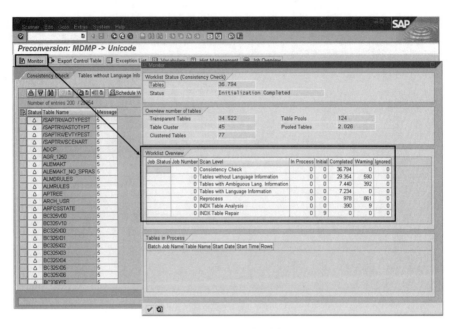

Figure 3.8 Scan Monitor in Transaction SPUMG

Start of Scan Phases

Initialization of the worklist

In the next step, the worklist for the consistency check (and thus for all of Transaction SPUMG) is constructed. All the tables in the nametab are entered into the table list for the consistency check. At the end of the initialization, all database tables with a gray status (not yet processed) are displayed in the area of the consistency check. If new tables are introduced into the system, the worklist can be adjusted accordingly (**Update Worklist**). This means that all new tables not yet known are included in the scans, and the various scans can be performed again for these tables.

Exception lists

It may be desirable for a number of reasons for certain tables either not to be considered in the SPUMG scans or for the content of those tables to be assigned exclusively to one code page in the SPUMG scans. Thus there is the option of adding a table to the so-called *exception list*. Here, you can define which source code page should be used to convert the entire contents of the table.

You can reach the exception list using the **Exception List** button in Transaction SPUMG. In Figure 3.9, you can clearly see how a table is entered into the customer-specific exception list. Using the **Insert**

Entries button, you can insert arbitrary tables into the exception list. Then you must enter the table names, and if necessary the language key field, the table category (see below), and the code page that should be used for all table entries.

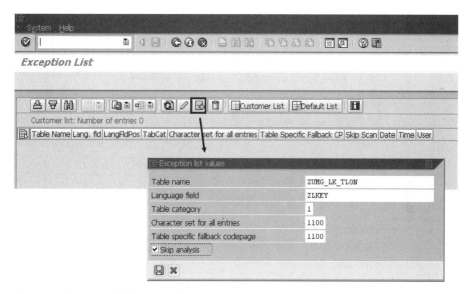

Figure 3.9 Entering a Table into the Exception List

Using the flag **Skip analysis** you can specify whether the table should still be handled in the SPUMG scans. If you check this flag, the table will not be scanned. Of course, you should be sure that all entries in the tables inserted into the exception list are actually supposed to be assigned to one code page, or that the content in these tables which may deviate from the conversion code page really isn't needed any longer.

In addition to this list, there is also a *default exception list* into which a series of tables are entered by default. These are chiefly SAP tables which are no longer used as of SAP Web AS 6.20.

Entry of a table in the exception list simply means that that table will be left out of the SPUMG scan if the **Skip Analysis** flag is turned on. It will still be included in the export and the import. Complete exclusion of a table from export can only be achieved by deleting it entirely or by removing the entries for the table from the R3load export control file. This should naturally only be done for customer tables, and only if it is absolutely clear that the table is no longer used. Alternatively, you can also delete the contents of the table, so that the conversion of the table causes only a minimum of effort.

In the subsequent consistency check, spot checks are made to check whether the data in each table is readable. Moreover, there is a division of the tables into the following two categories:

- ▶ **Category 1**
  All tables containing code-page-dependent data that have language keys with activated text language flags

- ▶ **Category 2**
  All tables containing code-page-dependent data that do not have language keys with activated text language flags

In the following scans, the category of a table can still change. If Transaction SPUMG determined that the table has no special characters, the category is updated to 3:

- ▶ **Category 3**
  Tables which only contain US-7-ASCII data and are thus code-page-independent

Generally, the content of tables in Category 2 is the largest part of the system vocabulary. Those tables are therefore particularly important.

In the *export control table*, all tables are stored with their categories and other relevant properties. The export control table is basically the repository of Transaction SPUMG. You can jump to the export control table using the **Export Control Table** button in Transaction SPUMG.

In Figure 3.10, you can see an excerpt of the export control table. Here you can already see that many SAP standard tables are assigned to Category 3 (**TabCat** column); that is, that they may not have any language key but this is actually not needed, as no special characters are used.

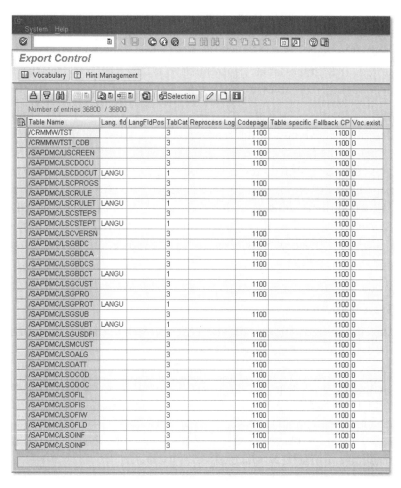

Figure 3.10 Excerpt from the Export Control Table

Scans to Construct the System Vocabulary

After the consistency check comes the scan of the tables in Category 2: the language-independent tables. This scan fills the system vocabulary with words containing special characters. The greater part of the system vocabulary is inserted during this scan. This is also the scan that generally takes the longest time.

Scan of the language-independent tables

In the next step, language-dependent tables are analyzed that contain ambiguous language keys. Here, too, all words from corresponding entries with special characters are inserted into the system vocabulary.

Scan of tables with ambiguous language information

INDX-type table
analysis

The scan of the INDX-type tables is the last of the series of scans responsible for the construction of the system vocabulary. INDX-type tables have a transparent area and a binary area in which data is stored. INDX-type tables can also have a language key. Language-dependent INDX tables are not scanned.

The transparent areas of INDX-type tables are handled in the scans described above and in the reprocessing scan. The INDX scan only examines the binary area (content of the field CLUSTD) of the tables. This area also normally stores the code page used in the record (code page information EXPORT TO DATABASE/IMPORT FROM DATABASE). In MDMP systems, however, this code page is not always correctly derived; that is, the entry may be incorrect. The scan of INDX-type tables extracts words with special characters from the entries listed and inserts it into the system vocabulary.

System Vocabulary

General
description

During the conversion of the database, *for each table entry* (for each row), the source code page must be determined. It would be easy to conclude that a large directory with all relevant table entries is created without language keys and that for each table entry the language keys are assigned in Transaction SPUMG. But because that would lead to an extremely large number of different entries for large databases that probably could only be edited per table, the decision was made to construct a *word-based system vocabulary*.

That means that in each scan from the texts in the database entry, so-called "words" are extracted and then written into the system vocabulary. Repeated words are thus written to the vocabulary only once. If, for instance, an entry contains the text string FRANK MÜLLER, MÜNCHEN, then this string is broken down into three words:

▶ FRANK

▶ MÜLLER

▶ MÜNCHEN

The last two words are written to the vocabulary because they contain special characters. This assumes that the system is not an MDMP system for Eastern and Western Europe only (Latin-1 and Latin-2). In that special case, the German special characters (umlauts) are included in both code pages, and with the standard settings German words will not be written to the vocabulary. It makes no difference whether the Eastern or Western European code page is used for the conversion.

Figure 3.11 shows a diagram of word extraction and the insertion of these German words into the vocabulary using the concrete example of an entry in the CDPOS table.

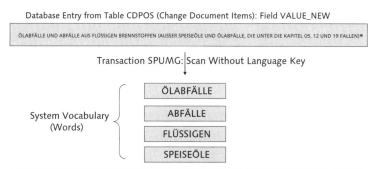

Database Entry from Table CDPOS (Change Document Items): Field VALUE_NEW

ÖLABFÄLLE UND ABFÄLLE AUS FLÜSSIGEN BRENNSTOFFEN (AUSSER SPEISEÖLE UND ÖLABFÄLLE, DIE UNTER DIE KAPITEL 05, 12 UND 19 FALLEN)*

Transaction SPUMG: Scan Without Language Key

System Vocabulary (Words)

ÖLABFÄLLE

ABFÄLLE

FLÜSSIGEN

SPEISEÖLE

* OIL WASTE AND WASTE FROM LIQUID FUELS (EXCEPT FOR EDIBLE OILS AND OIL WASTE THAT APPLIES TO CHAPTERS 05, 12, AND 19)

Figure 3.11 Extraction of Words with Special Characters from the CDPOS Table

The advantages of this *word-based* process in contrast with the listing of database entries are obvious. The volume of data to be edited is significantly smaller (as repeated words are used only once), and all words can be written to a central table and edited there relatively easily. This table can also be reused in other SAP systems without serious limitations. Database entries made after the scan process and containing only words known and edited in the system vocabulary cause no additional effort.

After the system vocabulary has been edited, the code page information for each *word* must be transferred back to the table entry level. This takes place during the conversion using the tool R3load. This uses the edited system vocabulary to determine during database export which source code page should be used to convert the entire database entry.

Figure 3.12 shows the corresponding process for the example of CDPOS from Figure 3.11: R3load determines the source code page for the conversion based on the language assignment of the words found in the database entry, using special characters in the edited system vocabulary.

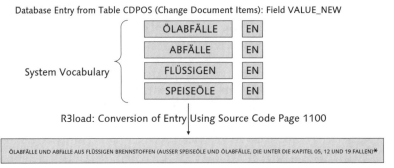

Database Entry from Table CDPOS (Change Document Items): Field VALUE_NEW

R3load: Conversion of Entry Using Source Code Page 1100

ÖLABFÄLLE UND ABFÄLLE AUS FLÜSSIGEN BRENNSTOFFEN (AUSSER SPEISEÖLE UND ÖLABFÄLLE, DIE UNTER DIE KAPITEL 05, 12 UND 19 FALLEN)*

* OIL WASTE AND WASTE FROM LIQUID FUELS (EXCEPT FOR EDIBLE OILS AND OIL WASTE THAT APPLIES TO CHAPTERS 05, 12, AND 19)

Figure 3.12 Transfer of Language Information from the System Vocabulary

Here, there can be problems; in some cases these occur because entries in the system vocabulary haven't been edited or unknown words have been added since the database scan. The reprocess phase and subsequence manual editing of the reprocessing log should automatically correct most of the errors occurring in the Unicode system in Transaction SUMG, however.

Editing the System Vocabulary

Scan of the language-dependent tables

The subsequent scan of the language-dependent tables serves to assign languages to words in the system vocabulary. If this step finds a word in a language-dependent table whose hex byte combination is identical to an entry in the system vocabulary, then the corresponding language key is assigned to the word in the system vocabulary. The prerequisite for a correct assignment is that only words with correct code pages are included in the entries. If the scan finds the German word "München," for instance, with both German and Russian language keys, then there is a *vocabulary collision*.

> **Note**
>
> The scan of the language-dependent tables is optional, so it can be omitted if there are many problematic entries in the language-dependent tables.

In the following list, several options for automatic or semiautomatic vocabulary maintenance are shown. Depending on the code page combination, it can be that the editing sequence suggested here must be adapted. The top priority is to reduce manual editing to a minimum.

▶ **Vocabulary transfer**

It is possible to transfer vocabulary contents between SAP systems. The table UMGPMDIT is introduced for this purpose, which basically serves as a buffer for edited vocabulary entries. If a transfer of vocabulary entries is to be performed, it takes place only using this table (in Transaction SPUMG, we speak of an "external vocabulary" in this case). You can import the contents of the table—which then generally comes from another system—into the system vocabulary, or export the edited entries from the system vocabulary into the UMGPMDIT table.

Exchanging contents of vocabulary between systems

The import takes place using the class CL_UMG_AL_IMPORT and the **Auto Assign** button in vocabulary maintenance. The export, on the other hand, can simply be started with the **Export** button (see Figure 3.13).

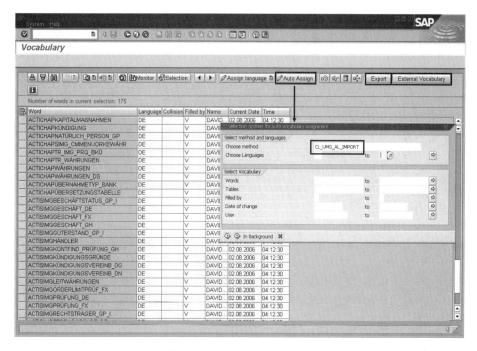

Figure 3.13 Export and Import in Vocabulary Maintenance

To transfer the contents of the UMGPMDIT table—i. e., the external vocabulary—into a different system, there are two options:

▷ Using a local upload and download, the data can be placed on the front-end. Local *.vocabulary files are created in this step.

▷ Alternatively, the table contents can also be transferred to the other systems using a normal transport order.

Figure 3.14 shows an excerpt from the view of the external vocabulary stored in table UMGPMDIT. In vocabulary maintenance, the **External Vocabulary** button takes to this view. Figure 3.14 shows the **Upload** and **Download** buttons in a frame: Here is where the vocabulary can be transferred locally. In this view, too, the standard tools for selection and the monitor are available.

A vocabulary transfer makes sense after vocabulary editing in other SAP systems (such as the sandbox system) have already concluded. The vocabulary can then be reused, for instance in the production system. Any other MDMP systems in the system landscape can be supplied with this system vocabulary as well (see also SAP Note 756535).

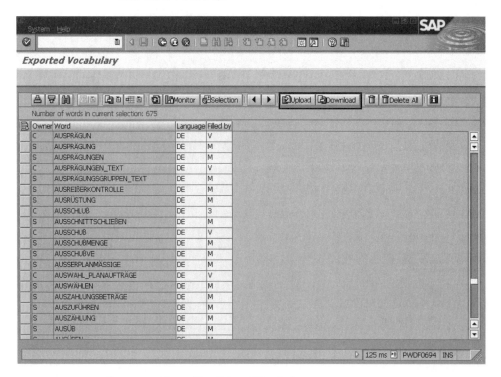

Figure 3.14 View of the External Vocabulary

In a typical scenario, vocabulary transport works in such a way that a Unicode conversion is tested in a sandbox system SBX. This results in an edited system vocabulary. This is then exported in Transaction SPUMG on the SBX into table UMGPMDIT. The content of the UMGPMDIT table is saved in a transport order before the conversion of the SBX system. This transport order can be imported into the development system DEV. After conclusion of the INDEX scan in DEV, the contents can now be imported from the external vocabulary in Transaction SPUMG.

▶ **SAP standard tools for language determination**
The Japanese code page Shift-JIS uses certain hex code ranges which are not occupied by other SAP standard code pages. This can be utilized by the CL_UMG_AL_TECHNICAL_PROPERTIES class. As a result, in this case the code page can be determined simply on the basis of technical attributes.

Using automatic SAP tools, you can assign a part of the vocabulary

Using statistical means, it can be determined with a certain probability which code page was used for a corresponding word. For this to work, you need statistical data for the languages involved. This option is used by the classes CL_UMG_AL_NA_CHARSTAT (for Single-Byte languages) and CL_UMG_AL_YA_CHARSTAT (for Asian languages).

▶ **Vocabulary processing with so-called "patterns"**
Certain hex-byte combinations are typical for specific languages. For instance, in German there is a typical component "keit," that occurs in only a few other languages. If you search the system vocabulary for *keit*, the probability that only German words will be selected is relatively large. In the appendix to SAP Note 871541, corresponding components (patterns) are listed for numerous languages. The SAP Note also includes an introduction to how the appendices should be used.

Use of patterns can contribute to vocabulary maintenance

As with all other semiautomatic or automatic methods for vocabulary processing, however, customers should always check whether the result is correct.

▶ **Report UMG_VOCABULARY_STATISTIC**
The UMG_VOCABULARY_STATISTIC report is used to identify tables with the most unedited words, namely entries without language keys assigned, in the system vocabulary. These are generally the tables for which the use of hints (to be discussed shortly) will pay off best. However, they may also be tables with language keys for

Identification of tables with many unedited language keys

which the text language flag is not set. In that case, you should check whether the flag should be set and the table then will be removed from the scan of language-independent tables.

As an alternative to this report, the table information can also be used in Transaction SPUMG which is called using **Extras · Table Information**. That provides a still more detailed overview for either individual tables or for all tables.

For tables with many vocabulary entries, hints can reduce the effort of manual mainte-nance

▶ **Use of "hints"**

Transaction SPUMG draws a distinction between language-depen-dent and language-independent data based on the existing lan-guage key and the associated text language flag. Other indicators, like the company code or the country, on the other hand, are ignored. So it is possible to use hints based on arbitrary indicators to perform an "automatic" assignment in the system vocabulary.

For instance, if a table has 10,000 entries without language keys but with a country code JP (Japan), you could define a hint on that table which, when executed, would assign all the corresponding words in the system vocabulary JA.

Just like the vocabulary, hints can either be transferred via table contents or by using a local upload and download.

The following examples of fields generally provide some informa-tion about the source code page of the data contained:

▶ Country field (field with data element LAND1) over table T005
Example table: PA0006-LAND1

▶ Company code (field with data element BUKRS) over table T001
Example table: BSEG-BUKRS, PA0001-BUKRS

▶ Plant number (field with data element WERKS_D) over table T001W
Example table: MSEG-WERKS, LIPS-WERKS

Manual editing of the vocabulary

After all the automatic or semiautomatic methods for vocabulary editing described above are exhausted, the remainder of the vocabu-lary not yet assigned a language key must be edited manually. SAP urgently recommends that employees who know the corresponding language very well do the editing. Ideally, it should be done by native speakers who grew up in a country with the language involved.

Moreover, for languages from different code pages (according to the MDMP rules) it is absolutely essential for the editors of the vocabulary to log on in the correct language, as otherwise the texts will not be displayed correctly and will thus not be identifiable. For instance, Russian editors must log on in Russian (RU). For languages within one code page (like French, Spanish, and Dutch, for instance) it is enough to log on in any one of those languages.

The display of the unassigned words in the vocabulary is performed by selecting the language Blank in the selection criteria in the vocabulary view. Figure 3.15 shows the selection options in the system vocabulary. The current default settings limit the display to 500 words.

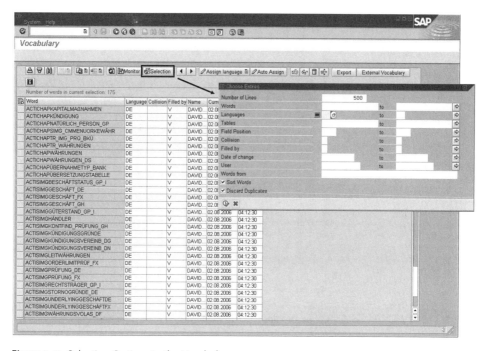

Figure 3.15 Selection Options in the Vocabulary

Words currently being edited are not locked; there is currently no blocking mechanism when editing the vocabulary.

The system vocabulary should be edited as completely as possible at the end of manual processing; that is, there should be only very few words without an assigned language key. Under some circumstances, unassigned words may cause additional effort in reprocessing.

Fill categories For final control of how maintenance of vocabulary entries is maintained, each is assigned a fill category. This allows a check to be performed of which process caused each language entry. In Table 3.4, the fill categories and their meanings are listed. These entries show the possible variants of vocabulary maintenance.

Value	Meaning	Comments
2	Automatically generated entry (scan of language-independent tables)	Initial entry: language field in system vocabulary is empty
A	Automatically generated entry (scan of tables with non-unique language keys)	Initial entry: language field in system vocabulary is empty
I	Caused by analysis of INDX-type tables	Initial entry: language field in system vocabulary is empty
R	Manual reset	There is no initial value; the language field was reset to empty
3	Automatic assignment (scan of tables with language keys)	Lang key was determined by entry in language-dependent table
H	Hint	Language key was determined by hint
M	Manual assignment	User determined language key
V	Vocabulary transfer	Lang assignment was performed in a different system and then imported by vocabulary transfer
C	Technical properties	Language assignment using CL_UMG_AL_TECHNICAL_PROPERTIES method
S	Assignment by character statistics	Language assignment using CL_UMG_AL_NA_CHARSTAT or CL_UMG_AL_YA_CHARSTAT methods

Table 3.4 Fill Categories and Their Meanings

Scans after Vocabulary Editing

Repair of INDX-type tables The scans after vocabulary editing describe the only step in which data on the non-Unicode source system is actually changed by Transaction SPUMG.

This phase performs any repair necessary of the code page for binary entries in the language-independent INDX-type tables. That means the existing number of the code page (e. g., 1100) is replaced by the correct number (e. g., 1401 for an Eastern European text). Analogous to the reprocessing scan (see below), in this step a so-called *INDX log* is written, in case information from the system vocabulary is not unambiguous or is contradictory. The INDX log should be edited analogously to the reprocessing log, so that automatic repairs can be made in Transaction SUMG on the target system.

After conclusion of the previous scans, there may still be entries in the database that have not been assigned. But it can also be the case that the info from the system vocabulary is contradictory. For instance, suppose that one word from a database entry has been identified as German and another from the same data entry as Japanese. This is why the step of *reprocessing* was introduced. Here is where all entries of words are handled which were assigned no language key in the vocabulary (that is, non-edited vocabulary entries). But there are also entries in the reprocessing log for words whose lengths are shorter than the minimum word length specified in the settings.

Reprocessing

The reprocessing log is inherently different from the vocabulary: It is not word-based, but rather shows database entries (or more precisely, code page-dependent parts of database entries) for each table.

In Figure 3.16, you can see reprocessing logs from the CSKU table. In the left column is the **Key**, in the middle part the actual **Text**, and in the right part the **Reason** why this entry was written to the reprocessing log. In the example shown, the entries in the system vocabulary were not edited (**Reason=3**), and that's why this table entry was written to the log. In Figure 3.16, you can also see the other reasons which can lead to an entry. In the **Language** column on the far right, you can also assign the corresponding language.

R3load does *not* use the information from the reprocessing log during conversion. The data is instead automatically repaired afterwards in the Unicode system in Transaction SUMG. To do so, the information about the source code page used during conversion of the corresponding entry during export from R3load is written to *.xml files. These are then evaluated afterwards in Transaction SUMG together with the reprocessing log.

Information from the reprocessing log can also be transferred between non-Unicode SAP systems. However, in that case this works only through local upload or download.

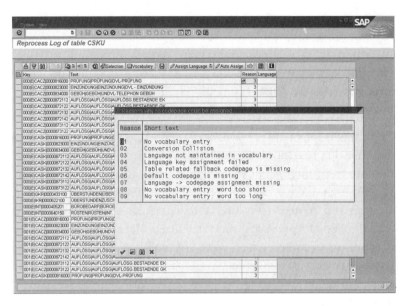

Figure 3.16 Reprocessing Log for Table CSKU

After the reprocessing logs have been edited as completely as possible, the SPUMG-specific tasks of the Unicode conversion are complete.

Delta Problems

Handling of texts that enter the database after the SPUMG scan Because Transaction SPUMG is a tool which is normally run during production operation, there is a possibility that data might be created which is not caught by the SPUMG scan. Here, we can distinguish between two areas:

- ▶ **New or changed tables**

  If new tables are transported into the system (for instance, by support packages), these must absolutely be made known to Transaction SPUMG. In addition, the necessary scans for the tables affected must be repeated.

  This is quite possible, but for many tables along with their contents it may take some time. Thus SAP strongly recommends a transport freeze on DDIC changes during the time from the last SPUMG scan in the production system until production conversion.

▶ **New data entries with special characters**

New data entries in existing tables are converted with the global fallback code page as source code page, if an assignment is not possible using the existing vocabulary. For this case, an entry is made in the corresponding XML log, and the text may need to be repaired manually in Transaction SUMG.

To keep the problems with new database entries to a minimum, the SPUMG scans on the production system should be finished as closely as possible to the start of the database export. At least one test run of Transaction SPUMG should be performed on the production system, as this is the only way to estimate the length of the SPUMG scan.

R3load

The actual Unicode conversion is performed outside SAP Web Application Server. That means that you cannot perform the export or import using an SAP transaction like Transaction SPUMG, but rather must manage it with different tools on the operating system level. Since the SAP Web AS must be taken down during the export for consistency reasons, the export can naturally not be controlled by an SAP transaction. For the import, there is generally not even an SAP system available that can run it, so no SAP transaction would be possible.

Tool on the operating system level

As the main export/import tool on the operating system level, the program R3load is used for Unicode conversion, while R3ldctl and R3szchk also exist for special tasks. R3load is comparable to the transport tool R3trans, which also must be run directly at the operating system level with the corresponding parameters. Besides those parameters, R3load is also controlled by a number of control files.

To make it less onerous to generate those files by hand, SAP provides the front-end tool SAPinst, so that the necessary entries can be made using appropriate windows. One of these windows which is important for the Unicode conversion is shown in Figure 3.17. Here, under the point **Data File Code Page**, depending on your CPU type, you must enter either **4103** (UTF-16 Little Endian) or **4102** (UTF-16 Big Endian).

SAPinst

Figure 3.17 SAPinst Input Window for Determination of the Unicode Format and the Number of R3load Processes

R3load can be parallelized by calling the program n times with different control files. Different tables are then exported at the same time. Each call is called an *R3load process*. In Figure 3.17, you can also see that you can use the **Number of Parallel Jobs** field to determine how many parallel R3load processes should be started. The number of processes possible is generally limited by the number of CPUs used. As a rule of thumb, each CPU can run two to three R3load processes.

SAPinst and R3load, by the way, are also used during new installations and OS/DB migrations, so they are not Unicode-specific tools.

R3load export– MDMP-specific behavior and interplay with Transaction SPUMG

During export, R3load is used to convert all language-dependent tables corresponding to the existing unique language key. If R3load detects an ambiguous language key (e. g., a blank language key field) in the same table and special characters are contained in the database entry, the corresponding words are searched for in the system vocabulary.

▶ If they are found in the vocabulary and also have a language key there, R3load converts this database entry with the source code page belonging to the language key detected.

▶ If all associated words have not been edited in the vocabulary, R3load uses the global fallback code page and writes a log entry into the corresponding XML log.

All entries in the tables in Category 2, that is, the language-independent tables, are treated analogously to the entries with ambiguous language keys.

The `R3load` import does not distinguish between an MDMP and a single code page system; there are no MDMP-specific steps. The conversion is after all already finished in this phase, and the Unicode data "only" need to be imported into the system.

R3load import

SUMG Processing in the Unicode System

After conclusion of the database import in the Unicode system, the repair of incorrectly converted data takes place in Transaction SUMG. First, the XML logs written by `R3load` are loaded into the transaction. If reprocessing log entries with language keys exist here, Transaction SUMG can automatically repair these database entries. If no reprocessing log or only a non-edited log (without language keys) exists, then the corresponding entry must be edited manually. This applies as well to the delta entries described above.

Using Transaction SUMG, incorrectly converted texts can be automatically or manually repaired

In manual editing, there also can be hints created which can automatically repair a great number of entries.

Example of SPUMG Functionality

In the following, SPUMG functionality is shown based on a very simple example. Here, the database is reduced to the contents of two test tables: one language-independent and one language-dependent table (INDX-type tables are omitted for simplicity's sake).

SPUMG functionality

We assume that this is a system with Western European, Eastern European, and Russian data (code pages 8859-1, 8859-2, and 8859-5; in SAP notation those are 1100, 1401, and 1500).

In Figure 3.18 and Table 3.5, the language-independent entries of table UMG_TEST_10 are shown; Figure 3.18, however, only shows the view of these tables with logon language EN in Transaction SE16. You can see that the Russian and Polish names do not appear correctly. In Table 3.5, on the other hand, the hex codes are listed as they appear in an MDMP system in the database, with the correct characters in the first column.

PERSON	TOWN
FRANK MÜLLER	MÜNCHEN
PETRŮ LUKÁ©	PRAHA
½ ⁰³/₄»⁰¹ ⁰³/₄²⁰»µ²	MOSCOW

Figure 3.18 MDMP View (Logon Language EN) of the Contents of the Language-Independent Example Table UMG_TEST_10

F	R	A	N	K		M	Ü	L	L	E	R	
46	52	41	4E	4B	20	4D	DC	4C	4C	45	52	
P	E	T	R	Ů		L	U	K	Á	Š		
50	45	54	52	D9	20	4C	55	4B	C1	A9		
Н	И	К	О	Л	А	Й		К	О	В	А	Л	Е	В
BD	B8	BA	BE	BB	B0	B9	20	BA	BE	B2	B0	BB	B5	B2

Table 3.5 Hex Codes in the Standard MDMP System

Figure 3.19 makes it clear how table UMG_TEST_10 has to look in the Unicode system after correct conversion. In contrast to the MDMP system, all texts are correctly displayed here. In the corresponding Table 3.6, you can now see the hex codes of the first column in the table, as they are used in a UTF-8-type database.

PERSON	TOWN
FRANK MÜLLER	MÜNCHEN
LUKÁŠ PETRŮ	PRAHA
НИКОЛАЙ КОВАЛЕВ	MOSCOW

Figure 3.19 Contents of the Language-Independent Example Table UMG_TEST_10, as It Should Appear in a Unicode System

F	R	A	N	K		M	Ü	L	L	E	R	
46	52	41	4E	4B	20	4D	C39C	4C	4C	45	52	
P	E	T	R	Ů		L	U	K	Á	Š		
50	45	54	52	C5AE	20	4C	55	4B	C381	C5A0		
Н	И	К	О	Л	А	Й		К	О	В	А	Л	Е	В
D09D	D0B8	D0BA	D0BE	D0BB	D0B0	D0B9	20	D09A	D0BE	D0B2	D0B0	D0BB	D0B5	D0B2

Table 3.6 Hex Codes in the UTF-8 Format

The conversion of table UMG_TEST_10 into Unicode thus consists of "transferring" the hex code from Table 3.5 into the hex codes from Table 3.6 (with the assumption that this is a UTF-8-type database). To achieve this, the table is scanned by Transaction SPUMG.

The content of the language-dependent table UMG_TEST_6 is shown in Figure 3.20. Here, you can again see typical MDMP behavior, because Figure 3.20 was created with the logon language set to English. This table, too, is scanned by Transaction SPUMG.

NAME	SPRAS	MORETEXT
MOSCOW	R	$^{03}/_4{}^{2°}$»µ²
PÜMPER		KÖLN

Figure 3.20 Contents of the Language-Dependent Example Table UMG_TEST_6 as Shown in the MDMP System

In the first step (consistency check) the tables are categorized. In the second step (scan of language-independent tables), the table UMG_TEST_10 is scanned. This leads to the corresponding entries in the system vocabulary.

SPUMG execution

The word "FRANK" is not entered into the system vocabulary, for instance, because this only contains characters from the US-7-ASCII range (that is, no special characters), and is therefore code-page independent. The Russian name "КОВАЛЕВ" or the German name "MÜLLER", on the other hand, reaches the system vocabulary, as they contain special characters.

Next is the scan of tables with ambiguous language information. Because table UMG_TEST_6 also contains entries with blank language keys and special characters, these entries are also written to the system vocabulary.

Figure 3.21 shows different views of the system vocabulary entries by logon language after the scan of the tables with ambiguous language information. At left is the logon with EN, in the middle the logon with PL, and on the right the logon with RU. The result is intentionally shown here in a "triple view."

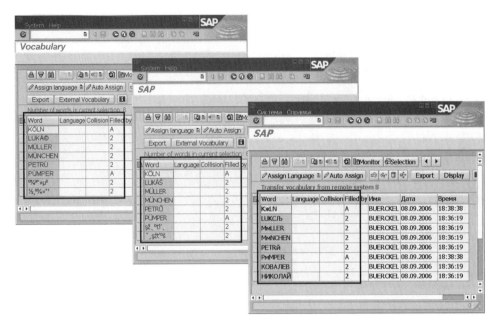

Figure 3.21 Entries in the System Vocabulary

To maintain the texts, a Russian employee must log on in Russian; otherwise the texts cannot be identified. The same applies to the Polish employee.

Finally, the scan of the language-dependent tables is performed. Because the word "КОВАЛЕВ" appears in both table UMG_TEST_6 and in UMG_TEST_10, the language key RU of that entry from UMG_TEST_6 is written to the system vocabulary (in Figure 3.20 you only see an "R" in field SPRAS, as this view shows only the one-character language key). As a result, this word need not be entered manually. This is visible in Figure 3.22 (entry RU for "КОВАЛЕВ"); for simplicity's sake, in this figure only the view with logon language RU is shown.

Figure 3.22 thus shows the state of the system vocabulary at the end of the main scan. At that point, the other options for system vocabulary editing must have been exhausted. At this point, all words should have been assigned, and R3load can convert the corresponding table entries with the correct source code page. In the Unicode system, then, the desired result appears, as shown in Table 3.6 or Figure 3.19.

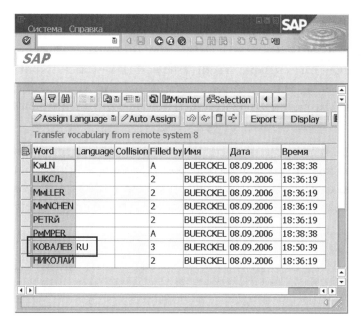

Figure 3.22 Entries in the System Vocabulary after the Scan of Language-Dependent Tables (Logon Language RU)

3.2.3 Export and Import

After all preparations are finished, the actual Unicode conversion takes place. The entire SAP system is exported in a database-independent format and converted into Unicode at the same time. This process is controlled by a series of R3load control and log files. In the previous section, the process and the MDMP-specific behavior of the tools were already explained. A good and detailed description of the process and the files can be found in *The SAP OS/DB Migration Project Guide* (SAP PRESS Essentials, 2005).

Description of the R3load process

Note

As of SAP NetWeaver 2004, texts from the Java stack may also need to be exported and imported. The Jload utility is used to do so (as a follow-on to R3load). A Unicode converstion is not necessary for these texts, however, because they were already created in Unicode.

SAP Note 795264 gives more detailed information on the handling of Java texts in a system copy or Unicode conversion.

It is natural to ask whether the existing database can be converted within a downtime tolerable to the application. Unfortunately, this question cannot be answered satisfactorily in the great majority of cases without corresponding testing, as the actual downtime is influenced by a large number of parameters. Using SAP Note 957081, customers can perform rough estimates of export or import times depending on the hardware in use.

Figure 3.23 shows a series of actual conversion times (start of export to end of import; preparation and post-processing times are not taken into consideration) depending on customer database size. As you can clearly see, there is no particular regularity to be discerned.

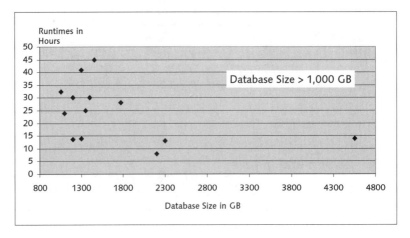

Figure 3.23 Examples of Export/Import Conversion Runtimes

Reasons for rather poor throughput or conversion times can be very different for each system.

▶ The customer only used one server; that is, the non-Unicode system was deleted and then the Unicode system was implemented on the same server.

▶ A customer has a relatively large downtime window, so that the necessity of performance optimization was rather low.

▶ On the non-Unicode side there was slow hardware, so the export times were longer.

▶ There were extremely large cluster tables that could not be broken down into smaller R3load packages (no table split).

Reasons for good conversion times can be derived from the following aspects:

▸ Very good hardware was used, possibly because corresponding servers with many CPUs were already planned for other systems (but those systems don't exist yet).

▸ The options for performance optimization were used; e. g., a table split or an unsorted export.

As a matter of principle, the majority of customers who have systems larger than a terabyte will be executing the import on separate hardware, since in this case the export and import can run in parallel. This is also a prerequisite for the use of other optimization methods, such as the *distribution monitor* or the *IMIG procedure*, which will be introduced below.

Possibilities for Runtime and Performance Optimization

The export/import procedure can in principle be performed in two different ways. On the one hand, it is possible to do first the export on a server, then to delete the non-Unicode system after completion, then construct the new Unicode system on the same hardware. On the other hand, you gain a lot of time if you can perform the import on a new, separate server. In that case, the export and import can at least partly be performed in parallel. Moreover, the old Unicode system is available for the time after the conversion as a reference system.

It is therefore recommended to use this *two-server method* for very large databases or for MDMP conversions. In support, SAP provides a so-called *migration monitor* (see SAP Note 784118). This ensures that completely exported packages are imported as quickly as possible on the Unicode side.

Because there are large requirements for CPU resources during a Unicode conversion, it is possible to use additional CPU modules to start more R3load processes and thus to increase the export speed.

> **Optimization of database parameters**
>
> The standard settings of the database parameters recommended by SAP apply for the normal operation of an SAP system. The export/import procedure, however, places very different requirements on the database, so that adaptation of the parameters can be used to improve the speed. In SAP Note 936441, there are some suggestions for the improvement of performance for Oracle databases listed.

Optimization of R3load Distribution and Table Split

Long-running exports and imports

When using the SAPinst standard settings, the tables of the SAP system are divided into about 15 packages according to a default schema, which are then each assigned an R3load process. In this scenario, it is very probable that some of the packages contain particularly large tables, while the rest of the packages are filled with smaller tables. As a result the R3load processes with the larger packages become long-running processes, while the other processes are finished very quickly. At the conclusion of the export process, there is frequently still one process running and the server is not running with a full load. This problem naturally propagates to the import, given that long-running exports are typically also long-running imports.

Ultimately, only a few large tables determine the conversion times. The situation might be amenable to improvement if the SAPinst option for the use of separate packages for the 50 largest tables is activated. Here, an additional 50 packages are created which each contain one of the 50 largest tables.

Figure 3.24 shows the SAPinst input window responsible for this setting. You can activate this package split under the point Largest Tables in Separate Packages.

Table split

Under some circumstances, however, this measure is not at all sufficient, as there are still very large individual tables determining the run times. In that case, so-called *table splitting* must be used. In this method, a large table is split into parts as close together in size as possible, which are then exported and imported separately by different R3load processes. The challenge in this case is to set up suitable *selection criteria* to make sure that more or least equally large parts of the tables are selected. These criteria are also called WHERE clauses and can be specified in the R3load control files.

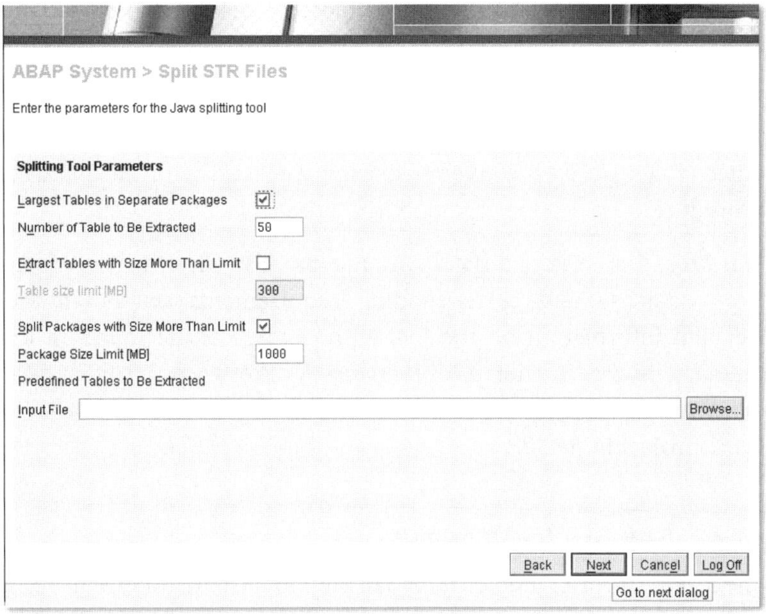

Figure 3.24 SAPinst Input Window for Package Split

There is partial tool support for this process from SAP; more information is available in SAP Note 952514. In large part, this is the split tool `R3ta`, which derives appropriate selection criteria. A good overview of the tools available can be found in the Media Library at the SAP Service Marketplace in the *http://service.sap.com/systemcopy* area.

Using the Distribution Monitor

A Unicode conversion places high requirements on the CPU areas of the hardware. By default, however, export and import are limited to one server. The distribution monitor can allow the use of additional existing application servers for the Unicode conversion. In SAP Note 955772, the procedure for using the distribution monitor is described.

Distribution monitor

Incremental Migration

The procedure of *incremental migration* (IMIG) converts a part of the database before the actual conversion on a weekend. Here, the largest tables—the so-called *IMIG tables* in the system—are exported and

IMIG procedure

converted during production and imported back into a second Unicode system.

All changes to the IMIG tables are logged starting at the beginning of the export and are "mirrored" by RFC on the Unicode system. The other tables are then converted on the weekend with the standard procedure.

This procedure is very difficult and is generally only of use with very large database and corresponding requirements for downtime. Detailed information on the IMIG procedure can be found in the Media Library in the SAP Service Marketplace (*http://service. sap.com/systemcopy*). SAP Note 693168 describes the procedure of an IMIG project in detail.

3.2.4   SAP GUI for Windows

Front-end view— SAP GUI

The SAP GUI for Windows is by far the most frequently used front-end tool to access SAP systems. SAP GUI for Windows has two modes: a Unicode mode that is automatically activated upon access to a Unicode system, and the "normal" non-Unicode mode. In addition, there is also the so-called *I18N functionality* (discussed later), which eliminates the dependency of the SAP GUI on the Windows settings (regional and language options) under Windows XP. The interplay between these settings, the I18N functionality, and the Unicode behavior of the SAP GUI will be presented in this section.

Regional and language options in Windows XP

In Microsoft Windows XP under **Settings • System Control • Regional and Language Options**, general settings regarding localization of the system can be made. On the **Extended** tab under **Language for programs that don't support Unicode** you see the language which determines the systemwide default for code page handling in the non-Unicode case. For simplicity's sake, we will call this the *Windows System Locale*. On the same tab under the point **Code page conversion tables** you have the options of activating support for additional code pages (e. g., Asian).

Thus, if a PC is to be used in support for multiple regions, such as Asia and Europe, all the necessary code pages should be installed here. Figure 3.25 shows the extended Windows language options.

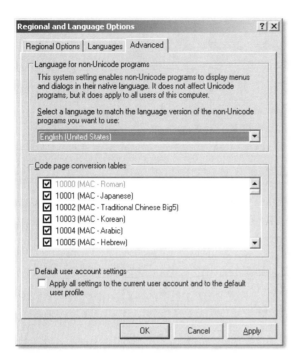

Figure 3.25 Language Settings Under Windows XP

During SAP logon as of SAP GUI Release 6.40, attributes can be adjusted under the **Systems** tab for every system entry. As you can see in Figure 3.26, to do this you select the system desired and then click the **Change entry** button. On the code page tab you can also find language settings and the upload/download encoding.

Settings in the SAP logo

The **Language** field is not relevant in Unicode systems. You shouldn't set the **Unicode Off** flag. In the **Encoding** field (available only in SAP GUI 6.40) you can specify the encoding format to be used for documents in front-end upload or download.

SAP GUI 4.6C for Windows introduced a new functionality, that of "I18N" (*Internationalization*[3]). In the non-Unicode case, I18N functionality is optional, and in the standard case (non-Unicode) it is normally not activated. An exception is the front end of users using an Asian version of Windows. Here, I18N is automatically activated.

I18N mode of the SAP GUI

---

3 The "18" in I18N stands for the 18 letters in the word "internationalization" between the starting I and the final N.

Figure 3.26 Code Page Settings on SAP Logon

In an SAP GUI session, I18N can be activated using **Adaptation of local layout Alt F12 • Options • I18N • Activate multi-byte functionality**. It then remains active after restarting the SAP logon and all SAP GUI sessions for the corresponding front end. If I18N is not activated on the corresponding front-end and the user accesses a Unicode system, I18N is automatically activated for that session.

In the area **Adaptation of local layout Alt F12** there are then additional entries: For comparison, Figure 3.27 shows the function without activation of I18N, and in Figure 3.28 I18N is activated (in the non-Unicode system). The entry **Character set** in the Unicode case serves for variable specification of the input character set. In the MDMP case (non-Unicode), this entry may not be changed, although this cannot be prevented technically. In the area **Fonts (I18N)** the fonts used can be adjusted. The area **Options (I18N)** is described in the SAP GUI help (locally available under **Adaptation of local layout Alt F12 • SAP GUI Help**).

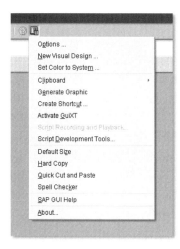

Figure 3.27 SAP GUI Without Activation of I18N Functionality

Figure 3.28 SAP GUI with Activation of I18N Functionality

Figure 3.29 shows a diagram of the three possible cases regarding the code page setup:

Case 1 ▸ **Unicode with I18N**

In the Unicode case, I18N is automatically activated. The database, the application server, and the SAP GUI each use Unicode with partly differing encoding schemes. The Windows system locale has no meaning for most areas when I18N functionality is used.

I18N and the keyboard (software and hardware) determine the character set in which data is entered. This character set (I18N and keyboard) can be changed, so that Japanese characters, for instance, can also be entered under an English logon.

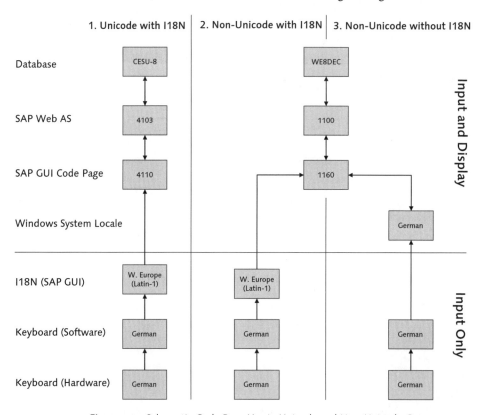

Figure 3.29 Schematic Code Page Use in Unicode and Non-Unicode Cases

Case 2 ▸ **Non-Unicode with I18N**

In the non-Unicode case, it is still no problem to use I18N. Analogous to the Unicode case, the database, the application server, and the SAP GUI each uses its own specific code page. The database code page, however, is determined by SAP (for Oracle, WE8DEC) and independent of the code page used on the application server.

On the input side, I18N and the keyboard are still used. However, changing the character set with a fixed logon language is not allowed. Within the character set used, the keyboard may be adapted (e. g., from German to French). In the case of MDMP, it is absolutely necessary to log on with Japanese if you want to enter Japanese characters. However, this can be done (using I18N) on the same front end.

▸ **Non-Unicode without I18N**

In the non-Unicode case, I18N does not need to be activated. However, only the input of characters from the Windows system locale is then supported. No Japanese characters can be entered on a machine set up with Windows under German, even though it is possible from a technical standpoint. If the user simply switches the keyboard to Japanese, Japanese can still be entered (illegally). This is then a "fool the system" case (see Section 2.2.1), and users should absolutely be trained to avoid it.

Case 3

The concept of I18N thus enables parallel use of logon sessions on both Unicode and non-Unicode systems on a front end. Mixed landscapes are supported as well.

As a matter of principle, we strongly recommend using SAP GUI 6.40 (or release 7.10 if available) with Unicode systems. Use of SAP GUI 6.20 is also possible, but some limitations must be taken into consideration. If Asian users access the system, SAP GUI 6.40 (or a later version) is absolutely necessary.

Release 6.20 vs. release 6.40

If Unicode tests in the SAP GUI result in errors, it may be necessary to load a later SAP GUI patch. As with any other patch, the probability of error is reduced if the latest possible level is used.

> **Note**
>
> The notes provided in this section are described in detail in the appendix to SAP Note 316903 with corresponding screen shots, as well as in SAP Note 508854. When in doubt, the SAP Notes take precedence.

3.2.5 Printing in the Unicode System

Basically, printing in the Unicode system behaves analogously to data output in the SAP GUI: There is a conversion from the code page of the application server to the SAP GUI code page (see Figure 3.29), and during printing there is an analogous conversion from the code page of the application server (or of the document) to the code page of the device type.

If characters are printed which are not included in the code page of the device type, they are printed as # characters; this applies for both non-Unicode and Unicode systems. The result is that Unicode conversion only requires a few adaptations to defined printers.

While previously, for example, a conversion from 1100 to 1116 (printer code page) took place, in the Unicode case a conversion from 4102 (Unicode) to 1116 is needed. The result is the same, as long as only characters supported by the printer code page (in this case, Latin-1) are printed. In Figure 3.30, this is shown in the upper region. In this way, all defined printers can still be used after the Unicode conversion with the old code pages.

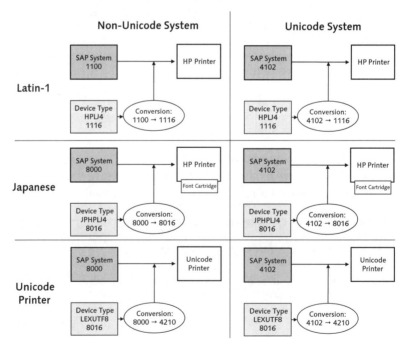

Figure 3.30 Printer Behavior in Non-Unicode and Unicode Systems

For new printers to be used in the Unicode system, the same rules apply as in the non-Unicode system. The prerequisite for use is that a corresponding device type exists in the SAP system. Information on standard device types can be found in SAP Note 8928.

If the restriction to the old code pages is not enough for a print job, there is the option of using special Unicode printers that can save Unicode fonts (for instance, on a built-in hard drive). An advantage of this is that when these printers are used, all supported Unicode characters can be used while printing. Furthermore, that printer can also be specified as the default for all countries, as all the characters needed are supported. A disadvantage is that these printers only offer a limited selection of fonts. Furthermore, Unicode printers can also be used with a non-Unicode system. Examples of supported Unicode printers can be found in SAP Notes 215015 and 750219.

Unicode printers

Another option for printing special characters from multiple "old" code pages is the *cascading fonts method*. Here, a so-called *cascading fonts configurator* can be used to assign different SAP subfonts — i. e., portions of SAP fonts — to other SAP fonts.

Cascading fonts

For instance, if the font DB Mincho is assigned to the font Times New Roman, this allows a print job to use both Japanese and Western European special characters. With this construct, for example, you can use front-end printing to print special characters from multiple old code pages, or characters which aren't supported at all under non-Unicode (such as Vietnamese). Detailed information on the cascading fonts method can be found in SAP Note 812821.

3.2.6 Transport between non-Unicode and Unicode Systems

Over the course of a conversion project, it is sometimes necessary to transport between a Unicode and a non-Unicode system. For instance, this can be the case when the development system has already been converted to Unicode, but the consolidation system is still based on non-Unicode, and urgent maintenance tasks make a transport necessary from the development system.

Transports between identical releases

Basically, communication between Unicode and non-Unicode systems is possible, with the following limitations:

- ▶ **Characters are not supported in the target code page**
  In a data transfer from Unicode to non-Unicode there are always problems when the data sent is not supported on the non-Unicode side. An example would be the transmission of a Japanese charaacter to a Latin-1 system. Generally, the character is converted into a # sign.

- ▶ **From Unicode to MDMP or from MDMP to Unicode**
  If the non-Unicode side is an MDMP system, the familiar conversion problems with language-independent data will arise: Using the transport parameter `Charset` (see SAP Note 80727), customers can specify the basis on which this data will be converted. Here, too, characters from other code pages are converted into # characters. The data in tables with language keys, on the other hand, are converted corresponding to the settings in Transaction SPUMG or the standard settings.

Transports between releases Transports from Unicode systems to systems with releases up to SAP R/3 4.6C are currently not possible technically (see SAP Note 330267); that is, transport will fail. But even a transport of ABAP objects from SAP R/3 4.6C into a Unicode system is extremely problematic, since these objects are not necessary Unicode capable and thus may not be executable.

3.2.7 Conversion of SAP NetWeaver BI and SAP CRM Systems

Conversion of non-ERP systems The standard migration tools assume that all information about tables in the SAP system is stored in the nametab or in the DDIC. These are read out and written into the R3load files during export.

For SAP NetWeaver BI systems, this assumption is incorrect. For instance, there are temporary tables generated in the /BIO/* namespace without nametab entries, which can cause problems during export. Another example is the use of partitioning in an Oracle database. This information, too, is invisible by default for R3load.

As a result, when converting SAP NetWeaver BI systems, additional steps must be taken into consideration. This is analogous when converting SAP SCM systems.

> **Note**
>
> As of SAP NetWeaver 2004, the functionality of SAP NetWeaver BI is auto-matically integrated into the ABAP stack. Thus, these additional steps are needed for all systems based on SAP NetWeaver.
>
> The procedure for such systems is described in detail in SAP Note 543715. Additional steps in the conversion of a SAP CRM system can be found in SAP Note 902083.

3.2.8 Summary

The Unicode architecture selected by SAP guarantees a high degree of integration of non-Unicode and Unicode in system landscapes. All character-type data in the Unicode system is stored as Unicode data, to which stricter syntax restrictions apply.

The Unicode conversion of an SAP system is based on the system copy. That means that the entire system must be exported and then imported again after conversion. This procedure takes place during the downtime and may therefore need to be runtime optimized. Prior to this, all language-independent data in an MDMP system must be scanned and assigned using Transaction SPUMG.

3.3 Upgrades and Unicode Conversion

Many large global SAP systems are still at old SAP release levels that are already outside SAP standard maintenance or will shortly run out. For example, the standard maintenance for SAP R/3 4.6C ended in December 2006. This is also true for other components of the SAP Business Suite, such as SAP CRM. In the following paragraphs, we will concentrate on the R/3 and ERP product family from SAP. The discussions and recommendations for single code page systems can be used in analogous manner for all the components of the SAP Business Suite in ABAP, particularly regarding aspects of single code page and Unicode conversion.

Current problem

Many of the 4.6C systems are very often operated with an MDMP or blended code-page configuration in order to support many countries and languages even before a Unicode-capable release. Some global MDMP project organizations are even planning to implement additional countries and languages in the next two to three years in SAP

R/3 4.6 C, even though the standard support for it ran out at the end of 2006.

Even if the current SAP R/3 4.6C system can get by with a single code page, it can be assumed with high probability that additional code pages will be added, so that finally an MDMP system under SAP R/3 4.6C will be the result.

Roll-out in BRIC countries requires new languages A currently very popular topic is the rollout in China or Russia, where even small and medium companies want to or have to expand their activities, often very soon, in order to profit from general economic growth in those countries. Since in BRIC countries (Brazil, Russia, India, China) the use of the local language is legally required, the SAP system must be extended with these languages using new code pages.

Since June, 2006, the new release SAP ERP 2005 (SAP ECC 6.0/SAP NetWeaver 2004s) is generally available. Customers with MDMP systems under SAP R/3 4.6C generally want to upgrade directly to this newest release. Some actually have to, given that the previous release SAP ERP 2004—the last release with MDMP support— doesn't have several SAP industrial solutions available. This results in the following challenges:

▸ The new target release SAP ERP 2005 supports neither MDMP nor blended code pages

▸ The global MDMP systems under SAP R/3 4.6C are mostly very large

▸ The downtime during the upgrade and the Unicode conversion can't be very long

Because SAP R/3 4.6C is not yet Unicode-capable, but an MDMP system is no longer supported in SAP ERP 2005 (see SAP Note 79991 for more details), these customers will need to perform the upgrade from SAP R/3 4.6C to SAP ERP 2005 *and* the Unicode conversion at the same time. As it is not realistic to expect an upgrade in two levels, such as from SAP R/3 4.6C to SAP R/3 Enterprise, followed by a Unicode conversion and another upgrade to SAP ERP 2005, customers must look for different and easier ways to achieve the goal.

Accordingly, SAP has developed combination procedures for upgrade and Unicode conversion in a single downtime: the combined procedure "CU & UC" (*Combined Upgrade and Unicode Conversion*) on the one hand and the combined procedure "TU & UC" (*Twin Upgrade and Unicode Conversion*) on the other. Please refer to SAP Note 928729 and references to see the current release status of both procedures.

Combined procedures for upgrades and Unicode conversion

▶ **CU & UC procedure**
The CU & UC procedure makes it possible to upgrade a non-Unicode SAP system with an MDMP configuration from a starting release of SAP R/3 4.6C, SAP R/3 Enterprise or SAP ERP 2004 in combination with a Unicode conversion. The procedure also enables upgrades of single code page systems to SAP ERP 2005 together with a Unicode conversion at an acceptable downtime.

> **Note**
>
> For blended code pages (BCP) special conditions and restrictions are valid; for details please refer to SAP Note 928729 and references. It is recommended that you contact SAP in this case. In this section, therefore, we will restrict our discussion to MDMP systems.

▶ **TU & UC procedure**
The TU & UC procedure, which uses a different approach, enables the conversion of start releases under SAP R/3 4.6C or special release 6.10, used by components of the SAP Business Suite as well as SAP CRM 3.0.

> **Note**
>
> Because the MDMP and blended code-page configuration is only designed for SAP R/3 and its successor SAP R/3 Enterprise or SAP ERP 2004, we will not go into further detail regarding other components of the SAP Business Suite. If an MDMP or blended code page system based on components other than SAP R/3 needs an upgrade and Unicode conversion, SAP should be contacted for clarification of the further procedure.

Since single code page systems are still supported by more recent SAP systems, the SAP standard upgrade to SAP ERP 2005 can first be done, and then a decision can be made whether the Unicode conversion will be performed immediately or only at a later date. Note at this point that many SAP applications today no longer run in only

Single code page system as starting release

one single system, but rather are distributed across multiple SAP components, which communicate with one another. An example is the *SAP Employee/Manager Self-Services* (ESS/MSS) if the SAP NetWeaver Portal is used as the central user interface.

The portal sends the data to the R/3 back-end system after user input and preparation, which then runs the application and sends the results back to the portal. The SAP NetWeaver Portal is implemented in Java and thus runs in Unicode. If the SAP back end is a non-Unicode system, the data must be converted during communication between Unicode and non-Unicode, which can lead to problems particularly for technically complex languages like the Asian languages (you can find details in Section 3.5).

So, when using Java-based Unicode applications integrated with an R/3 back end, you should convert the back-end system to Unicode immediately after or as shortly as possible after the upgrade. This is particularly true for Asian single code page systems, because Java always works under Unicode and not all characters are round-trip capable between Unicode and the Asian single code page system. This means that that after two opposing conversions (e. g., first from Unicode (SAP NetWeaver Portal) into single code pages (SAP R/3 and back) a character may be incorrect.

Currency symbol for the Euro only under Unicode

Even with a Latin-1 single code page system there can be this kind of problem. The currency symbol for the Euro (€) is not included in the SAP Latin-1 single code page 1100, but it is in Unicode. So there may be problems with this symbol when exchanging data between SAP NetWeaver Portal or ESS/MSS and the R/3 system. You can find more details in SAP Note 73606 and the corresponding references.

If an SAP system with starting release SAP R/3 4.6C or later and a single code page configuration is to be upgraded to SAP ERP 2005 and then immediately thereafter converted to Unicode, the CU & UC combined procedure may be considered as well as the sequential procedure.

In the following, the various procedures for combining an upgrade of an SAP system with a non-Unicode starting release to SAP ERP 2005 and a Unicode conversion will be described and compared in conception and methods. We will limit ourselves largely to the case of a starting release of SAP R/3 4.6C or lower with an MDMP configuration. There are also CU & UC and TU & UC combined procedures for systems with more recent starting releases or with single code-page configurations, but they function for the most part identically to the older starting releases. Moreover, for systems at SAP R/3 Enterprise or later there is always the option of first converting to Unicode and then (even at a later time) executing the upgrade.

3.3.1 Sequential (Separate) Upgrade and Unicode Conversion

The procedure of sequential upgrades is characterized by the fact that the upgrade and Unicode conversion are fully separate and independent projects.

Independent projects

First, an SAP standard upgrade is performed with all the necessary preparation and post-processing. After the upgrade, the SAP system is still running on the same code page configuration as in the starting release; that is, MDMP. But because MDMP is no longer supported in SAP ERP 2005, the only target release possible for a production system is SAP ERP 2004.

If the target release must be SAP ECC 6.0 and if no combined procedure can be used, for special cases there is a transitional rule with some limitations. This is described in more detail in SAP Note 79991. This procedure, with starting release SAP R/3 4.6C (MDMP) and target release SAP ECC 6.0, is only possible for test systems and development systems developed with a master language[4] and with no, or very little, multilingual language processing. In preparation for the combined upgrade and Unicode conversion (CU & UC), this procedure is also used for the Unicode enabling of custom development, as described in more detail in the following section.

3.3.2 Combined Upgrade and Unicode Conversion

To be able to upgrade an MDMP system under SAP R/3 4.6C directly to SAP ERP 2005—together with a Unicode conversion—the special CU & UC combined procedure was developed. This enables both steps to be performed during a single downtime phase (usually a

CU & UC combined procedure

---

4 The *master language* is the language in which a new development object is created and in which text elements are created. In a large global system, English is recommended as the master language.

long weekend or holidays). Naturally, this is a complex project, since even an upgrade to a large SAP system is a lot of work.

You may have assumed that the Unicode conversion would take place during the upgrade. This is unfortunately not the case, as the technology of the upgrade and the Unicode conversion are completely different. While the downtime for the upgrade after all optimizations only depends indirectly on database size, for the Unicode conversion it is very dependent, because in this procedure the database must be exported after the upgrade and imported into the new Unicode database.

Concepts of the procedure   With the combined CU & UC procedure, different preparation and post-processing steps for Unicode conversion can be combined advantageously with various upgrade steps to reduce downtime overall.

In general, this combined procedure is primarily intended for customers who may no longer run MDMP in production in SAP ECC 6.0. However, it is also possible to use the combined procedure for single code page systems and for non-Unicode systems with starting release SAP R/3 Enterprise and SAP ERP 2004. Although in the latter the Unicode conversion can be performed before the upgrade, the combined procedure offers some advantages. Information on these variants can be found in SAP Note 928729 and the corresponding references.

Preparations for Conversion

CU & UC procedure   The significant preparations for a Unicode conversion of a non-Unicode MDMP system are described in the following bullet points and presented in Section 3.2 as well:

- ▶ MDMP-specific preparation with editing of the vocabulary and reprocessing logs (Transaction SPUM4 analogous to SPUMG)
- ▶ Unicode enabling of custom development (ABAP enabling)
- ▶ special steps, like the generation of the Unicode nametab

The longest preparation time, besides the Unicode enabling of custom development, is taken by vocabulary maintenance. Depending on the size of the database and the number of different code pages, several hundred thousand entries (possibly even in the million range) are possible. It generally takes a few weeks for all entries to be assigned.

So that the vocabulary maintenance can take place before the start of the upgrade, Transaction SPUMG has been ported down to SAP R/3 4.6C under the name of SPUM4. The steps in Transaction SPUM4 are almost the same as in Transaction SPUMG, and Transaction SPUM4 can be run on the production system up to several weeks before the start of the upgrade. The tools for SPUM4 are imported into the R/3 system during execution of the upgrade preparation tool PREPARE loaded from the upgrade master DVD. Afterwards, SPUM4 can be started along with the other upgrade preparations.

SPUMG and SPUM4

The Unicode syntax adaptation of custom development is significantly more difficult, as described in Section 3.4 in more detail. Unfortunately, there is no way to port Transaction UCCHECK used for Unicode enabling in SAP Web AS 6.10 and later down to SAP R/3 4.6C and to adapt custom development in SAP R/3 4.6C before the upgrade in that way. You may already be familiar with this problem from basic upgrades, particularly for upgrades across large release level gaps. For the upgrade alone, every custom development must be tested and possibly adapted in the target release before the actual upgrade of the production system, as the new target release generally provides new functions and applications which should be used.

Working with custom developments

Custom SAP extensions (for instance, append structures) and modifications must also be adapted in the target release using Transactions SPDD and SPAU, which are used during every upgrade to compare with the SAP standard. In order to detect, process, and test the SPDD, SPAU, and other adaptations necessary for each upgrade in a timely manner, a test or development system must first be upgraded to the target release before work can being. That is the same approach used for Unicode enabling of custom development. Because for Transaction UCCHECK a Unicode-capable system must be available, this prerequisite is perfectly satisfied by the upgraded development or test system. The Unicode enabling of custom development thus take place in a way similar to that of upgrade adaptations, and they can even be done at the same time to achieve synergistic effects. This way, every needed code change to a custom development due to the upgrade is also automatically executed with the new Unicode syntax check and, if necessary corrected immediately (see Section 3.4 for an overview of the Unicode syntax).

If all custom developments have been adapted to Unicode, they are put into a collective transport (or several transports) like the upgrade adaptations, which integrates them during the subsequent upgrade, so that after its completion all the custom developments are prepared for Unicode without additional post-processing work. The ideal procedure must be determined individually for every project, as it depends on many factors.

RADCUCNT Some special steps for Unicode preparation, like the generation of the Unicode nametab with the RADCUCNT report (see Section 3.2.1) are performed during the upgrade, so that the run time for these jobs, which can last several ours, is eliminated for the Unicode preparation.

In all, the CU & UC combined procedure primarily differs from the sequential approach in that the special MDMP vocabulary processing has been ported down to SAP R/3 6.4C and some runtime-intensive jobs in the Unicode conversion can be performed during the upgrade. The Unicode enabling of custom development, however, must be performed in an SAP system with at least SAP Web AS 6.10/6.20. We recommend that the development or test system be upgraded to a release level of SAP ERP 2005/SAP ECC 6.0, which would have to happen anyway due to the upgrade. Another possible approach, to import custom development in SAP R/3 4.6C via a transport order into release 6.20 or a higher system, is generally only possible in simple cases and is unrealistic for a large number of custom developments.

CU & UC phases during the upgrade We will sketch the Unicode-specific phases before and during the upgrade with the CU & UC procedure. The details can be found in the following documents and SAP Notes, generally available only in English.

▸ SAP Note 928729 with questions and answers as well as the document *Combined Upgrade & Unicode Conversion SAP R/3 4.6C–SAP ERP Central Component ABAP 6.0 (or higher Support Release)* and other information and references.

▸ SAP documentation for the upgrade to SAP ERP 2005/SAP ECC 6.0, which you can find in the SAP Service Marketplace at *http://service.sap.com/instguides*. There is an *Upgrade Master Guide* for upgrade planning and general preparation, as well as an Upgrade

Component Guide for the current platform, with details about the execution of the upgrade.

▶ Document for Unicode conversion, *Unicode Conversion Guide–SAP NetWeaver Application Server 2004s, which you can find in the* SAP Service Marketplace at *http://service.sap.com/unicode@sap* in the area **Unicode Library • Unicode Conversion Library • Unicode Conversion Guide** for the current basis support package.

Process of the CU & UC Combined Procedure

The CU & UC combined procedure is initially started like an SAP standard upgrade[5], with the two main tools PREPARE for preparation and SAPup[6] used for the actual upgrade.

First, the preparation phases are started with PREPARE, which can take place in the production system long before the upgrade. Here, the MDMP-specific Transaction SPUM4 is imported for vocabulary processing, which is done together with the other PREPARE activities. After the upgrade with SAPup, where some Unicode-specific activities also take place, the Unicode conversion is performed immediately and concluded with some post-processing, particularly Transaction SUMG.

The process schema for the CU & UC combined procedure looks like the following (these are the special phases):

▶ **Preparation and start of PREPARE**
This is where the preparation for the upgrade and import of the SPUM4 tools takes place. PREPARE can be run long before the downtime (up to several weeks) without influencing production operation. It can also be executed repeatedly, such as when transports into the production system take place after the first start.

Process schema for the CU & UC combined procedure

▶ **Query for standard upgrade or combined CU & UC upgrade**
UCMIG_DECISION phase (Module Initialization)

During initialization, PREPARE analyzes the code-page configuration of the system and in a dialog offers a choice between the combined and simple upgrade (see Figure 3.31). For an MDMP or

UCMIG_DECISION phase

---

5 These descriptions assume SAP ERP 2005 as the target release.
6 The upgrade tool R3up used for upgrades to SAP ECC 5.0/SAP NetWeaver 2004 was replaced by SAPup.

blended code page system (if supported, check SAP Note 928729)—corresponding to the explanations at the start of Section 3.3—the combined procedure must be selected, so that the Unicode conversion can take place immediately after conclusion of the upgrade. If that is not possible, SAP experts must be consulted as to what possible alternatives exist.

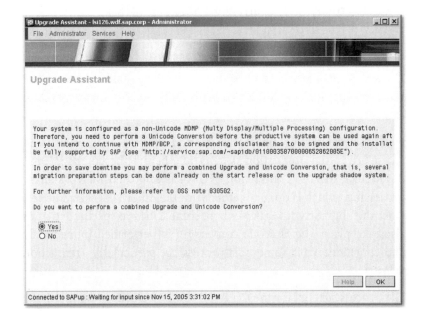

Figure 3.31 Upgrade Assistant—CU & UC

In the case of a single code page system, both options are possible. If the conversion to Unicode does not take place immediately after the upgrade, the standard procedure should be chosen.

TOOLIMP4_
UCMIG phase

▶ **Import of the tools for Transaction SPUM4**

TOOLIMP4_UCMIG phase (Module Import)

The tools for Transaction SPUM4 for vocabulary editing are imported; Transaction SPUM4 largely works like Transaction SPUMG under SAP Web AS 6.20 and higher releases. The editing of the vocabulary can take up to several weeks depending on the system, so it should be started appropriately early.

UCMIG_REQINC
phase

▶ **Import of custom developments adapted to Unicode from a different SAP ECC 6.0 system**

UCMIG_REQINC phase (Module Extension)

This is an important phase for integration of custom developments adapted for Unicode (Unicode ABAP enabling). Here, a collective transport or several individual transports are specified which were created during Unicode enabling of custom developments and setting of the Unicode flag. The programs adapted for Unicode are then integrated directly into the upgrade, so that after completion of the upgrade no further action is required (see Figure 3.32).

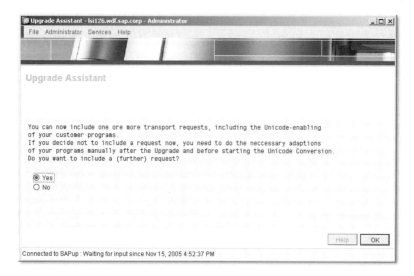

Figure 3.32 Upgrade Assistant—Transport Requests to Include

▶ **Execution of database scans and editing of vocabulary with Transaction SPUM4**
After PREPARE is started and the necessary entries made, the central transaction for vocabulary processing, SPUM4, is manually processed. Analogously to Transaction SPUMG, different scans of the database are performed in sequence to fill the initial vocabulary. Then automated tools and custom-written hints assign as many entries as possible, and at the end the remaining assignments of entries to languages is performed with native speakers or translators. Vocabulary editing is generally done during system uptime or, as described in Section 3.2, is first done in a sandbox system and then transported into the production system so that only a delta must be processed.

Transaction SPUM4 can be performed efficiently along with other preparations for PREPARE which belong to the upgrade, and should be completed no later than when the shadow system is started.

▶ **Additional preparations**

For the Unicode conversion subsequent to the upgrade, some additional important preparation steps are required which can be performed during the PREPARE upgrade phase. These include all measures for reduction of database size, like archiving and removal of unneeded data (temporary data, log entries, etc.)

These steps include the generation of the DDIC attribute **Text language** for customer tables using the special job UM4_TXFLAG_UPLOAD (see SAP Note 931615), and also the consistency check of critical SAP cluster tables according to SAP Note 89384.

Phase UCMIG_
STATUS_CHK1,
UCMIG_STATUS_
CHK21/22/23

▶ **Checking of Transaction SPUM4**

UCMIG_STATUS_CHK1, UCMIG_STATUS_CHK21/22/23 phase

A check is run to determine whether the SPUM4 activities are all finished. If not, a warning (CHK1) or an error message (CHK21/22/23) occurs, depending on the upgrade strategy selected.

JOB_UM4_COPY_
RESULTS phase

▶ **Transfer of SPUM4 results into target tables in SAP ECC 6.0**

JOB_UM4_COPY_RESULTS phase

The vocabulary and all SPUM4 tables are written into the tables of the target release SAP ECC 6.0, so that all MDMP-specific tables for the Unicode conversion after the upgrade will be available. It is generally not possible to process the vocabulary with Transaction SPUMG after the upgrade and before the Unicode conversion.

JOB_RADCUCNT_
ALL phase

▶ **Generation of the Unicode nametab during the upgrade**

JOB_RADCUCNT_ALL phase

The Unicode nametabs needed for the later Unicode system are generated. It is recommended that you pay close attention to the fact that no changes or imports of dictionary objects should take place after this point, although the upgrade is still in the uptime phase.

Upgrade downtime
phase

▶ **Upgrade in the downtime phase**

In the downtime phase, besides numerous upgrade phases, additional Unicode-specific phases are carried out, of which the most important are:

▶ JOB_UM4_FILL_RLOAD phase

Because not all development objects have a master language or a language key in table REPOSRC, this phase ensures that the RLOAD components of this table are filled with the master language.

▶ JOB_RADCUCNT_NEW phase

This phase takes care of the regeneration of the Unicode nametabs, if changes have taken place after the JOB_RADCUCNT_ALL nametab phase.

▶ **Final upgrade tasks and preparation for Unicode conversion**

After the upgrade goes into the uptime mode by default at the end, in the case of a CU & UC combined procedure, the system must remain down for the end user and be prepared for the immediately subsequent Unicode conversion. Some preparatory actions cannot take place during the execution of PREPARE or the upgrade, and must therefore be performed directly after the end of the upgrade.

Conclusion and post-processing of upgrade

After some necessary final tasks for the upgrade, which you can find in the upgrade documentation for SAP ECC 6.0, there are several Unicode-specific preparatory actions that are described in the documentation in greater detail and generally don't take terribly long to run. The most important prerequisites for Unicode conversion, namely the vocabulary and the reprocessing log from Transaction SPUM4 before the upgrade and the custom developments adapted for Unicode, have already been completed, so that nothing more is standing in the way of the database export. At this point, we should clarify how the database statistics are performed (either as a post-processing step in the upgrade or within the SAPinst program).

Unicode preparation directly after the upgrade

Before the actual Unicode conversion, the optimum export/import method must be determined. Because of the combined downtime during the upgrade and the Unicode conversion, the SAP Distribution and Migration Monitor is generally the tool of choice, with at least two servers and a high degree of parallelization (see also Section 3.2).

▶ **Unicode conversion: database export and import**

The Unicode conversion takes place in the same way as for an SAP system which is already on a Unicode-capable release and is being

Conversion

converted to Unicode. The standard SAP tools SAPinst and R3load are used, together with the optimization strategy chosen (see Section 3.2). It should be noted again that the vocabulary and reprocessing log must be completed during the upgrade PREPARE and uptime phase.

Post-processing ▶ **Post-processing after the Unicode conversion**

After the database export and import with SAPinst and R3load as basic tools, and the distribution and migration monitor as optimization tool, some post-processing steps must be performed during the Unicode conversion itself before the system can be released for use in Unicode, including the important jobs UMG_POOL_TABLE for the special handling of pool tables and RUTTTYPACT for the activation of table types. Also very important are parameter adaptations for the new Unicode system (see SAP Note 790099) and the regeneration of generated objects that could not be handled during the Unicode enabling of custom development (see also Section 3.4).

Post-processing with SUMG
A larger post-processing step is Transaction SUMG, which repairs incorrectly converted texts. As with standalone Unicode conversion, first the automatic repairs from the reprocessing log language assignments are performed, and these still run during the downtime and can take up to several hours depending on the size of the reprocessing log. Then at any time later, even after the system is already in production, manual corrections can be made using Transaction SUMG.

Summary of the CU & UC Combined Procedure

CU & UC procedure in overview
In summary, the Unicode-specific steps for the CU & UC combined procedure can be presented as shown in Table 3.7: before, during, and after the upgrade.

Uptime	Downtime	Uptime
1. Unicode enabling of custom developments and conversion of custom code pages*	6. Upgrade with SAP tool SAPup	10. Manual post-processing in SAP ECC 6.0 (Unicode) including manual repairs
2. Collective transport order for integration of custom developments and custom code pages during upgrade	7. Consistency check, including nametab check in SAP ECC 6.0 (non-Unicode)	
3. Preparation of the upgrade with PRE-PARE, with import of the Unicode preparation tool SPUM4 for an MDMP system	8. Unicode conversion (as with standalone Unicode conversion or system copy with SAP-inst and usually with the migration and distribution monitor)	
4. Preparation of the Unicode conversion in SAP R/3 4.6C (consistency check, scans, vocabulary maintenance)	9. Unicode post-processing and automatic repair completion in SAP ECC 6.0	
5. Unicode preparation during upgrade (e.g. automatic generation of nametabs)		

* Please note that Unicode enabling is only possible with SAP Web AS 6.20 or higher. Thus the development or test system must be upgraded first. The adaptations are then directly integrated into the subsequent upgrades with a transport order.

Table 3.7 Process Schema from SAP R/3 4.6C (MDMP) to SAP ECC 6.0 (Unicode)

3.3.3 Twin Upgrade and Unicode Conversion

Although the majority of large global SAP systems that are not yet on SAP R/3 Enterprise or higher are only using SAP R/3 4.6C, the number of MDMP systems with releases lower than SAP R/3 4.6C is still not negligible. A direct upgrade to SAP ECC 6.0 is technically possible even from starting release SAP R/3 3.1I, so that customer with systems at such releases and MDMP or blended code page configurations will want to make use of that.

TU & UC combined procedure

Unfortunately, the CU & UC combined procedure described in Section 3.3.2 cannot be ported down to releases lower than SAP R/3

4.6C, particularly because Transaction SPUM4 already ported is based on object-oriented ABAP programming, which is not available, or insufficiently mature, on those releases.

To support customers with a lower starting release with a direct upgrade to SAP ERP 2005/SAP ECC 6.0 and subsequent Unicode conversion in a reasonable downtime, the TU & UC combined procedure is provided, which is based on a different approach from that taken in the CU & UC combined procedure.[7]

Process of the TU & UC Combined Procedure

Differences in the combined procedures

The main difference from the CU & UC combined procedure is that in the starting release system there is no tool for vocabulary maintenance like that provided by the SPUM4 tool. To achieve a combined solution with an upgrade and Unicode conversion in a suitable downtime despite this, the following approach is taken in this procedure.

First, a system copy of the production system (a *twin*) is made, as close as possible to the start of the project. This copy is upgraded using the SAP standard upgrade to SAP ERP 2005, although it still has an MDMP or blended code-page configuration. Then in the system copy, the most important MDMP Unicode preparations, namely the Unicode enabling of custom development with Transaction UCCHECK and vocabulary processing, together with the database scans by SPUMG, are performed just as for a standalone MDMP Unicode conversion.

The difference from the CU & UC combined procedure is that the vocabulary processing and all the database scans needed don't take place before the upgrade in the PREPARE phase, but rather is transported from the twin system into the production system *after* its upgrade. This means that the production system can start the Unicode conversion of the database relatively quickly after the upgrade, without needing to spend a lot of time on the database scans and vocabulary maintenance.

---

7 For details on the current availability status of this procedure please refer to SAP Note 959698 and references, and you can contact SAP directly by sending your questions to *globalization@sap.com* and *internationalization@sap.com*.

The process schema for the TU & UC combined procedure is as follows:

Process schema for the TU & UC combined procedure

▶ **Creation of a system copy of the production system as the twin system**
The twin system should be created as close as possible to the time of upgrade, in order to have the latest production data, and it should include as much as possible of the custom development used in production, which must be adapted for Unicode. After the system copy, a freeze or at least reduction of custom development should take place.

▶ **SAP standard upgrade to SAP ERP 2005/SAP ECC 6.0 on the twin system**
The twin system is upgraded according to the standard SAP upgrade procedure to target release SAP ERP 2005/SAP ECC 6.0, and this takes place with the existing MDMP or blended code-page configuration still used in the starting release. The custom developments are neither adapted to ABAP or Unicode and they don't have the Unicode flag set.

▶ **ABAP Unicode enabling and vocabulary maintenance**
In two relatively independent subprojects, the ABAP Unicode enabling and the MDMP-specific activities with the SPUMG tool are carried out. After completion of the ABAP Unicode enabling, just as for the CU & UC combined procedure, a collective transport is created that directly integrates the adaptations to the custom development during the upgrade of the production system.

▶ **Transport of the Unicode adapatations of custom development and SPUMG table contents into the production system**
The big difference from the CU & UC combined procedure is in the approach to the MDMP-specific database scans, vocabulary maintenance, and the reprocessing logs: In the TU & UC combined procedure, the data from the SPUMG tables (i.e., all relevant table contents from SPUMG in the twin system) are imported into the productive system after upgrade and before the Unicode conversion in a way similar to that used for the Unicode-adapted custom development into the production system after the upgrade. This is much faster than the execution of the SPUMG database scans needed for a standalone Unicode conversion of an MDMP system, which take some time to run.

► **Unicode preparation, conversion, and reprocessing**
Then comes the required Unicode preparation, followed by the Unicode conversion of the database, again done with the SAPinst and R3load along with the migration and distribution monitor.

Postprocessing in the TU & UC Combined Procedure

Post-processing after the upgrade and Unicode conversion

After the Unicode conversion, the post-processing must be performed, similarly to the CU & UC combined procedure. You can expect greater difficulty than with the CU & UC combined procedure when it comes to manual repair of unassigned words using the SUMG tool. This is because the twin system is "older" than the production system at the time of the upgrade and the Unicode conversion, all the new vocabulary and reprocessing words cannot be determined (the delta problem). During the database export with R3load, there is no conversion information available for these words, so that an XML log file is created with a corresponding entry. Its contents may be, for instance, that only the global fallback code page could be used for conversion (see Section 3.2).

The tables with these words are then flagged in the worklist in Transaction SUMG in the Unicode system as requiring manual repair after the automatic repair job. Thus, after the Unicode conversion, some manual repair can be expected with Transaction SUMG.

3.3.4 Comparison of the Combined Procedures

CU & UC vs. TU & UC

While in a standalone Unicode conversion with the CU & UC combined procedure the vocabulary alone can be transported into the new system, the runtime-intensive database scans must still be performed in every system independently of the vocabulary transfer. In the TU & UC combined procedure, by contrast, all the scan data is transported from the twin system into the production system. While the CU & UC combined procedure is only usable for starting release SAP R/3 4.6C with MDMP (for blended code page systems see SAP Note 928729) and also for SAP R/3 Enterprise and SAP ECC 5.0—the TU & UC combined procedure will be available for SAP starting releases below SAP R/3 4.6C as well as SAP Web AS 6.10 and all Unicode-capable target releases.

The main feature of the TU & UC combined procedure, namely that the very runtime-intensive database scans stored in many UMG tables (*Unicode migration*) are transported from the twin system into the production system, may seem trivial to you. You may be asking why this couldn't also be used for standalone Unicode conversions. However, despite the obvious simplicity of the procedure, this process shouldn't be underestimated. There are a great number of detailed problems and there isn't much experience yet from customer projects. However, SAP is making every effort to continue to improve this procedure and to extend it to more scenarios if possible. For more information, see SAP Note 959698.

Finally, in Table 3.8 we summarize the different options for upgrading SAP R/3 or ERP systems to higher ERP releases (production systems) depending on code-page configuration. For non-R/3 single code page components in the SAP Business Suite, analogous options apply for the upgrade and Unicode conversion (without combined procedures), which can be derived from the comparison of the underlying SAP Basis component with the corresponding R/3 or ERP system. For example, SAP CRM 4.0 uses the SAP basis with release 6.20 and thus corresponds to SAP R/3 Enterprise, which also uses that SAP basis.

Overview: Upgrade and Unicode conversion options

Starting release / Upgrade method	Direct upgrade to SAP ERP 2005	Direct upgrade to SAP ERP 2004	Unicode conversion before upgrade	Combined Upgrade and Unicode Conversion*
< SAP R/3 4.6C	yes	yes	no	no
SAP R/3 4.6C	yes	yes	no	CU & UC
SAP R/3 Enterprise	yes	yes	yes	CU & UC
SAP ERP 2004	yes	–	yes	CU & UC

* For availability details please refer to SAP Note 928729.

Table 3.8 Upgrade Options for a Single Code Page System to SAP ERP

For the upgrade and Unicode conversion of an MDMP or blended code page system to SAP ERP 2005/SAP ECC 6.0, the limitation of the direct upgrade especially applies, because MDMP and blended code-page configurations will no longer be supported as of SAP

NetWeaver 2004s with basis release 7.00. This also applies for all other components of the SAP Business Suite with a target release based on SAP NetWeaver 2004s (for instance, SAP CRM 5.0). Table 3.9 illustrates this relationship.

Starting release	Upgrade method	Direct upgrade to SAP ERP 2005	Direct upgrade to SAP ERP 2004	Unicode conversion before upgrade	Combined upgrade and Unicode conversion**
< SAP R/3 4.6C		no*	yes	no	TU & UC
SAP R/3 4.6C		no*	yes	no	CU & UC
SAP R/3 Enterprise		no***	yes	yes	CU & UC
SAP ERP 2004		no***	–	yes	CU & UC

   *   Special options and restrictions in SAP Notes 79991 and 896144.

  **   For availability details please refer to SAP Note 928729 and 959698.

*** Unicode conversion before upgrade recommended.

Table 3.9 Upgrade Options for an MDMP System to SAP ERP

3.4 ABAP and Unicode

ABAP and Unicode The introduction of the SAP Web Application Server 6.10/6.20 heralded a new era for the SAP standard programming language ABAP. Besides numerous new features that had been planned for a long time, the greatest driver was the complete support of Unicode in all SAP applications, which required significant changes to ABAP, especially for text processing.

New technologies and concepts, especially from object-oriented programming and communications with Internet-based applications, made it necessary to change and extend ABAP as well. It was also time to ban very obsolete ABAP constructs (still valid for reasons of compatibility) that sometimes allowed very shaky programming. So the "new ABAP" as of SAP Web AS 6.20 also contributes to significant general quality improvements to programs, which benefits SAP customers and SAP alike.

We will now present the most important changes and new features in ABAP that are necessary for the Unicode enabling of custom development and modifications. The tools and recommended procedures for adaptation will also be addressed.

After many Unicode conversion projects, it proved the case that program which had already been programmed "cleanly" already largely fulfilled the new Unicode rules, and thus required very little effort to change. On the other hand, all the locations where greater changes needed to be performed usually indicated error-prone and thus questionable programming practices. Just as in ABAP Objects the older, dangerous language constructs were declared obsolete and were no longer permitted to be used, the rules for Unicode programs offer increased security when programming, for example when working with character fields and mixed structures. This is particularly true of the storage of external data, such as the file interface, which was completely reworked for use in Unicode programs.

Low adaptation effort due to good programming style

Tip
If you are in an Unicode-capable SAP release we recommend that you always mark new programs as Unicode programs upon creation, and convert older programs to Unicode step by step.

3.4.1 Overview

A deciding factor in the interplay of ABAP and Unicode is that as of SAP Basis 6.10 and 6.20 the ABAP source code in a Unicode system and a non-Unicode system are identical. So there are no different ABAP versions or additional data types in a Unicode system. Differences show up in the different interpretation of character-based data type C, N, D, T, STRING, which have a length of one byte in a non-Unicode system, but 2 bytes in a Unicode system. The SAP kernel and the database also differ, as they are in Unicode format in a Unicode system. Figure 3.1 in Section 3.1 already illustrated this property.

To enable a transition between old and new ABAP syntax, a so-called *Unicode flag* was introduced which specifies whether the new or old ABAP syntax check applies to that program. This flag is a new program attribute which is edited in the ABAP Workbench when editing the attributes of development objects. Figure 3.33 shows the ABAP Editor (Transaction SE38) with the program properties of an example program RFUMSV00. The field **Unicode checks active**, representing the

Unicode flag

Unicode flag, is checked here; that is, the new Unicode syntax is active for RFUMSV00.

A Unicode-capable ABAP program is therefore a program for which the Unicode flag is set and all Unicode checks are active. Such a program in a non-Unicode system returns the same results as in a Unicode system. To perform the corresponding syntax checks, the Unicode flag must be set in the dynpros of the program and class properties, as shown in the example in Figure 3.33.

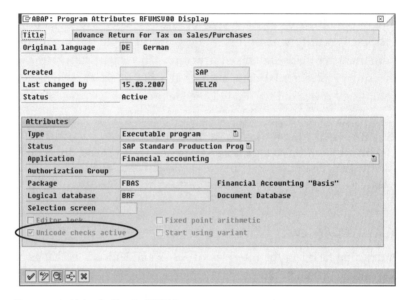

Figure 3.33 Unicode Flag in ABAP Programs

Unicode flag in Unicode and non-Unicode systems

In a Unicode system, only those programs may be executed that have the Unicode flag set, while a non-Unicode system permits programs with or without the flag. If the Unicode flag is set, syntactic checks and program execution follow the new syntax rules, whether the system is a Unicode system or a non-Unicode system. SAP applications are only supplied with the Unicode flag in both non-Unicode systems and Unicode systems.

If the Unicode flag is not set, the program can only be run in a non-Unicode system. For such programs, the new syntactic and semantic changes have no effect. However, all language extensions can be used which have been introduced with the transition to Unicode.

The changes and limitations associated with the Unicode flag have the effect that programs in the Unicode system and non-Unicode system are executed with the most similar semantics possible, although in a few cases differences can still occur, especially when programming with bytes and offsets. Programs that should run in both systems should therefore be tested in both the non-Unicode system and the Unicode system.

3.4.2 Unicode-Relevant Changes and Additions in ABAP as of SAP Web AS 6.10/6.20

> **Note**
>
> In the following part of this chapter, the most important concepts of the "new ABAP syntax" as of SAP Web AS 6.10/6.20 are presented, although we can't cover all the details. For further information, you should make use of the copious documentation on this topic (see Appendix C). A pragmatic approach is followed here.

Why are existing ABAP programs from release SAP R/3 4.6C or earlier not already Unicode capable? The main reason lies in the fact that without Unicode a character has always been considered equivalent to a byte, and that the corresponding layout of data structures has relied on that fact. Asian Double-Byte languages simply use 2 bytes per character, hence the name "Double-Byte."

One of the main technical properties of Unicode, however, is that a character may occupy a different number of bytes in the system. For example, the global character set in a UTF-16 system occupies 2 bytes per character and in UTF-8 only 1, while a Korean character in UTF-16 has 2 bytes and in UTF-8 has 3, so the equivalence of characters and bytes can simply no longer be used.

This led to a significant change in ABAP: Character-type and non-character-type data types are now strictly separate. Thus, there weren't any new data types introduced because, after all, the same ABAP code should still run in a non-Unicode system and a Unicode system. Rather, a better and more transparent interpretation of the data types was introduced. Thus many of the syntactic ABAP changes and extensions follow from the main rule: "One character is not one byte!"

Unicode: One
character is not
one byte!
This new rule especially has effects on programming with the Asian Double-Byte languages: In the non-Unicode system, a character is assigned 2 bytes, while the permitted length of a field is reduced by half. For instance, in a non-Unicode system a name written in Chinese may only be 10 characters long in a character-type table field of length 20. In a Unicode system, however, each character is treated the same (regardless of language), so this name can be 20 characters long.

**Data types and
structures**
ABAP distinguishes the following data types and structures:

▸ *Character-type* data types and structures are:

  ▹ C: Characters (letters, numerals, special characters)

  ▹ N: Numeric characters (numerals)

  ▹ D: Date

  ▹ T: Time

  ▹ STRING: Character string

  ▹ Character-type structures are structures which contain only fields of types C, N, D, or T, either directly or in substructures.

▸ *Numerical* flat data types are F, P, and I. Variables of types X and XSTRING are called *byte-typed*.

**Structures under
Unicode**
▸ *Structures* are distinguished according to the following features:

  ▹ *Flat structures* contain only fields of the elementary types C, N, D, T, F, I, P, and X, or structures of those types.

  ▹ *Deep structures*, in addition to the elementary types, contain strings, internal tables, and field or object references.

  ▹ *Nested structures* are structures that themselves contain substructures as components.

  ▹ *Non-nested structures* are structures that do not contain other structures.

In the new syntax, there must be a strict distinction drawn between character-type and non-character-type variables. Especially if structures with fields of mixed data types are used, adaptations and changes can be expected, because here the new rules make themselves especially strongly felt.

In the following, some selected changes and extensions are described with small examples which can often be observed during Unicode enabling in concrete projects. For a complete description, please consult the corresponding documentation.

Character and Byte-Oriented Processing

In a Unicode system, a syntax distinction must be made between character and byte-based processing using syntax extensions.

▶ Example of character processing:

```
CONCATENATE cf1 cf2 TO cf3IF cf1 CS cf2 ... .
```

▶ Example of byte processing:

```
CONCATENATE xf1 xf2 TO xf3 IN BYTE MODE.
IF xf1 BYTE-CS xf2 ... .
```

Difference between character and byte-based processing in Unicode ABAP

While the CONCATENATE command with character-type data types needs no addition, thus can remain unchanged, in the second case the addition IN BYTE MODE and BYTE-CS must be used for comparison operations, whereby only operands of the types X and XSTRING are permitted.

Specification of Field Length of Data Objects

The DESCRIBE statement is used to specify the properties of data objects of elementary data types. To calculate the length directly occupied in memory, the LENGTH addition is used, which must now be specified in bytes or characters:

Field lengths in Unicode ABAP

```
DESCRIBE FIELD ... LENGTH ...
  IN (BYTE | CHARACTER) MODE
```

In these statements, the developer must decide whether the length or offset should be measured in characters or bytes. The following example shows this statement:

```
FORM write3 USING fld TYPE c.
DATA: fldlen TYPE i.
DESCRIBE FIELD fld LENGTH fldlen IN CHARACTER MODE.
IF fldlen >= 3.
  WRITE: / fld(3).
ENDIF.
ENDFORM.
```

The new distinction between characters and bytes in the Unicode system also has a significant effect on programming with offsets and lengths in structures. In general, this method was not recommended long before Unicode, as it contributes to a lack of transparency and is error-prone.

Programming with offsets and lengths in Unicode ABAP

In general, offset and length specifications are critical, because the length of the individual characters is platform-dependent and thus initially it is not clear for mixed structures whether the unit "byte" or "character" is meant. So partly significant limitations are now required, offset and length access continues to be possible if you follow certain rules, as will be shown below. This rule affects accesses to individual fields and structures, passing of parameters to subprograms, and also working with field symbols.

Primarily, this is the same rule of distinguishing between characters and bytes. For offset and length access to individual fields, with character-type access the offset/length values are given in characters, and for X and XSTRING in bytes.

Limitations on offsets and lengths in structures

Offset and length programming are critical for structures in which significant limitations apply in the Unicode system. This technology is only permitted for flat structures, and offset and length access calculated in characters may only apply to character-type fields from the start of the structure; that is, it may not jump over any byte-based or numerically based fields. Besides the undesirable programming style with offsets, a significant reason is in the memory layout of Unicode systems, in which alignment gaps occur so that structure fields are not always stored in sequential storage space.

Figure 3.34 shows a structure with fields of mixed data types. Offset and length access in characters is possible in the first two fields, because both are character-type. Access to the last field is not possible because the next-to-last field, as X(3), is byte-oriented and thus this would be a disallowed jump.

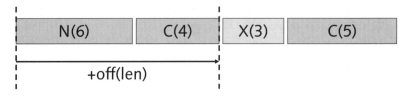

Figure 3.34 Offset and Length Access in Structures

Assignments Between Fields, Structures, or Mixed Types

The last rule has other effects, particularly in assignments between incompatible fields, structures, or mixed types. The strict separation of character- and byte-type and numerical data types means that direct assignments between variables of mixed data types is no longer possible.

Assignments in structures with fields of mixed data types

The following example shows two structures, CSTRU and XSTRU, with three fields apiece, where the second field of XSTRU has the byte-type data type X:

```
DATA:
BEGIN OF cstru,
  first(10) TYPE c,
  tab(1) TYPE c,
  last(10) TYPE c,
END OF cstru
DATA:
BEGIN OF xstru,
  first(10) TYPE c,
  tab(1) TYPE x VALUE '09',
  last(10) TYPE c,
END OF xstru.
```

The following assignment in the Unicode system is erroneous, because the second field of XSTRU has type X and thus this violates this rule:

```
cstru = xstru.   "Unicode Error!
```

You will surely be asking yourself at this point how this kind of case is solved. Although we can't go into more detail, we do want to give you the following recommendations.

Recommendations for programming

▶ **General avoidance of mixed structures**
The best approach is to avoid mixed structures in general, so that these problems never arise. However, this is not always possible, as we can see in the case of container programming (described a bit later).

▶ **Assignment through individual fields**
When assigning through individual fields, instead of an assignment between entire (mixed) structures, the strucure fields should

be directly, explicitly specified and assigned (that is, according to the concept of MOVE CORRESPONDING). If necessary, corresponding logic can be built in. This method is somewhat costlier than direct assignment between structures, but it is much more transparent and safer.

▸ **Type casting**
If fields of different types are assigned, the use of field symbols may be of use. The ABAP statement ASSIGN ... CASTING makes it possible to view the contents of a field through a field symbol as a value of a different type. One application of this statement, for example, is to provide different views of a structure using casts to different types.

Container Technology

A popular programming technology, but one which is unfortunately rather complicated, is *container technology*. This is used to "pack" multiple data objects of different types into a kind of black box, represented by a long field of type C. A particular operation is then performed, such as a data transfer, and then the data is unpacked again and provided to the application. Thus different data types must be assigned to a long field of type C.

A familiar example involves the IDocs in the SAP ALE technology, in which the segments of the application data are stored in the EDID4-SDATA field of type C with length 1000. Particular rules apply to container programming, which will be described in greater detail in the next section.

Container Alignment for Asian Double-Byte languages

If a character-type structure is stored in a simple field C or STRING and this is transported from a non-Unicode to a Unicode system or vice versa, then when using Asian Double-Byte languages (JA, KO, ZH, ZF) a special alignment of the structure is performed: the *Container Alignment*. The purpose of this is to compensate for the different character processing of these languages in non-Unicode and Unicode systems.

The SAP standard applications are already equipped with the Container Alignment except for a few exceptions, so these are primarily custom developments. An example should illustrate the problems.

A structure s with two fields c4 and c3 of data type C and with four or three elements is assigned a variable container of data type C with seven elements:

Container Alignment program in Asian languages

```
DATA: BEGIN OF s,
        c4(4) TYPE c,
        c3(3) TYPE c,
      END OF s,
container(7) TYPE c.
* Assign the structure to container before
* transfer Non-Unicode to Unicode or vice versa
container = s.
* < Transfer from Non-Unicode to Unicode or vice versa >
* Assign container to the structure in partner system
s = container.
```

If the processing happens between non-Unicode and Unicode systems, the cases shown in Table 3.10 may occur for Asian Double-Byte languages.

Description	Content of s and container
Content of s in the Asian non-Unicode system: ▸ c4 = 中石 (2 characters with 2 Double-Byte characters each) ▸ c3 = ABC	|中石|ABC|
Content of container after assignment in non-Unicode: container = s	中石ABC
Content of container after transport into a Unicode-system (RFC/File/R3trans): Since Asian characters in the Unicode system are stored like any other characters, the first two characters container now only occupy 2 units of memory (and not 4, as in the non-Unicode system); therefore 2 blanks ∪ are inserted.	中石ABC ∪ ∪ (∪ = blank)
For an assignment in the Unicode system s = container without correction, the fields c3 = 中石AB and c4 = C∪∪ would have the wrong values.	|中石AB|C∪∪|

Table 3.10 Container Problem in Non-Unicode/Unicode Scenarios

Description	Content of s and container
The correction (Container Alignment) adjusts the structure lengths in container to that of the non-Unicode system.	中石∪∪ABC
With the Container Alignment, the assignment s = container delivers the right values again: c4 = 中石∪∪ (2 additional blanks) c3 = ABC	|中石∪∪|ABC|

Table 3.10 Container Problem in Non-Unicode/Unicode Scenarios (cont.)

This container problem can occur when using Asian languages under the following conditions.

▶ A container transfer is performed with RFC between a Unicode and a non-Unicode system or vice versa.

▶ A container transfer is performed using a file between a Unicode and a non-Unicode system or vice versa.

▶ The ABAP statement IMPORT FROM DATABASE reads a container in a Unicode system when was written on a non-Unicode system.

▶ After a Unicode conversion, a container is read which was written previously in the non-Unicode system.

▶ Containers are transported with R3trans between a non-Unicode and a Unicode-system or vice versa.

Container Alignment: Solutions

To solve this problem, as of SAP Web AS 6.20 there have been special classes which support Container Alignment: The alignment always takes place in the Unicode system. The following bullet points describe three possible solutions, initially just for the situation where the Unicode system read the container from a non-Unicode system and assigns it to the structure,

▶ Correction takes place when the content of the container is assigned to the structure. The class CL_NLS_STRUC_CONTAINER and method CONT_TO_STRUC can be used for this.

▶ The correction occurs "in place" before assignment of the container to the structure. The class CL_NLS_STRUC_CONTAINER_SNAME and method CONT_TO_STRUC can be used for this purpose. The name of the structure is needed, which must be defined in the ABAP Dictionary.

▶ If only the field lengths of the structure (nametabs) are known, then in the generic case the class CL_NLS_STRUC_CONTAINER_ OFFS and method CONT_TO_STRUC can be used.

SAP Note 510882 and corresponding references can provide more details.

For the reverse direction, whereby the Unicode system sends container data to a non-Unicode system, the same classes can be used with the method STRUC_TO_CONT instead of CONT_TO_STRUC. Thus alignment happens during or after assignment of the structure to the container.

To be able to program the adjustments described in Section 3.5 in MDMP-Unicode scenarios efficiently for Container Alignment as well, the methods CONT_TO_STRUC and STRUC_TO_CONT have a language parameter LANGU which works well with the NLS_GET_LANGU_ CP_TAB function to determine the code page of an MDMP system.

The following Container Alignment programming example in Listing 3.1 shows the use of the CL_NLS_STRUC_CONTAINER class for Container Alignment in a Unicode system which receives data from a non-Unicode system my_dest whose code page configuration is determined using the function NLS_GET_LANGU_CP_TAB.

Container Alignment: programming example

```
DATA:
  my_dest  TYPE rfcdest VALUE 'my_dest',
  my_tab   TYPE TABLE OF t100,
  cp_tab   TYPE nls_langu_cp_tab,
  cc       TYPE REF TO cl_nls_struc_container,
  stru     LIKE t100u.
FIELD-SYMBOLS <fs> TYPE t100.
* Do the remote function call.
CALL FUNCTION 'MY_F' DESTINATION my_dest
  TABLES
    tab = my_tab.
* Get the code page information.
CALL FUNCTION 'NLS_GET_LANGU_CP_TAB'
  EXPORTING
    destination = my_dest
  TABLES
    cp_tab = cp_tab.
* Create an instance of the alignment correction class.
cc = cl_nls_struc_container=>create( cp_tab = cp_tab ).
```

```
* Process contents of my_tab.
LOOP AT my_tab ASSIGNING <fs>.
* Convert the container <fs>-text into the structure stru
* with correct alignment, taking into account the language
* key <fs>-sprsl.
  cc->cont_to_struc( EXPORTING langu = <fs>-sprsl
                               cont  = <fs>-text
                     IMPORTING struc = stru ).
* Continue processing stru ...
ENDLOOP.
*-----------------------------------------------------------
* If just the name of the structure (but not a
* structure variable) is available when the alignment
* correction is done, the class
* CL_NLS_STRUC_CONTAINER_SNAME can be used:
*-----------------------------------------------------------
* Create an instance of the alignment correction class;
* needs the name of the structure.
cc = cl_nls_struc_container_sname=>create
( cp_tab      = cp_tab
  struc_name = 'T100U' ).
* Correct the alignment of the container <fs>-text,
* taking into account the language key <fs>-sprsl.
DATA cont like t100-text.
cont = <fs>-text.
cc->cont_to_struc( EXPORTING langu = <fs>-sprsl
                   CHANGING  cont  = cont ).
```

Listing 3.1 Example Program for Container Alignment

Enhancements of SAP Tables and Structures

Customer enhancements

SAP standard tables and structures can be enhanced by customers using appends or customizing includes. The enhancements do not just refer to the structures or tables themselves, but also to dependent structures which take the enhancement as an include or reference structure. Append structures, which appear only at the end of the starting structure, can lead to offsets within structures in the case of dependent structures.

With the new Unicode syntax, arbitrary enhancements are no longer possible. Thus the selection of an enhancement category is necessary, since in programs without active Unicode checking enhancement of tables and structures can lead to syntax and runtime errors.

In programs with active Unicode checking, assignments, operand checks, and accesses with offset and length are all problematic. Difficulties may arise, for instance, when numerical or deep components are inserted into a purely character-type structure and the structure therefore loses its character-type nature.

In the ABAP Dictionary of a table or structure (Transaction SE11/SE12) the possible enhancement categories particularly needing consideration in the case of custom enhancements are displayed using the menu item **Extras • Enhancement category** depending on the structure definition, as follows:

▶ **Can be arbitrarily enhanced**
The structure and its enhancements may contain components with arbitrary data types.

▶ **Can be enhanced — character and numerical type**
The structure and its enhancements may not contain deep data types (tables, references, strings).

▶ **Can be enhanced — character-like**
All structure components and their enhancements must be character-typed (C, N, D, or T). The starting structure and all enhancements by customizing includes or append structures are subject to this limitation.

▶ **Cannot be enhanced**
The structure may not be enhanced.

▶ **Unclassified**
There is no information available about enhancements.

Figure 3.35 shows the enhancement category of the SAP table MARA, which permits appends with character-type and numerical data types.

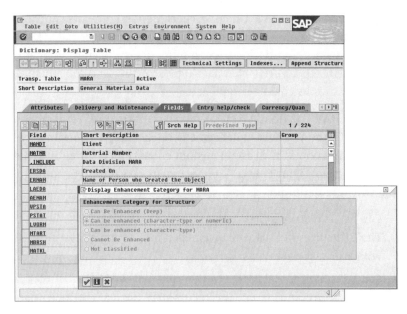

Figure 3.35 Enhancement Category for Appends

File Interfaces

If a Unicode system communicates with another system, one of the central questions is whether the other system is running with or without Unicode. Section 3.5 covers this topic in detail. However, because there are important syntactic changes in the ABAP file interface and these are very often used in custom development, we will take a look at them here.

File transfer through the application server

To process files on the application server, the new syntax requires knowledge of the code page of the file; that is, when a file is opened it should be known whether it is a Unicode or non-Unicode file with a code page to be supplied. The syntax of the OPEN DATASET statement was extended for this purpose, so the reading/writing of texts in the Unicode system can look like this:[8]

```
OPEN DATASET dsn IN TEXT MODE
        ENCODING (DEFAULT | UTF-8 | NON-UNICODE)
        REPLACEMENT CHARACTER c
        IGNORING CONVERSION ERRORS.
```

---

8 The full syntax of the OPEN DATASET statement can be found in the documentation.

The ENCODING addition required in the Unicode system determines the character set with which the data is to be processed. DEFAULT is always UTF-8 in the Unicode system; in the non-Unicode system it is the current code page. The specification NON-UNICODE cases the single code page of the logon language to be used for the file, which can also be directly set using the SET LOCALE LANGUAGE statement.

The additions REPLACEMENT and IGNORING are important for Unicode/non-Unicode (SAP system/file) conversion. The addition REPLACEMENT CHARACTER determines the replacement character to be used when a character is not present in the target character set during conversion. Without this specification, the replacement character (#) is used. The addition IGNORING CONVERSION ERRORS suppresses runtime errors when reading or writing the file, in case a conversion error occurs. These two additions are also available for RFC Unicode and non-Unicode communication in Transaction SM59 under **Special Options**.

In the following code example, the reading and writing of arbitrary text and binary data in the non-Unicode system format is illustrated:

Processing of non-Unicode files with legacy mode in Unicode system

```
OPEN DATASET dsn IN LEGACY (TEXT | BINARY) MODE
                        (LITTLE | BIG) ENDIAN
                        CODE PAGE cp.
```

Legacy mode makes it possible to treat the file as in a non-Unicode system. This is especially interesting when no (or few) code-page and format changes to the files used so far should occur during Unicode enabling. TEXT MODE and BINARY MODE specify the text or binary mode of the file. LITTLE ENDIAN and BIG ENDIAN replace the obsolete statement TRANSLATE NUMBER FORMAT.

The addition CODE PAGE is a replacement for the obsolete statement TRANSLATE ... CODE PAGE and acts as follows: Without this addition, a conversion takes place between Unicode (SAP system) and the single code page of the file as specified by the logon language or by the value of SY-LANGU in the Unicode system. With the CODE PAGE addition, there is always a conversion between this code page and Unicode. To avoid incorrect conversions, it is generally recommended that the single code page of the file be given explicitly.

File Transfer Through the SAP GUI

File processing on the front end with GUI_UPLOAD and GUI_DOWNLOAD

Another popular custom development is the upload and download of local files between the SAP system and the PC of the user using the SAP GUI as the front end. For instance, ABAP lists of SAP reports can be loaded onto the PC and edited further with Microsoft Office programs. Because all enterprises have their own formats and processes, this is an area where a particularly large number of customer programs have been developed.

The traditional function modules WS_UPLOAD and WS_DOWNLOAD are obsolete because of the number of Unicode changes, and have been replaced by the new components GUI_UPLOAD and GUI_DOWNLOAD, described in detail in the documentation. Alternatively, you can also use the following new class methods:

```
CL_GUI_FRONTEND_SERVICES=>FILE_OPEN/SAVE_DIALOG
```

This makes it possible to use the parameter WITH_ENCODING = 'X' in SAP GUI 6.40 and up to select a code page interactively during uploads and downloads.

To convert between Unicode (SAP system) and the local file, the same rules apply as for file transfer with the application server. It is possible to specify an explicit code page for the file, replacement characters for conversion errors, and an ignore parameter to prevent stops on conversion errors. Please refer to Section 3.5 for more information.

Utilities Classes

ABAP utilities classes for special characters

For more functions for Unicode programming, there are utilities classes available that should always be used in the development of new programs and in Unicode enabling wherever possible, in cases where they aren't already required. In the following paragraphs, we'll describe some important classes. You can find detailed descriptions in the class documentation and other references.

The class CL_ABAP_CHAR_UTILITIES provides attributes and methods relevant to the properties of individual characters. For instance, control characters are provided as attributes—such as newline or horizontal_tab—which are often used in file processing and are usually encoded in hexadecimal in the non-Unicode system. The following ABAP example replaces a tab with a space in a text of type STRING:

```
CLASS cl_abap_char_utilities DEFINITION LOAD.
DATA: text TYPE string.
REPLACE cl_abap_char_utilites=>horizontal_tab
WITH space INTO text.
```

The attribute charsize determines the length of a field C(1) in bytes, that is, one byte in a non-Unicode system and two in a Unicode system. This attribute can easily be used to decide whether an SAP system is running in Unicode or non-Unicode and is therefore used in many applications which need to distinguish between Unicode and non-Unicode environments. The field **Unicode system yes/no** cannot be directly used from the system status.

The following example shows an excerpt from the RFFORI99 include from the SAP-FI application Payment Medium International, in order to see general subroutines which handle file transfer differently in Unicode and non-Unicode:

```
i = cl_abap_char_utilities=>charsize.
IF i = 1.   " Non-Unicode system
  OPEN DATASET hlp_filename IN BINARY MODE FOR OUTPUT.
ELSE.   " Unicode system
  OPEN DATASET hlp_filename IN LEGACY BINARY MODE
   FOR OUTPUT.
ENDIF.
```

Depending on whether the system is a non-Unicode system (cl_abap_char_utilities=>charsize = 1) or a Unicode system (charsize = 2), different statements are used to process the file. If the system is a Unicode system, the LEGACY BINARY MODE is used to process a non-Unicode file with a single code page, which in the absence of other specifications is derived from the logon language, into the Unicode system. During this processing, conversion between single code page and Unicode is performed automatically. In the case of a non-Unicode system, the file is opened IN BINARY MODE FOR OUTPUT, so that the data can be written to the file in binary with no conversion.

ABAP utilities
classes for arbitrary
conversions
between Unicode
and single code
page

To enable numerous conversions between Unicode and non-Unicode, there are special utilities classes available which are very powerful and can conversion between Unicode and all known single code pages. They also replace the obsolete TRANSLATE statement.

▸ The class CL_ABAP_CONV_IN_CE allows the reading of data from a container and conversion to the system format. It is also possible to fill structures with data.

▸ CL_ABAP_CONV_OUT_CE converts data from the system format into an external format and writes it into a container.

▸ CL_ABAP_CONV_X2X_CE enables an arbitrary conversion of data from an external format to a different external format.

▸ In this context, we should also mention the class CL_ABAP_CONTAINER_UTILITIES, which supports the reading and writing of containers. This has changed due to the new syntax rules and the separation between characters and bytes.

▸ Another class, CL_ABAP_LIST_UTILITIES, is of interest in list output with Eastern Asian texts. In the Unicode system, an Asian character is treated exactly like a European one; that is, there is no longer any distinction between Single- or Double-Byte as in the non-Unicode system. Nonetheless, an Asian character is significantly wider than a European one. During display or printing, therefore, it may well play a role in whether a character is Asian or not; especially when lists or tables with a fixed column length are involved (alignment). In a Unicode system, all characters, including Eastern Asian ones, fit in one memory cell, but the Eastern Asian characters on ABAP lists require two screen columns, while European characters only occupy one.

This class includes methods to achieve a correct column alignment for display of Eastern Asian scripts. Such characters are used especially in the languages Chinese, Japanese, and Korean. At this point, we should mention that this alignment problem should also be taken into consideration for list-type output on printers and other output media.

3.4.3 Tools for Unicode Enabling

To perform Unicode enabling of custom development as efficiently as possible and accelerate it further, the following special tools are available:

UCCHECK, SCOV, SCI

- ▶ **Transaction UCCHECK**
  The *Unicode Syntax Check* (Transaction UCCHECK) is used centrally for Unicode enabling.

- ▶ **Transaction SCOV**
  The *Coverage Analyzer* (Transaction SCOV) measures the actual usage of custom developments in the production system and supports testing.

- ▶ **Transaction SCI**
  The *Code Inspector* (Transaction SCI) examines the source code of custom development for critical or inefficient code and suggests appropriate hints for its improvement.

Besides Unicode enabling, these tools also permit a general improvement of the overall quality of your custom development. In the following sections, we will take a closer look at these tools.

Unicode Syntax Check

With Transaction UCCHECK (*Unicode syntax check*), customer programs can be centrally adapted to the new Unicode syntax. Several selection criteria are possible, of which especially the checkbox **Only examine programs without activated Unicode flag** is of interest, which if set checks all programs without a Unicode flag.

UCCHECK in detail

The programs are checked for Unicode-relevant syntax errors and displayed in a results list with the traffic light colors green, yellow, or red. For syntax errors in red, the program can jump from the list directly into the ABAP Editor in order to make the changes needed. Yellow shows that a complete check is impossible due to runtime dependencies, so that additional analysis and tests will be necessary in the Unicode system. Green means that the program is syntactically correct, but it cannot say anything about whether it is semantically correct or will run correctly; this can only be ascertained by testing.

From the results list, you can automatically create transport orders and set the Unicode flag in batches. In addition, some application-specific checks are integrated which can highlight the points in programs which are not Unicode capable. Figure 3.36 shows a result list from UCCHECK.

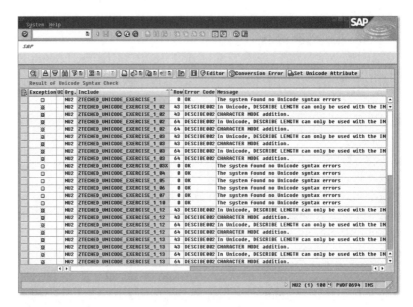

Figure 3.36 Results of the Unicode Check by UCCHECK

We highly recommend developing exclusively in the new Unicode syntax throughout the non-Unicode system if the existing custom development has all been adapted to the new Unicode syntax but the system hasn't yet been converted to Unicode. To develop in this way, the special instance profile parameter abap/unicode_check can be configured as follows:

abap/unicode_
check for system-
wide configuration
of the new
Unicode syntax

▶ **Instance profile parameter abap/unicode_check**
To determine throughout a non-Unicode system whether the new syntax is always active or only if the Unicode flag is set, the instance profile parameter abap/unicode_check can be configured as follows in Transaction RZ10 for profile maintenance:

  ▶ on
  For each ABAP program, the new Unicode checks will be performed regardless of the Unicode flag. Thus the system behaves as though the flag were always set.

  ▶ off (default)
  Unicode checks are only performed if the Unicode flag is set.

This is the recommended value before the Unicode enabling of customer programs. After adaptation (but before Unicode conversion) the parameter should be set to on so that development continues only with the new syntax.

In a Unicode system, the Unicode checks are always performed, so this parameter has no effect.

▸ **User exits and modifications**
As of SAP Web AS 6.10/6.20, all SAP standard programs are Unicode-capable and are delivered with the Unicode flag set in both the non-Unicode system and the Unicode system. If such an SAP program contains customer coding in a user exit, BAdI, or a modification and it is not Unicode-capable, syntax errors will occur. Thus user exits, BAdIs, and modifications must always have the new syntax, even in the non-Unicode system.

Enabling of user exits and modifications

If a user exit or BAdI is newly created in a non-Unicode system, the Unicode flag is already set, and right from the start the new syntax is used, so there will be no problems. In the case of an upgrade, however, this can be problematic. This is because the user exit or modification from the old release may be syntactically not yet Unicode-capable, but the Unicode flag may already be set in the associated SAP program or function group during the upgrade, so that an error occurs even during the upgrade. This applies for upgrades without a later Unicode conversion as well, since the set Unicode flag in the non-Unicode system and Unicode system always checks the new syntax.

There is no generally valid solution for the upgrade case. We recommend that you adapt the erroneous user exits or modifications to the new syntax after the first test upgrade and integrate them into the other adapted programs in a collective transport during the next upgrade. Additional information can be found in the SAP Notes and the Unicode documentation.

▸ **Generated programs**
Programs and other development objects generated by applications—for instance, by customizing—represent a special case. Because they are generated, they don't count as customer programs and are not looked at by Transaction UCCHECK. They must be regenerated for the Unicode system in order to set the Unicode flag automatically and use the new syntax.

Adaptation of application-specific generated programs

One example are applications maintaining conditions. Without regeneration, they may crash in the Unicode system with an error message such as "The program "/1SBDF12L/RV14AKxy" is not Unicode-capable." SAP Note 497850 describes a solution for regeneration in that case. Because the number of regenerations greatly depends on the configuration and customizing for the applications used, we won't go into any further detail here. Information on regenerations can be found in the corresponding Unicode conversion guides and SAP Notes, and should be carefully taken into consideration during the Unicode conversion.

Example programs for UCCHECK

Every SAP system at SAP Web AS 6.20 or higher includes example programs with exercises and solutions to make the differences between old and new syntax clear. The programs `TECHED_UNICODE_EXERCISE_x` (x = 1, 2, …, 22) and `TECHED_UNICODE_SOLUTION_x`, which are derived from various SAP TechEd events, contain examples and exercises with syntax errors and their solutions[9]. The programs 1 through 10 are internal applications and programs 11 through 20 include examples of interfaces and communication between Unicode and non-Unicode systems. You can access these programs directly in your SAP system by calling the ABAP Editor with the names above. They are mostly self-explanatory and include additional commentary.

Coverage Analyzer

Analysis of degree of utilization of custom development

It is often the case that certain custom development, when it is examined more closely, turns out not to be used in production. These are mostly old development or have been rewritten due to many changes, but are still in the production system and thus initially are considered relevant for Unicode enabling. There is not enough information to reliably determine which custom programs are actually used in production and often has no reliable answer, so all programs must be adapted.

As of SAP Web AS 6.20, there is the Coverage Analyzer (Transaction SCOV), which can analyze the runtime behavior of applications. The Coverage Analyzer allows an evaluation of the utilization of ABAP programs, so that especially custom developments can be analyzed.

---

9 Names and numbers might change in later SAP releases.

The Coverage Analyzer is started at a certain time and records the execution of programs, together with other useful information. The data can be consolidated and displayed graphically with detailed information. After a certain time has passed, the result is concrete and reliable information regarding which custom programs and parts of programs are truly being used in production. It is then possible to exclude obsolete programs from the Unicode enabling, which reduces the effort required. Moreover, the analyzer also provides other evaluation possibilities for testing and general quality improvement.

Figure 3.37 shows an example of a Coverage Analyzer report over a period of nine quarters in the years 2004 through 2006.

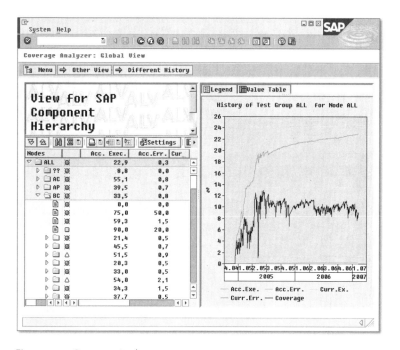

Figure 3.37 Coverage Analyzer

Code Inspector

Another useful tool which is of great use during the Unicode enabling is the Code Inspector (Transaction SCI), which is also available as of SAP Web AS 6.20. While the Coverage Analyzer largely analyzes the runtime behavior of ABAP programs, the Code Inspector combined different static tests of programs (see Figure 3.38). Syntactical and semantic correctness are checked as far as possible, and among other

Analysis of critical program code

things, potential performance problems due to suboptimal code are indicated. So using the Code Inspector is not just helpful for Unicode enabling but also for general quality improvement. Extended ABAP syntax check with Transaction SLIN is integrated into the Code Inspector.

Figure 3.38 Code Inspector

Recommended Procedure for Unicode Enabling

Tips for adaptation of custom development

To convert custom-developed programs on Unicode systems, the following general procedure is recommended. This must be individually designed for each project due to differing background conditions and prerequisites. In the case of complex system landscapes with many dependencies and possible distributed development, special investigations must be performed, which will not be described here.

▶ In the case of a massive volume of custom programs (typically 1,000 or more) you should clarify before the Unicode enabling which programs are used in production and which are obsolete. It has often proved the case in practice that only a certain percentage are used in production and that may old programs still exist unused in the production system. The Coverage Analyzer can be used for this; however, there are other procedures and special SAP services for this purpose.

▶ First, Transaction UCCHECK should be started in the non-Unicode system, whereby in addition to other selection criteria the checkbox **Examine only programs without activated Unicode flag** should be checked. This way, all still-unadapted programs without the Unicode flag will be checked.

▶ The combination of upgrade and Unicode conversion is problematic if the starting release is earlier than 6.10 or 6.20, for instance SAP R/3 4.6C (see also Section 3.3). Because the new ABAP syntax only exists as of release 6.10/6.20, the upgrade of a development or test system must be performed first before UCCHECK and the adaptations can be performed.

▶ After all syntax errors have been corrected, the Unicode flag can be set for every program directly using UCCHECK, or it can be set manually. All adapted programs are entered into transport orders for further transport. In case of a combined upgrade of SAP R/3 4.6C (or lower) and Unicode conversion, they are entered into the upgrade-specific collective transports. This integrates the adapted programs directly into the upgrade for later upgrades.

▶ Now the adapted programs must be tested in the non-Unicode system and the Unicode system. In the case of a combined upgrade and Unicode conversion or in the case that the adapted program is not used in production in the non-Unicode system, testing is only required in the Unicode system. The goals of the test are the detection of runtime errors and proof of the correctness of the results in both systems. In order to eliminate runtime errors in advance, field symbols and parameters should always be typed, so that problematic locations can already be detected during syntax checking.

Testing the Unicode programs

▶ After the Unicode enabling, the instance profile parameter `abap/unicode_check` in the non-Unicode system should be set to `on` so that throughout the system only the new syntax will be used. Moreover, programs still not adapted or needing regeneration will be identified quickly during testing, since they will no longer be executable.

3.4.4   Summary

The ABAP programming language has been changed and extended in several ways for operation in a Unicode system. The central change is the new strict separation of characters and bytes. Custom development from a non-Unicode system that is not Unicode-capable must be adapted as part of the Unicode project. The same ABAP coding in a non-Unicode system and a Unicode system is syntactically the same and semantically almost always equivalent.

Besides syntax adaptation, a Unicode-capable program must set the Unicode flag as an attribute. Transaction UCCHECK is the central tool for the enabling of custom development to the new Unicode syntax.

Experience from many Unicode projects has shown that for a good programming style in custom development, an enabling rate of several thousand lines per day per developer can be achieved. Furthermore, it has been shown that the cost of interface programming is generally higher than for internal programs, such as reports.

3.5   Communication and Interfaces

Global business processes via the Internet

Today, a global enterprise generally operates worldwide, or at least in multiple countries, so customers, suppliers, delivery firms, and other business partners are distributed across different countries and must exchange data between all their computer systems. The Internet has created a significant technological breakthrough in this regard, so that business documents no longer need to be exchanged on paper, but can be exchanged electronically instead. It is expected or even legally required for these documents to be translated into the various national languages of the partners.

Figure 3.39 shows a typical scenario in which SAP and non-SAP systems exchange arbitrary data over the Internet and other communications media between business partners with different roles for different currencies on different continents.

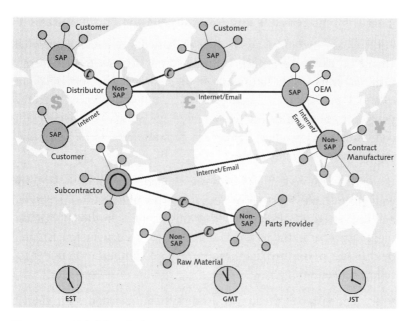

Figure 3.39 Global Data Exchange

A great challenge for the IT systems is the technology of communica- **Global data** tion and data exchange. Although during the time of Big Iron and **exchange** afterwards only a few, usually simple, interfaces were the rule, nowadays arbitrary data exchange in arbitrary formats is a must. In addition to the existing challenges posed for data communication by different technologies, network protocols, data formats, and application protocols, now there is another: Language. If texts from different character sets and languages must be exchanged—imagine a German automobile supplier expanding into China and therefore needing German and Chinese—then all texts and languages must be correctly and unambiguously transmitted between all the systems involved.

That is only possible without limitation between Unicode systems, given that non-Unicode single code page systems can only process languages from a single character set. MDMP systems have a similar problem, as they only know languages of the code pages configured. Even more challenging is the fact that MDMP is only known in SAP systems and there are significant limitations and even exclusions when communicating with non-SAP systems.

3.5.1 Homogeneous and Inhomogeneous Communication

For language exchange, an ideal global network of global enterprises would be one where only Unicode-based systems from different manufacturers would communicate together (*homogeneous communication*). Unfortunately, this is a wish that will only be possible a few years from now. In reality, we largely have networks in which Unicode and non-Unicode systems must communicate with one another (*inhomogeneous communication*[10]).

Using different code pages between Unicode and the non-Unicode code pages, texts must be correctly and unambiguously interpreted and converted. Regardless whether this happens in the application, middleware, or in the technical interface, such a conversion can only be correctly performed in inhomogeneous communication under the following conditions.

► The code page of the non-Unicode system determines the characters which can be correctly transmitted.

► The code page of the non-Unicode system must be unambiguous and known to the Unicode system.

► The Unicode system must be able to determine the code page of the non-Unicode system from parameters or configuration data.

► For the transfer, conversion routines between Unicode and all non-Unicode single code pages used must be available.

The following example in Table 3.11 should illustrate the conversion process. It includes the text "Alex" in the German, Russian, Japanese (Katakana), and Thai (shown in a simplified form) languages. In the code page columns, you can see the corresponding encoding in hexadecimal code for UTF-16 and UTF-8 as Unicode on the one hand, and for ISO, SJIS, TIS, and Microsoft Windows as single-code-page on the other.

---

10 The term *heterogeneous communication*, also used, is equivalent.

Language	Word (translated)	Code page encoding			
		UTF-16 Big Endian ▸ 2 bytes per character	**UTF-8** ▸ one byte: asc ▸ 2 bytes: nas ▸ 3 bytes: as	**ISO SJIS TIS** ▸ one byte: nas ▸ 2 bytes: as	**Microsoft Windows** ▸ one byte: nas ▸ 2 bytes: as
German	Alex	0041 006C 0065 0078	41 6C 65 78	41 6C 65 78	41 6C 65 78
Russian	Алекс	0410 043B 0435 043A 0441	D090 D0BB D0B5 D0BA D181	B0 DB D5 DA E1	C0 EB E5 EA F1
Japanese	アレックス	30A2 30EC 30b3 30AF 30B9	E382A2 E383AC E38383 E382AF E382B9	8341 838C 8362 834E 8358	8341 838C 8362 834E 8358
Thai	อเลกซ	0E2D 0E40 0E25 0E01 0E0B	E0B8AD E0B980 E0B8A5 E0B881 E0B88B	CD E0 C5 A1 AB	CD E0 C5 A1 AB
asc = ASCII, as = Asian, nas = non-Asian					

Table 3.11 Unicode/Non-Unicode Conversion

From this little example, we can already derive a few important facts.

Unicode/non-Unicode conversion

▸ There are different encodings between Unicode and non-Unicode code pages.

▸ There are some differences in encoding between the ISO and Microsoft Windows single code page (here, in the Russian).

▸ The number of bytes for a character is different, depending on the language and the character set. Very important is the difference between the Asian languages JA, KO, ZH, and ZF. In non-Unicode they occupy 2 bytes per character, in contrast to the other single-byte languages, while in UTF-16 all languages occupy 2 bytes. Thus, the Asian languages are particularly problematic in inhomogeneous communication.

▸ The UTF-16 format is dependent on the endianess of the platform (CPU). Depending on the hardware used, the encodings of characters are available in Big Endian or Little Endian and must be converted during data exchange under some circumstances. The UTF-8 format, on the other hand, is independent of the hardware and always gives the same encoding for a character regardless of platform. When communicating between SAP and external systems with different CPUs and different endianess; therefore the UTF-8 format is preferred.

▶ A character should be interpreted independently of the bytes encoded. This is particularly important for custom interface programming.

Homogeneous communication Figure 3.40 shows an ideal scenario with a global SAP ERP system in the middle. All partner systems are Unicode-capable and can be SAP or non-SAP systems. Because of the different Unicode formats possibly used in the partner systems, settings and parameters (usually simple ones) may be necessary for the interfaces.

Moreover, the scenario offers the following advantages:

▶ Conversions are take place algorithmically (1:1 relation)

▶ There are unambiguous data and texts

▶ There is no data loss

▶ All business texts are available everywhere at any time

The most important insight from this scenario is that arbitrary characters from arbitrary languages can be transmitted correctly and unambiguously.

Inhomogeneous communication Matters are quite different in a scenario with inhomogeneous communication between Unicode and non-Unicode systems (see Figure 3.41). The greatest difficulty is avoiding corrupt texts, which could occur, for instance, if a Unicode system (SAP ERP) were to send Chinese texts to a Latin-1 system (SAP NetWeaver BI). Also very problematic is transfer between a Unicode and an MDMP system, because during the data transfer several conversions between the Unicode and MDMP single code pages are necessary.

Furthermore, the following problem areas need to be handled:

▶ Conversions are made between incompatible code pages

▶ Only the global character set is uniquely exchangeable

▶ There is a risk of data loss

▶ Access to business texts is limited

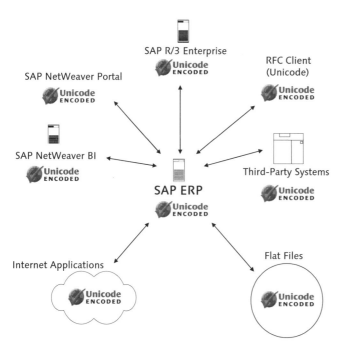

Figure 3.40 Ideal Communication Scenario

It follows directly that in most cases such a scenario requires special adaptations with a lot of effort in the interfaces.

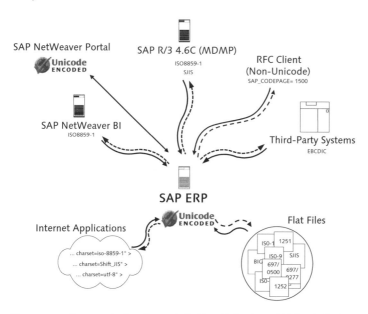

Figure 3.41 Communication Scenario in Non-Unicode and Unicode Systems

Communications
scenarios So how does SAP support the different communication scenarios? The homogeneous case can be answered very easily: It is fully supported. If the partners have different endianess (Big/Little Endian) or even different Unicode formats (UTF-16 or UTF-8), an unambiguous algorithmic conversion takes place automatically.

The inhomogeneous case is much more difficult and is treated in more detail in the following section, when communication with Remote Function Calls and with files is examined in more detail. The mechanisms and functions available in the SAP standard interfaces for this needed conversion will be explained.

3.5.2 Communication with RFC

For the direct communication of ABAP applications and components with other systems, RFC is almost always the technology used. Even with the increasing number of Java-based applications, RFC is important, as the communication between the ABAP and Java stacks takes place through the *SAP Java Connector* (JCo), which connects the ABAP and the Java worlds using RFC technology. Other connectors, like the *SAP .NET Connector*, the *SAP Business Connector* or even the RFC and IDoc adapters important for *SAP NetWeaver Exchange Infrastructure* can be traced back to RFC technology.

RFC Unicode/non-
Unicode functions RFC technology has been extended with numerous functions for Unicode, with particular value being placed on the support of inhomogeneous communication scenarios (Unicode/non-Unicode). The most important functions are:

▶ Automatic switch between homogeneous (Unicode/Unicode or single MDMP code page/single MDMP code page) and inhomogeneous communication (Unicode/non-Unicode)

▶ Automatic conversion between Unicode and a single code page system

▶ Several mechanisms for automatic detection and configuration of the single code page of the partner

▶ Different options for error handling in case of transmission of invalid and/or unconvertable characters

▶ Parallel, line-by-line conversion of table structures with language keys, where each line is converted between Unicode and the single code page assigned to the language key (suitable for Unicode/MDMP transfers)

Overview of Communication with RFC

In a SAP Unicode system, all characters on the application server are processed in UTF-16 format; that is, each character has a length of 2 bytes. In a non-Unicode system, each character has a length of one byte from a technical standpoint (the Asian Double-Byte languages use 2 bytes per character, which can be seen as 2 x 1 byte). Here, the notion of length is very important (charlen). The SAP Unicode system always has length 2; the non-Unicode system always has length 1. We speak of homogeneous or inhomogeneous communication if the length between the partners is identical or different. Thus the two cases Unicode/Unicode and single code page/single code page are homogeneous, since both partners have a length of 2 bytes in one case, and 1 byte in the other.

RFC communication architecture

In the case of inhomogeneous RFC communication, any needed data conversion always takes place on the receiving side[11], so that the sending system always sends the original format. The receiver then converts the data—if necessary—and any errors are displayed on the receiving end. In contrast to this, in inhomogeneous communication between Unicode and non-Unicode, the conversion is always performed on the Unicode system, regardless of whether it is the sender or the receiver.

The behavior and format of the data during transmission thus varies. A significant reason for this is the fact that the Unicode system has the necessary functions and tools to convert between Unicode and non-Unicode, which is especially important in the case of different releases between the partners. For instance, if the sender is an SAP non-Unicode system running SAP R/3 4.6C and the receiver an SAP Unicode system with Basis 6.40, the sending system doesn't have the ability to perform the right conversion from non-Unicode to Unicode, so that can only happen on the receiving end.

---

11 You can find details in the RFC documentation in the SAP Help Portal (*http://help.sap.com*) and in the SAP Service Marketplace (*http://service.sap.com/nw2004s*) under **SAP NetWeaver in Detail • Application Platform • Connectivity • Connectors • RFC Library**.

RFC conversion
behavior Figure 3.42 shows the RFC conversion behavior for both cases. It is assumed that the two Unicode systems have different endianess, so that even in the Unicode/Unicode case there is an endianess conversion (exchange of byte order) to be performed. If both systems are non-Unicode systems, then this is a homogeneous case. If the two systems have different single code pages, as here the left system code page 1100 Latin-1 and the right system code page 8000 Japanese, RFC must convert between 1100 and 8000.[12] Proper conversion between the two non-Unicode systems can only be performed for the global character set (ASCII), because the upper regions of the two SAP code pages 1100 and 8000 are completely different.

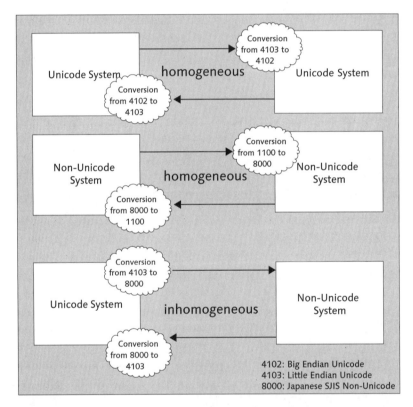

Figure 3.42 RFC Conversion Behavior for Homogeneous and Inhomogeneous Communication (Non-Unicode System Left 1100, Right 8000)

---

12 We assume standard code pages and current RFC versions, so that the conversion takes place using the RFC-F1 converter and no CDP files are needed (see, for instance, SAP Note 53665).

During conversion, RFC distinguishes between two groups of ABAP data types, which are handled differently (see also Section 3.4.2).

▶ *Flat data types* are all the simple ABAP data types C, N, D, T, X, I, F, P and structures with fields of those types.

▶ *Deep data types* are the types STRING, XSTRING, table types, object references, and arbitrary structures with those types. They are also called *XRFC* in RFC jargon. Deep data types are also the case when simple tables are declared as IMPORT, EXPORT or CHANGING parameters in function calls.

In the inhomogeneous case—Unicode/non-Unicode—the two groups are handled differently:

▶ Flat data types are always converted on the Unicode system directly into the target code page (see Figure 3.42), which will be explained below. Here, only character-based data types are converted, that is C, N, D, and T. The numerical and byte-based types X, I, F, and P are unchanged.

▶ Deep data types are first converted on the sending side into an SAP-specific UTF-8 XML intermediate format and then converted by the receiver into the target code page. Deep data types are not suitable for the Unicode/MDMP case.

For inhomogeneous communication between Unicode and non-Unicode, in most cases it is the flat data types that are of interest; thus we will not go into the details of the deep data types here, referring you instead to the specialized documentation.

Homogeneous Communication

The single code page/single code page case doesn't initially have anything to do with Unicode, but it is important for the understanding of the inhomogeneous case. If the code pages of the two systems are different (as for example in Figure 3.42), RFC needs to convert from the sender's code page to the receiver's on the input side of the receiver. Only shared characters in the two character sets can be converted correctly in that process. To do this, RFC uses the *F1 converter*, which in current RFC versions knows all the SAP standard code pages. In special cases, so-called *CDP conversion files* must be generated which RFC can use to convert.

The RFC communication code page is initially determined by the code page of the sender (in the example above, 1100), then if necessary there is a conversion by the received from that (remote) code page to the local code page (1100 to 8000). The receiver then responds with its code page (8000), so the communication code page of the response changes and is converted to the code page of the original sender upon receipt (8000 to 1100).

The RFC communication code page is determined using table TCP0C from the logon language of the sender, and the local code page of the receiver is determined from the logon language of the RFC user. If the two code pages are different, then a corresponding conversion takes place on the receiving end, as for single code page systems.

MDMP/MDMP communication

But what happens in a transfer of data packets with texts of different code pages, as is common in MDMP systems? Here, the "tricky" property of RFC error handling for non-Unicode systems is used to ignore conversion errors and to pass the data in an unchanged (binary) format to the receiver.

> **Example**
>
> An example should illustrate this point. A user logs on in Russian to an MDMP system A with code pages 1100, 1500, and 8000, and sends text data in the languages English (EN), Japanese (JA), and Russian (RU) to another MDMP system B with the same code pages. The RFC connection in system A has an RFC user who logged on to system B with language EN.
>
> System A establishes the connection with code page 1500 (logon language RU) as a communication code page; system B has local code page 1100, so that an RFC conversion from 1500 to 1100 is necessary in system B. The actual erroneous conversions of Russian texts from system A into Western European characters in system B is ignored, so that the Russian texts stay correct in system B, and the same is true of Japanese texts.

Unicode/Unicode

This Unicode/Unicode case, on the other hand, is very simple. If the two Unicode systems have different endianess, RFC automatically detects that and converts correspondingly. It is important to note again that RFC identifies the Unicode system as format UTF-16 using the length 2 bytes. For the combination of an SAP Unicode system with an external non-SAP Unicode system, this may play a role under some circumstances.

Inhomogeneous Communication

If one system is Unicode-based, but the other is a non-Unicode single code page system—thus this is inhomogeneous communication—the Unicode system must perform the conversion to the single code page, regardless of whether it is the sender or the receiver.

Unicode/non-Unicode single code page

The important question is how the communication code page is determined between the Unicode and single code page systems. We distinguish among the following cases:

Determining the communication code page

► **Both partners are SAP systems**
If both partners are SAP systems, the Unicode system is able to configure itself, both as sender and as receiver, to the system code page of the non-Unicode SAP system, as one would expect. However, you must take into account the newest kernel patches and RFC versions necessary for both partner systems, and some peculiarities described in the corresponding SAP Notes.

► **SAP Unicode system is sender; non-SAP single code page system is receiver**
In this case, the communication code page is determined by the logon language, (session language) of the sending user or process in the Unicode system, by assigning the language to a single code page in Table TCP0C.

► **Non-SAP system single code page is sender; SAP Unicode system is receiver**
In this case, several options are possible, depending largely on the communication technology used. If an external C, C++, or similar program is the RFC client, using the RFC library, the value of the environment variable SAP_CODEPAGE determines the RFC communication code page. Other options will be described later.

► **SAP system single code page communicates with non-SAP Unicode system**
The case of an SAP single code page/non-SAP Unicode system is a special case. In general the non-SAP Unicode system must take care of the correct conversion between single-code-page and Unicode.

Once the communication code page is known—having been determined during the connection initialization handshake between the partners (client and server)—the RFC data transfer takes place during the existing connection with the conversion to/from Unicode appropriate for that code page. Note the following:

Single code page data transfer ► If the non-Unicode single code page system is sending, generally all the characters can be converted correctly and unambiguously into Unicode, given that Unicode is a superset containing every single code page character. However, if the transfer is in the other direction, then only those characters valid for the single code page can be converted correctly. For example, the Unicode system cannot send Russian text data to a Latin-1 single code page system.

Multilingual data transfer ► If the application sends texts with different code pages in one transfer step, under some circumstances data loss can occur, as shown in the following example.

Example

The Unicode system sends a data packet with texts in the languages German (DE), Japanese (JA), Thai (TH), and Korean (KO) to a Latin-1 single code page system. The texts in languages JA, TH, and KO are lost in the process and are converted to the replacement character # because they do not belong to the Latin-1 character set or code page 1100 (see Table 3.12). The application would need to filter the languages JA, TH, KO out of the data content to be sent before the transmission step.

Sender: Unicode (4102 Big Endian, 4103 Little Endian)	Language	RFC communication code page 1100	Receiver: Latin-1 single code page (1100)Single code page Latin-1
Ä	DE	valid	Ä
ß	DE	valid	ß
邔	JA	invalid	#
ฬ	TH	invalid	#
긹	KO	invalid	#

Table 3.12 Multilingual Data Transfer Between Unicode and Single Code Page 1100

It must be checked in detail whether the application has such filter mechanisms, and under some circumstances there must be special adaptations performed, for instance using user exits. RFC itself does not check content before sending it.

Unicode/non-Unicode MDMP transfer is the most difficult case and is handled in Section 3.5.4 in detail. Both partners must be SAP ABAP systems. In the following, the most important technical basis for RFC communication between a Unicode and MDMP system is covered.

Unicode/non-Unicode MDMP transfer

The main problem in this case is the question of how a data packet with texts in multiple code pages can be transmitted correctly between Unicode and MDMP. The basic RFC architecture only supports the Unicode/single code page case.

This gives rise to a workaround that may be the only solution in certain cases: The MDMP data packet is broken down into multiple single code-page data packets, and for each code page there is a separate RFC transmission step. In this step, as in the Unicode/single code page case, the Unicode system converts the each code page is converted from the logon language of the sender. If the application permits, several logical RFC connections—one per code page—can be configured, each of which is used for the transmission of one packet. This workaround requires some adaptation in the application and is therefore not very practical, and sometimes not even possible.

Breaking down into single code page data packets

RFC is equipped with a special feature to enable parallel conversion between Unicode and multiple single code pages for language-dependent tables and table structures (flat data type). If the table or structure has a field with a valid, active language key, RFC can convert during the transfer on a line-by-line basis between Unicode and the code page assigned to the language key. RFC switches to a different code page for each table line, so to speak. The languages must be configured in the MDMP system. In the case of missing languages, in the newer RFC versions and kernel patches the communication code page is used for conversion (see SAP Note 920831).

Parallel RFC conversion for language-dependent structures

The following prerequisites must be considered and must especially be supported in the applications.

▶ This RFC feature is only possible in an RFC connection between two ABAP-based SAP systems. Communication between an ABAP stack and a Java stack system cannot use this feature (for instance, the connection between SAP R/3 and the SAP NetWeaver Portal).

▶ A language-dependent table must have a field with data type LANG. In a basis system with release 6.20, the text language flag must be set for this field.

▶ The table or table structure must be transparent to RFC during the transfer, that is, RFC can particularly access the language key.

▶ The table or structure must be passed as TABLES parameter to an RFC function (RFM).

▶ The application must ensure correct filling with language data in the table.

Example

Parallel RFC conversion for language-dependent tables

The example in Table 3.13 illustrates parallel RFC conversion in language-dependent tables between a Unicode and an MDMP system configured for the languages German (DE, code page 1100), Japanese (JA, code page 8000), and Thai (TH, code page 8600). The language Korean (KO) is only supported in the Unicode system.

The Unicode system transmits data from a language-dependent table in the logon language English (EN)—using an RFC-capable function module (RFM)—in one step to the MDMP system, during which all texts in the languages DE, JA, and TH are correctly transmitted, while the language KO is invalid in the MDMP system and thus becomes #.

Sender/receiver: Unicode-System (4102 Big Endian, 4103 Little Endian)	Language key	Communication, code page-dependent on language key or default code page	Receiver/ sender: MDMP system (1100 Latin-1, 8000 SJIS, 8600 TIS620)
Ä	DE	1100	Ä
ß	DE	1100	ß
邰	JA	8000	邰
₩	TH	8600	₩
贓	KO	Default 1100	#

Table 3.13 Multilingual Data Transfer in a Language-Dependent Table from Unicode to MDMP

Configuration of RFC Connections

The right configuration for the RFC connections shown is very important, so we'll cover it in some more detail. After a Unicode conversion (see Section 3.2), all existing RFC connections must be checked and generally must be adapted. The settings for the RFC connections are done in Transaction SM59 (see Figure 3.43).

RFC configuration in Unicode and non-Unicode systems

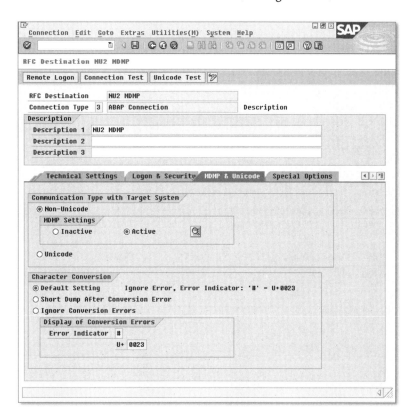

Figure 3.43 Settings for a Non-Unicode MDMP Partner System in Transaction SM59

To enable the various cases of homogeneous and inhomogeneous connections with appropriate conversion, the options in Transaction SM59 have been extended in an ABAP Unicode system. Up to and including basis release 6.40, there is a new tab **Special Options**, and as of release 7.00 there are two tabs: **MDMP & Unicode** and **Special Options**. In the following, the procedure under SAP ERP 2005 (release 7.00) is described, which could easily be adapted for a 6.20 or 6.40 system.

Communication
type selection
screen with the
target system

Tab MDMP & Unicode

Initially, the **Non-Unicode** option can be used to inform the RFC that the partner system has length (character size) 1 and thus is a non-Unicode system. In the **MDMP Settings**, the option must be set to **Inactive** for a single code page or **Active** for an MDMP system.

If the partner system is an MDMP system, then MDMP settings are performed using the detail icon next to the checked **Active** option. RFC on the Unicode system then reads the code page configuration of the MDMP system in order to determine the valid languages and code pages for the parallel conversion (see Figure 3.44). Additional information can be found in the user information (**i** button).

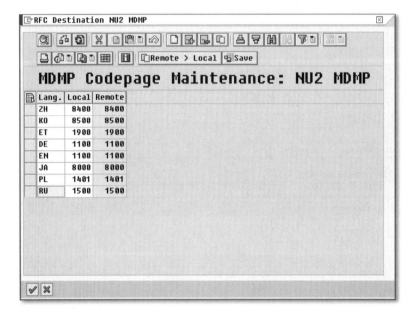

Figure 3.44 MDMP Settings

If the partner system is a Unicode system, the option **Unicode** is checked as communication type. RFC detects a Unicode system using the length (character size) 2, which can easily be tested using the **Unicode Test** button. With an SAP partner system, this test can easily be used to find out whether the partner system is running Unicode or non-Unicode (see Figure 3.45).

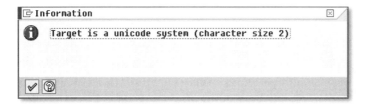

Figure 3.45 Unicode Text Pop-Up Menu in Transaction SM59

In a non-SAP system, however, you must carefully check in advance whether it is Unicode or non-Unicode: If the non-SAP system is running in UTF-8 Unicode format, the communication type **Non-Unicode** should be marked, given that UTF-8 is interpreted by RFC as length 1. There are also installation-dependent exceptions for Unicode for SAP components not based on ABAP; these can be found in the corresponding documentation.

Figure 3.46 shows the RFC settings for a Unicode partner system.

Figure 3.46 Settings for a Unicode Partner System in Transaction SM59

More RFC settings   In the **Character Conversion** selection screen, then, different options can be selected for how to proceed after an erroneous conversion. This is particularly of interest in case of "Unicode sending to non-Unicode system." By default, conversion errors are ignored and the erroneous character becomes the replacement character "#", but you can also force a failure (**Short Dump after Conversion Error**) or select a different replacement character.

Special Options Tab

Here, the **RFC Bit Option** button is of interest, which as of release 6.40 includes the option **Use Found Communication Code Page** (see Figure 3.47). If this option is selected, the logon language of the RFC user determined in Transaction SM59 is used to determine the RFC communication code page for a non-Unicode partner system, and not the local logon language in the Unicode system. Thus, the code page of the logon language of the RFC user determines the communication code page in the inhomogeneous case with a Unicode system as sender, if the option is selected. The hexadecimal value of this bit option is 0x00000200 and must be set in a Unicode system with release 6.20 as a hex value.

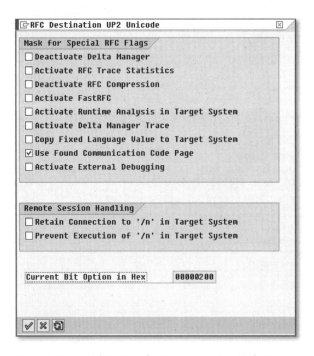

Figure 3.47 Special Options for Communication Code Page

3.5.3 Communication Using File Transfer

Besides direct electronic communication, data exchange using files plays a great role in a global enterprise. Many business partners for security reasons do not allow direct communication, or are still working with old IT systems that don't permit direct communication. Today, in most SAP systems, business data is usually exchanged with banks (funds transfers, for instance) using file communication, a typical SAP application for this being the *DMEE Workbench*.

Just as with the different communication scenarios for RFC, with file transfer there is also the important question of which code page mode—Unicode or non-Unicode—a file must be in so that it can be correctly processed by both partner systems. Because customer programs often are developed for communication via file transfer, for the general ABAP Unicode enabling (see Section 3.4) a precise analysis must be performed of the code page in which the files are processed.

Communication using files in Unicode and non-Unicode

It may very well turn out that the custom program must be extended with new dialog logic allowing the user to select whether the file should be processed in Unicode or non-Unicode. Furthermore it must be precisely clarified which code page the partner system understands. If it supports Unicode, the custom program must also generate a Unicode file; for Unicode files, the UTF-8 format is preferred for reasons of platform independence.

In the following subsections we will present concepts and tools complementary to those described in Section 3.4 that are provided by the SAP Unicode system in ABAP for file processing. File transfer on the SAP application server is discussed, along with the upload and download of files on the SAP GUI.

File Transfer on the SAP Application Server

As of SAP Application Server release 6.20, an ABAP statement for a file transfer looks like this:

Extended statement

```
OPEN DATASET ... IN <mode>.
  TRANSFER/READ ... .
CLOSE DATASET.
```

For <mode>, the following options are available:

- BINARY MODE

  All data is directly transmitted by the application server (without interpretation) to the file in unchanged order.

- TEXT MODE ENCODING UTF-8 | NON-UNICODE | DEFAULT

  In the file, text data is processed the code page of which is determined by the ENCODING addition. The alternative UTF-8 processes the file data in UTF-8 format. NON-UNICODE on a single code page system uses the system code page or for an MDMP system a code page derived from the logon language or the ABAP system variable SY-LANGU. The alternative DEFAULT takes the value **UTF-8** on the Unicode system and **NON-UNICODE** on the non-Unicode system.

- LEGACY TEXT | BINARY MODE

  This option generates a non-Unicode-compatible format in which text is always written in the non-Unicode format and non-character-based structures are permitted. TEXT, in contrast with BINARY, writes a line end marker.

For more details and options for this statement, you can consult the ABAP documentation.

Selection criteria for the file code page

Ultimately, this statement results in the following behavior:

- If the SAP system is a Unicode system, the option DEFAULT processes the file in UTF-8 Unicode (read and write access).

- If a single code-page file is to be processed by an SAP Unicode system, the options NON-UNICODE or LEGACY MODE can be used. Analogously to RFC communication, this enables the automatic conversion of Unicode/non-Unicode, and the single code page is determined either from the system code page or the logon language (MDMP). The code page can also be set using the system parameter SY-LANGU, which has the value of the logon language by default, using SET LOCALE LANGUAGE <LANG>.

- A good Unicode file-transfer format is TEXT MODE UTF-8, although only the content of character-type data objects (particularly flat data types) can be transmitted, not complex structures.

- The BINARY MODE should only be used in special cases. If this option is used from a Unicode system, the data will be read/written in platform-dependent UTF-16 Little Endian or Big Endian format.

▶ For Unicode/non-Unicode conversion, the same aspects apply as for RFC: In the case of invalid characters or those which cannot be converted, the replacement character "#" is generated.

▶ The OPEN DATASET statement specifies a certain code page for the file. If a selection is allowed—for instance in order to process the file in Unicode or as single code page—a corresponding logic must be programmed. This then contains multiple OPEN DATASET statements with different options, possibly in combination with the SET LOCALE <LANG> statement.

▶ If the file is to be processed in UTF-16 or another code page than the one derived, the following possibilities are available:

  ▷ Use of the GUI_UPLOAD/GUI_DOWNLOAD function in a custom ABAP program allows the upload and download of files between the SAP application server and front-end PCs, and includes the formal parameter CODEPAGE that can be set to the code page desired.

  ▷ Separate conversion is also possible with the ABAP program RSCP_CONVERT_FILE (see SAP Note 752859) or the system program sapiconv (see SAP Note 747615).

File Transfer on the Front End

For file transfer between an SAP system and the front end on a local PC (SAP GUI), the new functions GUI_DOWNLOAD and GUI_UPLOAD can be used. The earlier functions WS_UPLOAD and WS_DOWNLOAD are no longer permitted and will be flagged as incorrect during Unicode syntax checking with UCCHECK.

GUI_DOWNLOAD and GUI_UPLOAD offer numerous parameters and options, of which some are listed here:

GUI_DOWNLOAD and GUI_UPLOAD

▶ If a file is to be processed by an SAP Unicode system for a single code page, similar criteria to those used for RFC and server-based file transfer apply. The Single-Byte code page is determined from the logon language and can be changed using the SY-LANGU parameter with the SET LOCALE LANGUAGE <lang> statement. There is also a parameter CODEPAGE which can be set explicitly when calling GUI_DOWNLOAD and GUI_UPLOAD.

▶ As of SAP GUI 6.40, there is the possibility of an interactive file dialog using the class method CL_GUI_FRONTEND_SERVICES =>FILE_

OPEN/SAVE_DIALOG (with parameter WITH_ENCODING = 'X'). This means the PC user can select the code page interactively, as shown in Figure 3.48. An example is a situation where a file from an SAP Unicode system is going to be downloaded to a PC with conversion to the Windows code page Cyrillic (Microsoft 1251, SAP 1504).

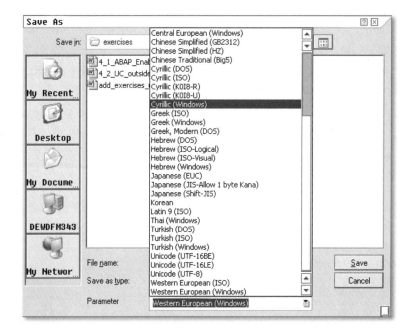

Figure 3.48 Code Page Selection in Front-End Download

▸ As of SAP GUI 6.40, the code page for the PC file can be preset by default by selecting the desired code page in **Options • Properties • Extended • Upload/Download encoding** in the SAP logon entry for the SAP system (there may be some variation between different SAP logon versions).

Summary

Finally, let's summarize the different communication cases involving Unicode and non-Unicode systems with the different interface types and look at some important implementation aspects. The special case of MDMP systems is covered in detail in the next section.

▶ **Unicode/Unicode**

Optimum case, where no conversion is necessary. The technical conversion between different Unicode formats like UTF-8 or Big Endian and Little Endian may be necessary.

▶ **Single code page/Unicode**

All single code page characters are unambiguously mappable to Unicode, so that conversion is technically very simple to perform.

▶ **Unicode/single code page**

This case requires a check or a filter, so that only allowed texts are transmitted to the single code page system. For instance, no Russian texts may reach a Western European single code page system from a Unicode system.

▶ **Unicode/MDMP and MDMP/Unicode**

This difficult scenario generally requires a high degree of adaptation and development in order to implement the multiple conversions necessary from Unicode into each single code page. The text data to be transmitted must be available in language-dependent data structures or tables for the transfer. Because this is often not the case, it must take place through corresponding adaptation. The effort depends on each application, the number of code pages in the MDMP system, the use of Asian Double-Byte languages, and the interface technology used.

Table 3.14 shows an overview of the communication technologies discussed for RFC and file transfer, with a focus on Unicode/non-Unicode partner systems.

Overview of communication technologies

Interface	Properties		Target code page	Structured data	MDMP suitable (ABAP/ABAP)
RFC	Flat data type	language-dependent	Language key table row	yes	yes
		not language-dependent	Communication code page/logon language	yes	no
	Deep data types		Communication code page/logon language	yes	no

Table 3.14 Overview of RFC and File Communication Between Unicode and Non-Unicode Systems

Interface	Properties		Target code page	Struc- tured data	MDMP suit- able (ABAP/ ABAP)
File trans- fer ABAP	TEXT MODE		SY-LANGU	yes (field by field)	sometimes
	LEGACY MODE	TEXT MODE	SY-LANGU	yes	sometimes
		BINARY MODE	SY-LANGU	yes	sometimes
File trans- fer SAP GUI	GUI_UPLOAD			yes	no
	GUI_DOWNLOAD			yes	sometimes

Table 3.14 Overview of RFC and File Communication Between Unicode and Non-Unicode Systems (cont.)

3.5.4 Communication Between SAP Unicode and SAP non-Unicode MDMP Systems

As you have already seen, things become very complicated when an SAP Unicode system must communicate with an SAP MDMP system. The basic difficulty is that business data are to be transmitted which may include texts from different code pages in one data packet.

Example

Imagine, for example, a material 4711 whose material texts are available in 10 languages with 10 different code pages. Now you want to transmit material 4711 with all its material texts, which are a fixed component of material. 4711, from a Unicode system to an MDMP system (with something like an SAP ALE application).

Because of the 10 different code pages, there must be 10 parallel conversions between Unicode and the right single code page. The interface or the application above it must thus be capable of detecting all the code pages and correctly converting them.

Because this communication scenario only happens between two SAP systems the RFC technology is largely used for direct communication. Communication between MDMP and external Unicode or non-Unicode systems is not supported and requires its own special project, so we won't address it here. If the applications of both communication partners are ABAP-based, the parallel conversion feature of RFC can be used.

As we have already seen, however, RFC can only convert in parallel if the data structure to be transmitted is language-dependent. By that we mean that a language key or another unambiguous parameter is available that makes the single code page of the individual rows with partial texts unambiguous and thus enables the parallel conversion between Unicode and MDMP.

Figure 3.49 shows an example of a material with different material texts which are to be transmitted between a Unicode and an MDMP system.

Example of transfer of a material with different material texts

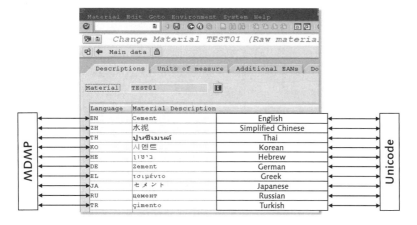

Figure 3.49 Material Descriptions with Different Code Pages

What options are there for correct transmission? Luckily, the material descriptions are stored in a language-dependent table MAKT with language key SPRAS, so that the prerequisites for a correct transfer with RFC are satisfied. For instance, if the transfer is performed with a call to an RFM, all texts would be correctly converted in parallel.

Unfortunately, the reality is different. Either the business data to be sent doesn't have a language key, or the business data is "packed" by the application or the middleware in special data structures for the transfer, so that any existing language key is invisible to RFC.

Dates without language key

Thus SAP ALE applications (*Application Link Enabling*) use the IDoc format (*Intermediate Document*) for data transfer; that is, the business data is buffered in the sending system from the original tables in a special segment-like hierarchical arrangement in the IDoc (*outbound processing*), transmitted using tRFC (*transactional RFC*), and passed to the application in the receiving system, which then writes the data from the IDoc into the original tables after successful posting (*inbound processing*). In the case of the example above, that means that the table MAKT with the material descriptions is stored in the IDoc along with the other material data (from other tables). The original language key from MAKT is quite well hidden in a segment. During transmission, RFC doesn't see a language key and thus converts only according to *one* communication code page between Unicode and non-Unicode.

Data exchange between components of the SAP Business Suite
Similar situations occur during data exchanges within the components of the SAP Business Suite. For instance, for transmission between SAP R/3 and SAP CRM or SAP SRM, so-called BDocs (*Business Documents*) are used. These amount to extensions of IDocs and use qRFC (*queued RFC*). During the data extraction from SAP R/3 to SAP NetWeaver BI, special transfer structures are also employed, which use *extractors*. All these transmission techniques share the fact that they almost never use the original structure of the business data, but rather use structures specially suited for the transfer, which allow any existing language key to become invisible.

In communication between ABAP and Java-based components, such as between SAP R/3 and SAP NetWeaver Portal, another difficulty compounds the situation. Java only knows Unicode, and not MDMP. In this case, the parallel RFC conversion feature cannot be used because the communication between the ABAP stack and the Java stack takes place through the *SAP Java Connector* (JCo) or a variant (JRFC). Usually, only a JCo connection can be configured, which exchanges all data with one RFC system user and one logon language. If the ABAP system is running under MDMP, therefore, only one code page, that of the JCo user, can be correctly transmitted without additional measures.

Solutions for the scenario
Keep in mind that such scenarios are inherently complex, and there is no general solution, partly because SAP is no longer performing active development of MDMP. Thus only solutions can be derived either through special configuration and behavior rules for end users or ultimately with custom development and modifications. The effort can vary greatly and can be intensive. As a result, even the costs of a Unicode conversion of the MDMP system involved in com-

munication may be lower over the middle or long term than for the adaptation effort needed for the Unicode/MDMP interface enabling.

Reduction to Unicode/Single Code Page Data Exchange

Before a Unicode/MDMP scenario is analyzed in detail and implemented, however, you first should try either to reduce the data transmission fully to single code page/Unicode or to break it down into multiple data transfers with one code page per data packet.

Reduction to "single code page with Unicode" communication

The advantages of such a simplification are clear. As already described, communication from single code page to Unicode works completely automatically and in the other direction as well, as long as valid characters for the single code page are used (automatic conversion using the RFC communication code page). There may need to be some filtration, which generally doesn't represent a great deal of effort.

If a technically configured MDMP system is to be connected to a Unicode system, that doesn't automatically mean that all data to be exchanged actually contains MDMP data; that is, texts with mixed code pages. For instance, between an R/3 and an SCM/APO system for Demand Planning, it is largely planning figures that are transmitted: numerical data and not much text. Because an SCM/APO system, due to the integrated BI components of SAP NetWeaver, does not support MDMP, it often is the case in a global system landscape that the SCM system has been converted to Unicode even before the MDMP system. The same applies to a BI system which must also run Unicode for global multilingual use.

Thus, if it is possible to reduce the data transfer to a single code page, the case as described above is the de facto situation. The greater part of the effort will then be focused on exchanging data from only one single code page, either using organizational measures or technical filters.

If the use of a single code page in the data packets cannot be supported, another simplification may still help to reduce the effort in comparison with a general Unicode/MDMP scenario. The data packets to be transmitted are broken down into packets with one single code page apiece, and then for each code page a separate RFC transfer step is performed with the correct RFC communication code page. Naturally, this means increased communication effort and

Decomposition into multiple Unicode/single code page transfers

load, but the advantages of this simplification are often far greater than a complex modification solution for MDMP/Unicode. In certain cases, this is the only solution.

If the application supports such a decomposition, this should be attempted in any case. Here are some examples of this approach.

▶ **SAP ALE with message type MATMAS for exchange of material master data**
The ALE distribution model includes a filter for one language group by default. This makes it possible to generate IDocs with only one language or code page, so that all other languages are filtered out. Thus, an ALE model can be designed that creates several RFC connections for different communication code pages. These transmit the material text several times with the suitable code page as single code page-to-Unicode communication.

▶ **Use of suitable filters in the middleware**
When coupling SAP R/3 with SAP CRM, the middleware offers filter functions for the transmission objects, the BDocs can often be used for this purpose, especially when there is a language dependency. Thus it is possible—for instance when exchanging data between R/3 materials and CRM products—to filter the material texts according to the language key in the middleware. Thus, either the single code page-to-Unicode case or the decomposition into multiple single code page with multiple transfers—though with additional RFC configuration—can be derived.

▶ **Communication with Multilingual Non-SAP Systems**
For communication between an SAP Unicode system and external multilingual non-SAP systems in non-Unicode, the case is particularly difficult. If the data or texts from an external system are not available in a Unicode format, then the decomposition into individual code pages with multiple transfers per code page and corresponding RFC connection (for file transfer with the corresponding upload/download conversion program) is the only solution. This includes external files as well which contain texts with mixed code page.

For instance, if an external RFC client sends multilingual texts over a registered RFC connection into an SAP Unicode system, the external RFC client program must break these texts down into the individual code pages. It then sends them to the SAP Unicode system in a loop with one transfer step each with the right value in the environment variable SAP_CODEPAGE[13].

Golden Rules for Communication Between Unicode and MDMP Systems

If a reduction to single code page or decomposition into multiple single code pages with multiple transfers is impossible, this is a case for communication between an SAP Unicode system and an MDMP system. Some important prerequisites must be ensured here for such a case to be implemented at all.

> **Note**
>
> As already noted, this case is very complex, and you can expect additional and perhaps extensive development efforts. There is not a solution for every scenario.

To make a solution possible at all for such a scenario, certain "golden rules" must again be introduced, oriented towards the RFC communication properties and the MDMP architecture. Almost all rules are determined by the MDMP system, which can be called the technically and linguistically weaker of the two systems.

These rules must be carefully analyzed and communicated early to all partners involved. They also generally require some organizational measures. For instance, the end users may not execute certain scenarios, such as sending a Russian document to the MDMP system using an English logon language in the Unicode system. In the following bullet points, the most important rules are listed.

▶ **Installation of all languages involved in the transfer**
All the languages included in the data packets must be installed on both systems (Unicode and MDMP system); the code page alone is not sufficient. It must be possible to log on in the languages on the system. As described in more detail in Chapter 5, a language may

Complete language installation

---

13 If an external RFC client is transmitting to an SAP Unicode system, the RFC communication code page is determined by the environment variable SAP_CODEPAGE or from the *remote connection string*. You can find additional information in the documentation for the RFC Software Development Kit at *http://service.sap.com/nw2004s* (**NetWeaver in Detail** • **Application Platform** • **Connectivity** • **Connectors** • **RFC Library**).

need to be installed by supplementation from another language (usually English).

Communication
code page with
RFC bit option
(SM59)

► **Transmission from Unicode to MDMP**

For RFC, the rule applies that the logon language in the Unicode system determines the communication code page. In such a scenario, this deserves very special attention, if there is no language key available in the data structure to be transmitted.

For instance, if an order with Russian texts is to be transmitted from a Unicode to an MDMP system, then this must take place with the Russian logon language on the Unicode system. This applies to the process initializing the RFC communication: If this is a background job, for instance, this can be its background job "step-language," which must be Russian.

In many cases it is possible to achieve some dynamism with this rule, which can lead to a great deal more flexibility: The RFC communication code page is determined using the logon language of the RFC user together with the special RFC bit option in Transaction SM59. It is 0x00000200 in Web AS 6.20 or the **Communication language** checkbox as of SAP Web AS 6.40. Here, the **Logon language** field of the RFC user is left blank, so that the logon language of the RFC user in the MDMP system and thus the active code page is inherited at runtime from the language of the calling Unicode system. This is particularly advantageous when only a single RFC connection can be configured between the two systems, for instance with SAP R/3 and SAP CRM.

► **Transmission from MDMP to Unicode**

Here, the rule strictly applies that the logon language of the calling process in the MDMP system determines the communication code page. For instance, it is not allowed to log on to the MDMP system in English and to send an order with Russian texts to the Unicode system. An RFC bit option such as in the Unicode system does not exist here as a client.

General Solution Scenarios for Unicode/MDMP Communication

The golden rules for Unicode-to-MDMP communication often cannot be obeyed, or only with difficulty. Often, texts in the data packets contain an arbitrary combination of different code pages which cannot be predicted, or only with great difficulty. In this case, a general approach must be found.

The only technically plausible variant would be the parallel conversion feature of RFC for language-dependent flat data structures, as already explained. Thus, we must ensure that during the Unicode-to-MDMP transfer the RFC data structure contains a language key with texts correctly filled in for each line.

Parallel RFC conversion as solution for Unicode/MDMP communication

The difficult work is to analyze the data structure used in the concrete scenario to determine whether a transparent language key exists with correctly populated rows. If this is not the case, generally custom enhancements or modifications must be made, which at heart all share the goal of creating a language key for the data structure and to ensure the correct row contents. The extent of the effort and the degree of modification must be examined in a special project.

An exhaustive description of the solution scenarios for SAP Unicode/MDMP communication can be found in SAP Collective Note 745030, which presents general solution approaches for many communication scenarios and the steps for the adaptations and modifications needed.

Solution scenarios for Unicode/MDMP communication

Here, we will describe the general solution approach with selected examples for the cases:

▶ ALE applications with communication between SAP R/3 Unicode and MDMP system (in detail including a prototype)

▶ Communication between the CRM/SRM components of the SAP Business Suite (Unicode) and SAP R/3 (MDMP)

▶ Communication between SAP NetWeaver BI (Unicode) and SAP R/3 (MDMP)

These scenarios often occur at global SAP customers who have had one or more, often very large and complex, R/3 systems (MDMP) in use for several years. These customers are planning to use or have already implemented new SAP Business Suite components in Unicode.

Scenario: ALE Application with ERP Unicode and R/3 MDMP System

Unicode/MDMP communication in ALE applications

The SAP ALE technology uses IDocs for transfer between partner systems. In the sending system, the IDocs are generated by the application from business data (*outbound processing*), sent asynchronously with tRFC, and then are passed to the application on the receiving system for *inbound processing* and posting. The data structures relevant to RFC are the IDoc-specific structures EDI_DC40 (control data) and EDI_DD40 (business data), which correspond to the database tables EDIDC and EDID4 in which the IDocs are stored. Unfortunately, by default these do not contain language keys, so IDocs with texts of mixed code pages are transferred between Unicode and MDMP correctly only for the communication code page, but incorrectly for all others.

Thus, an enhancement or modification must be made which extends the RFC IDoc structure EDI_DD40 with a language key and provides the logic for correct population of EDI_DD40. Because the structure and the content of the IDocs are determined by the ALE message types, this modification depends on the message type and thus on the underlying application. With a few hundred predefined SAP ALE message types, it will quickly be obvious to you that this can be done only with great development effort. If there is a possibility for simplification and reduction to single code page transfer, this should absolutely be considered first. SAP Note 613389 has some valuable information on this point.

IDocs with texts from multiple code pages

However, if it is unavoidable to transfer IDocs with texts of multiple code pages between a Unicode and an MDMP system, the IDoc enhancement and modifications to ALE components outlined will be necessary. The focus here is on enhancing the IDoc transfer structure with a language key and ensuring that the language-dependent IDoc structure rows are filled with the right language key and row content for the language before sending them with RFC and converting them row by row from or to Unicode.

> **Note**
>
> We should again explicitly note that this case requires significant modification to the SAP standard, so that you definitely should contact SAP before planning such a project.

Below, we describe a prototype of this concept of an IDoc enhancement based on the ALE transfer of multilingual material master data between SAP R/3 Enterprise (MDMP) and a Unicode system running SAP Basis 6.20 (Support Package 58). We will show the prototype and its associated, partly detailed ABAP components and explanations in the transfer direction from the Unicode to the MDMP system. For the reverse direction, the same components are used along with an addition for the special treatment of Double-Byte languages. The solution presented is naturally only one of various possibilities. You can find more details in the SAP collective notes 745030 and 656350, as well as the associated references. The following explanations also largely apply for SAP MDMP systems with releases 4.6C and 4.6D.

ALE prototype for material distribution with message type MATMAS

The ALE message type for material master data is MATMAS, with basic IDoc type MATMAS05.[14]

The material texts are stored in the language-dependent table MAKT. This does, in fact, have an active language key SPRAS, but in the base IDoc type MATMAS05 this is "invisibly" packed into the special segment E1MAKTM for RFC, so that a standard ALE transfer between Unicode and MDMP will only convert the code page texts of the RFC communication code page correctly. Moreover, there are also multilingual long texts maintained for materials; these are stored in an SAPscript object with a language key TDSPRAS and must also be transferred between the MDMP and Unicode systems correctly.

To understand the following procedure, a good knowledge of the ALE technology and ABAP programming skills are important; Figure 3.50 illustrates the situation.

In order to avoid making too many SAP standard modifications for the adaptations, but rather a solution using new additional programs—similar to add-ons—for the ALE layer in the prototype, only the collective ALE IDoc transfer was implemented when sending, that is, the IDocs are first stored collectively in the sending system according to the partner profile data, and then transferred using tRFC (*transactional RFC*)) by executing an adapted copy of the send program RSEOUT00. The ALE application generates a master IDoc before the actual transfer, from which, according to the previously configured ALE distribution model, a certain communication IDoc is generated for each receiving system.

Adaptations and custom development for the prototype

---

14 Basic IDoc types from previous versions, like MATMAS03, are also possible.

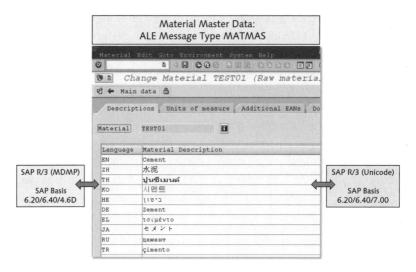

Figure 3.50 ALE Material Master Data Distribution Between an SAP Unicode and an SAP MDMP System

The master IDoc is generated in the ALE function MASTER_IDOC_DIS-TRIBUTE, which is called by the ALE application. Now comes the new code: Instead of the SAP standard program RSEOUT00, in the ALE Unicode/MDMP scenario, the newly created send program RSEOUT00_U is called; in an actual project, names from the customer namespace must be used. The program includes all the enhancements necessary, particularly the IDoc transfer structure EDI_DD40_U extended with the language key SLANGU (see Figure 3.51) and the logic to fill the rows of the material texts of this structure with the correct languages (segments E1MAKTM and E1MTXHM with subordinate segment E1MTXLM).

This allows the IDoc to be transferred correctly with the parallel code-page conversion feature of RFC between the Unicode and an MDMP system.

Extended IDoc structure with language key After receipt of the IDoc, the ALE inbound processing in the receiving system must be adapted accordingly. Instead of the standard ALE function IDOC_INBOUND_ASYNCHRONOUS, the enhanced new function IDOC_INBOUND_ASYNCHRONOUS_U is called, which processes the modified IDoc structure with the language keys and passes it to the application as shown in Figure 3.52.

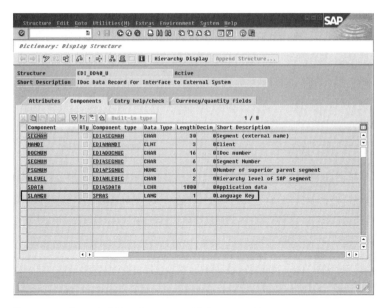

Figure 3.51 Extended IDoc Structure with Language Key

Let's look at these steps in detail. First, the program RSEUT00 is created as a new program RSEOUT00_U with the new include RSEOUTF0_U instead of RSEOUTF0. The program RSEOUTF0_U contains several changed or new form routines needed for this prototype (see Listing 3.2).

Custom development of the ALE prototype in detail

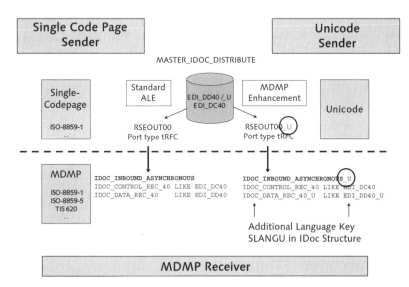

Figure 3.52 ALE Enhancements for the Unicode/MDMP Transfer of Material Master Data

```
REPORT RSEOUT00_U MESSAGE-ID E0.
* Enhancement of RSEOUT00 for transfer between a SAP
* MDMP and Unicode System
* status-values
INCLUDE RSECSTAT.
* Include for data definitions, tables, parameters
INCLUDE RSEOUTDT.
* New/replaced Include with formroutines for MDMP to
* Unicode transfer
INCLUDE RSEOUTFO_U.
*INCLUDE RSEOUTFO.
***********************************************************
*              M a i n    R o u t i n e
***********************************************************
START-OF-SELECTION.
* Selection of all important EDIDC-set
* and collect in internal table
PERFORM SELECT_ALL_EDIDC.
END-OF-SELECTION.
```

Listing 3.2 Collective Transfer of all Selected Multilingual IDocs

New function group for the prototype ALE/EDI routines

In the new include RSEOUTFO_U, the existing function calls to EDI_OUTPUT_NEW are replaced by the new function EDI_OUTPUT_NEW_U, which belongs to the new function group EDI7_U. This also includes the functions IDOCS_OUTPUT_TO_R3_U, IDOC_CONVERT_TO_EDI_DD40, IDOC_CONVERT_TO_EDI_DD40_U, and IDOC_INBOUND_ASYNCHRONOUS_U, which can be seen further below. These have been copied from the corresponding components of the standard SAP function group EDI_7 and enhanced (see Listing 3.3).

```
***INCLUDE RSEOUTFO_U.
* Formroutines
*----------------------------------------------------------*
*         FORM SELECT_ALL_EDIDC                            *
**----------------------------------------------------------*
* Fill internal table IDOCTAB  with all selected
* EDIDC-records   *
*----------------------------------------------------------*
...
* Adjustments for ALE MDMP - Unicode Scenario
* Replace Function Calls of EDI_OUTPUT_NEW
CALL FUNCTION 'EDI_OUTPUT_NEW_U'
    EXPORTING
      ONL_OPTION  = 'B'              "batch
```

```
    TABLES
     I_EDIDC     = COM_EDIDC
     I_EDIDD     = INT_EDIDD
    EXCEPTIONS
      OTHERS     = 1.
...
```

Listing 3.3 ALE/EDI Processing of Multilingual IDocs

It is important to select a uniform and self-explanatory naming convention in the concrete case of custom development. For instance, the customer name ZUEDI_7 for the copy and the enabling of the SAP function group EDI_7 would be suitable, or the name LZUEDI7F00 for an adaptation of the include LEDI7F00; the prefix "ZU" thus indicates that this is an adapted component for the ALE MDMP/Unicode scenario. Instead of using the customer namespace, we will use the special suffix "_U" in the interest of improved illustration.

Customer namespace

In the next include, LEDI7_UF00 which is a copy of LEDI7F00 in the form routine SEND_TO_R3, the call to IDOCS_OUTPUT_TO_R3 is replaced by the copied and renamed function IDOCS_OUTPUT_TO_R3_U (see Listing 3.4).

```
***INCLUDE LEDI7_UF00.
...
*------------------------------------------------------*
*     SEND_TO_R3                                        *
*------------------------------------------------------
FORM SEND_TO_R3 TABLES I_EDIDC STRUCTURE EDIDC
                       I_EDIDD STRUCTURE EDIDD.
IF DATA_EMPTY = 'Y'.
   CLEAR I_EDIDD.
   REFRESH I_EDIDD.
ENDIF.
IF IDOCPAKETERROR = 'M'.
   ERR_FLAG = 'M'.
ENDIF.
* ALE MDMP - Unicode Scenario Adjustment
CALL FUNCTION 'IDOCS_OUTPUT_TO_R3_U'
   EXPORTING
      NAST_RECORD       = NAST_REC
      ERROR_FLAG        = ERR_FLAG
      PORT_DESCRIPTION  = EDIPOA
      SEGMENT_RELEASE   = SEGRELEASE
      TABLES
```

```
            I_EDIDC        = I_EDIDC
            I_EDIDD        = I_EDIDD.
ENDFORM.
```

Listing 3.4 Preparing the Send Process

Filling the lan-guage-dependent IDoc structure
Now we have nearly reached the actual transfer or send step. The IDoc transfer structure now has fields with a language key, but they must be filled before sending with the correct texts from the language-relevant IDoc segments. This is achieved as follows by adaptations in the include LEDI7_UF12 (copy and adaptation of LEDI7F12):

In the old form routine SEND_DATA_TO_R3, the call to IDOC_INBOUND_ASYNCHRONOUS is replaced by two calls, first to the new function IDOC_CONVERT_TO_EDI_DD40_U, then one to IDOC_INBOUND_ASYNCHRONOUS_U, copied and adapted from IDOC_INBOUND_ASYNCHRONOUS (see Listing 3.5).

```
***INCLUDE LEDI7_UF12 .
...
*-----------------------------------------------------------*
*   SEND_DATA_TO_R3                                          *
*-----------------------------------------------------------*
FORM SEND_DATA_TO_R3 TABLES I_EDIDC STRUCTURE EDIDC
                            I_EDIDD STRUCTURE EDIDD.
...
* Adjustments for ALE MDMP - Unicode Scenario
* Extended structure EDI_DD40_U with language key
DATA EDIDD40_U LIKE EDI_DD40_U OCCURS 0.
* New function to process language dependent IDoc
* for message type MATMAS
CALL FUNCTION 'IDOC_CONVERT_TO_EDI_DD40_U'
   TABLES
      IDOC_CONTROL_REC_40 = ext_edidc_40
      IDOC_DATA_REC_40    = conv_edidd40
      IDOC_DATA_REC_40_U  = EDIDD40_U.
CALL FUNCTION 'IDOC_INBOUND_ASYNCHRONOUS_U'
   IN BACKGROUND TASK
   AS SEPARATE UNIT      " eine TID pro Ruf
   DESTINATION EDIPOA-LOGDES
   TABLES
      IDOC_CONTROL_REC_40 = EXT_EDIDC_40
      IDOC_DATA_REC_40_u  = EDIDD40_U.
...
```

Listing 3.5 Generation of Enhanced IDocs and Transfer

Here, we should highlight the declaration of the internal (IDoc) table EDIDD40_U, which takes on the data type of the IDoc transfer structure EDI_DD40_U enhanced with the language key. At this point, the language-dependent IDoc processing appears for the first time. The call to IDOC_CONVERT_TO_EDI_DD40_U is necessary in order to write the language-dependent texts from the segments of message type MATMAS or the basic IDoc type MATMAS05 into the internal table EDIDD40_U together with the right language key. Thus, this is the central location in the prototype, which is based on the predefined message type MATMAS.

Specific functions for each message type

While the adaptations described so far can largely also be used for other ALE message types in an ALE MDMP Unicode scenario, at this point we are dealing with the very specific message type MATMAS or basic IDoc type MATMAS05. For a development project with multiple message types, a separate specific function would have to be called for each message type, which must be developed beforehand. Thus a good idea would be to develop a wrapper function, which could call a specific function suitable for the message type in the function of a dispatcher. The specific function would then fill the extended IDoc transfer structure with the language-dependent texts. Due to its central importance, we will look at this function IDOC_CONVERT_TO_EDI_DD40_U in more detail (see Listing 3.6).

```
FUNCTION IDOC_CONVERT_TO_EDI_DD40_U.
*"----------------------------------------------------------
*"*"Local Interface
*"  TABLES
*"      IDOC_CONTROL_REC_40 STRUCTURE  EDI_DC40
*"      IDOC_DATA_REC_40 STRUCTURE  EDI_DD40
*"      IDOC_DATA_REC_40_U STRUCTURE  EDI_DD40_U
*"----------------------------------------------------------
DATA LS_IDOC_DATA_REC_40   TYPE EDI_DD40.
* IDoc structure with language key
DATA LS_IDOC_DATA_REC_40_U TYPE EDI_DD40_U.
* Language relevant IDoc segments of MATMAS05
DATA E1MAKTM LIKE E1MAKTM.
DATA E1MTXHM LIKE E1MTXHM.
DATA E1MTXLM LIKE E1MTXLM.
CLEAR IDOC_DATA_REC_40_U[].
* Loop to fill the IDOC transfer structure
LOOP AT IDOC_DATA_REC_40 INTO LS_IDOC_DATA_REC_40.
* Copy standard fields
```

```
      CLEAR LS_IDOC_DATA_REC_40_U.
      MOVE-CORRESPONDING LS_IDOC_DATA_REC_40 TO
      LS_IDOC_DATA_REC_40_U.
*   Assign language key from segments
*   statc / dynamic
      CASE LS_IDOC_DATA_REC_40-SEGNAM.
*   Segment E1MAKTM contains (short) material
*   descriptions from table MAKT
      WHEN 'E2MAKTM001'.
          E1MAKTM = LS_IDOC_DATA_REC_40-SDATA.
          LS_IDOC_DATA_REC_40_U-SLANGU = E1MAKTM-SPRAS.
* Segment E1MTXHM and subsegment E1MTXLM contain
* long texts of a material stored in a SAPscript text
* object with language key TDSPRAS
      WHEN 'E2MTXHM001'.
          E1MTXHM = LS_IDOC_DATA_REC_40-SDATA.
          LS_IDOC_DATA_REC_40_U-SLANGU = E1MTXHM-TDSPRAS.
      WHEN 'E2MTXLM'.
          E1MTXLM = LS_IDOC_DATA_REC_40-SDATA.
* Inherited
          LS_IDOC_DATA_REC_40_U-SLANGU = E1MTXHM-TDSPRAS.
      ENDCASE.
      APPEND LS_IDOC_DATA_REC_40_U TO IDOC_DATA_REC_40_U.
ENDLOOP.
*-------------------------------------------------
* Container Alignment
*-------------------------------------------------
* In case of multibyte (Double Byte) languages
* special container alignemnt for IDoc structure
* necessary in Unicode system before sending to
* MDMP system
DATA LV_RFC_DEST          TYPE RFCDISPLAY-RFCDEST.
DATA LT_LANGU_CODEPAGE    TYPE NLS_LANGU_CP_TAB.
DATA LS_LANGU_CODEPAGE    TYPE NLS_LANGU_CP_LINE.
DATA LV_IS_MULTIBYTE      TYPE BOOLEAN.
DATA LV_IS_UNICODE_SYSTEM TYPE BOOLEAN.
CLASS CL_NLS_CODEPAGE_PROPERTIES DEFINITION LOAD.
DATA CONT_NLS TYPE REF TO CL_NLS_STRUC_CONTAINER_SNAME.

* Check if this is a Unicode system
CLASS CL_ABAP_CHAR_UTILITIES DEFINITION LOAD.
IF CL_ABAP_CHAR_UTILITIES=>CHARSIZE = 1.
   LV_IS_UNICODE_SYSTEM = ' '.
ELSE.
   LV_IS_UNICODE_SYSTEM = 'X'.
```

```
ENDIF.
IF LV_IS_UNICODE_SYSTEM IS INITIAL.
* Non-Unicode system
   EXIT.
ENDIF.
* Take RFC destination of the caller from the IDoc
* control structure
READ TABLE IDOC_CONTROL_REC_40 INDEX 1.
LV_RFC_DEST = IDOC_CONTROL_REC_40-RCVPRN.
* Get language - codepage assignment of the called
* MDMP system
CALL FUNCTION 'NLS_GET_LANGU_CP_TAB'
   EXPORTING
     DESTINATION              = LV_RFC_DEST
   TABLES
     CP_TAB                   = LT_LANGU_CODEPAGE
   EXCEPTIONS
     SYSTEM_FAILURE        = 1
      COMMUNICATION_FAILURE = 2
      UNKNOWN_ERROR         = 3
      OTHERS                = 4.
IF SY-SUBRC <> 0.
* <own error handling >
ENDIF.
LOOP AT IDOC_DATA_REC_40_U INTO LS_IDOC_DATA_REC_40_U.
* Process only textrelevant segments
IF NOT LS_IDOC_DATA_REC_40_U-SLANGU IS INITIAL.
* Get codepage from language
READ TABLE LT_LANGU_CODEPAGE INTO LS_LANGU_CODEPAGE
   WITH KEY LANGU = LS_IDOC_DATA_REC_40_U-SLANGU.
IF NOT SY-SUBRC IS INITIAL.
* < own error handling >
ENDIF.
* Check, if it is a multibyte codepage
CALL METHOD CL_NLS_CODEPAGE_PROPERTIES=>IS_MULTIBYTE
   EXPORTING
     CODEPAGE = LS_LANGU_CODEPAGE-CODEPAGE
   RECEIVING
     VALUE    = LV_IS_MULTIBYTE.
* Container alignment only for multibyte codepages
IF NOT LV_IS_MULTIBYTE IS INITIAL.
   DATA LV_IDOC_FORMAT LIKE EDI_DC-TABNAM.
   DATA LV_SEGNAM LIKE EDI_DD40-SEGNAM.
   LV_IDOC_FORMAT = 'EDI_DC40'.
   LV_SEGNAM = LS_IDOC_DATA_REC_40_U-SEGNAM.
```

```
* Convert external name of segment to internal name
    CALL FUNCTION 'SEGMENT_INTERNAL_NAME_GET'
      EXPORTING
        SEGNAM                     = LV_SEGNAM
        IDOC_FORMAT                = LV_IDOC_FORMAT
      IMPORTING
        SEGTYP                     = LV_SEGNAM
      EXCEPTIONS
        SEGNAM_UNUSABLE         = 1
        CONVERSION_NOT_AVAILABLE = 2
        UNKNOWN_FORMAT          = 3
        OTHERS                  = 4.
    IF NOT SY-SUBRC IS INITIAL.
*       <own error handling>
    ENDIF.
    LS_IDOC_DATA_REC_40_U-SEGNAM = LV_SEGNAM.
*   Do the container alignment
    CONT_NLS =
CL_NLS_STRUC_CONTAINER_SNAME=>CREATE_FOR_FIXED_CODEPAGE
    ( CODEPAGE = LS_LANGU_CODEPAGE-CODEPAGE
      STRUC_NAME = LV_SEGNAM ).
    DATA T TYPE I.
    CALL METHOD CONT_NLS->STRUC_TO_CONT
      EXPORTING
        LANGU          = ' '
      IMPORTING
        TRUNCATION_FLAG = T
      CHANGING
        CONT           = LS_IDOC_DATA_REC_40_U-SDATA.
    FREE CONT_NLS.
  ENDIF.    " if block: Only multibyte codepages
  ENDIF.    " if block: Only text rekevant segments
  MODIFY IDOC_DATA_REC_40_U FROM LS_IDOC_DATA_REC_40_U.
ENDLOOP.
ENDFUNCTION.
```

Listing 3.6 Filling the Enhanced IDocs in the Sending System Before Transfer

IDoc preparation and Container Alignment for Asian Double-Byte languages

This function is broken down into two significant parts:

▶ **Filling of the language-dependent IDoc transfer structure with data and texts from the segments**
Using the TABLES parameter IDOC_DATA_REC_40, the IDoc data is passed to the function without language keys. There, in the first LOOP statement, the IDoc data is assigned by row and segment to the new IDoc structure IDOC_DATA_REC_40_U (also a TABLES param-

eter) with the language key field SLANGU. Besides the segment with the material short texts E1MAKTM, which originate from table MAKT with language key SPRAS, there are also enhanced texts for a material in segments E1MTXHM and E1MTXLM, available as SAPscript objects in the language TDSPRAS.

▶ **Container Alignment for Asian Double-Byte/multibyte languages**
As we already saw in Section 3.4, for inhomogeneous communication of the technically complicated Double-Byte languages JA, KO, ZH, and ZF, there must be specific additional measures if structure data with these languages are transmitted in containers between non-Unicode and Unicode systems. Because transfer of IDocs is done using container technology, this is exactly that case.

In this prototype, as described in Section 3.4.2, the class CL_NLS_STRUC_CONTAINER_SNAME is used for execution of the Container Alignment to allow the transfer of Asian languages (see also the programming example in Listing 3.1). After the method call CL_ABAP_CHAR_UTILITIES=>CHARSIZE has determined that this is a Unicode system, alignment is performed in another LOOP statement, in which only language- and text-relevant segments must be considered (IF NOT LS_IDOC_DATA_REC_40_U-SLANGU IS INITIAL). If that condition is satisfied, first the code page of the current segment is determined using language SLANGU and the method call CALL METHOD CL_NLS_CODEPAGE_PROPERTIES=>IS_MULTIBYTE is used to determine whether this is a Double-Byte code page from the languages JA, KO, ZH, or ZF. If this is also true, Container Alignment is performed using the statements CONT_NLS = CL_NLS_STRUC_CONTAINER_SNAME =>CREATE_FOR_FIXED_CODEPAGE and CALL METHOD CONT_NLS->STRUC_TO_CONT.

The function IDOC_CONVERT_TO_EDI_DD40_U returns the filled language-dependent IDoc transfer structure EDIDD40_U back to LEDI7_UF12. This allows the transfer of the IDocs from the Unicode to the MDMP system, which is done using the (remote) call to function IDOC_INBOUND_ASYNCHRONOUS_U in the receiving system with address DESTINATION EDIPOA-LOGDES. Thus, a tRFC connection is made from the Unicode to the MDMP system and the transfer performed in the receiving system (see Listing 3.7).

Multilingual IDoc data transfer

```
FUNCTION IDOC_INBOUND_ASYNCHRONOUS_U.
*"------------------------------------------------------
```

```
*"*"Local Interface
*"       TABLES
*"          IDOC_CONTROL_REC_40 STRUCTURE  EDI_DC40
*"          IDOC_DATA_REC_40_U STRUCTURE  EDI_DD40_U
*"-----------------------------------------------------------
DATA IDOC_DATA_REC_40 LIKE EDI_DD40 OCCURS 0.
* Convert to standard IDOC structure
  CALL FUNCTION 'IDOC_CONVERT_TO_EDI_DD40'
    TABLES
      IDOC_CONTROL_REC_40 = IDOC_CONTROL_REC_40
      IDOC_DATA_REC_40_U  = IDOC_DATA_REC_40_U
      IDOC_DATA_REC_40    = IDOC_DATA_REC_40.
* Call standard IDOC inbound with RFC destination NONE
  CALL FUNCTION 'IDOC_INBOUND_ASYNCHRONOUS'
    DESTINATION 'NONE'
    TABLES
      IDOC_CONTROL_REC_40 = IDOC_CONTROL_REC_40
      IDOC_DATA_REC_40    = IDOC_DATA_REC_40.
ENDFUNCTION.
```

Listing 3.7 Processing of the Enhanced IDocs after Receipt

Transfer from the extended structure back to the standard IDoc structure and inbound processing

The IDoc data are converted between the current code page and Unicode row by row based on the enhanced IDoc transfer structure according to the RFC language key. After the transfer, the IDoc data must be passed to the application through inbound processing using CALL FUNCTION 'IDOC_INBOUND_ASYNCHRONOUS'. However, first the IDoc data must be extracted from the language-dependent IDoc structure IDOC_DATA_REC_40_U back into the IDoc standard structure IDOC_DATA_REC_40, because otherwise more changes would be required to inbound processing, which we want to avoid.

This "back conversion" of the enhanced IDoc data is done with the CALL FUNCTION 'IDOC_CONVERT_TO_EDI_DD40' call, which returned the filled IDoc standard structure in IDOC_DATA_REC_40, so that the IDoc data can be passed to inbound processing with CALL FUNCTION 'IDOC_INBOUND_ASYNCHRONOUS' on the same system (DESTINATION 'NONE').

So the IDOC_CONVERT_TO_EDI_DD40 function is the counterpart to IDOC_CONVERT_TO_EDI_DD_U, which has the task of copying the IDoc data before sending, from the standard structure without a language key into the enhanced IDoc transfer structure with a language key. This is the reverse direction; that is, the IDoc data is copied in the receiving system from the enhanced IDoc structure into the standard structure before the actual inbound processing. If Asian Double-Byte languages are involved, we would actually expect a Container Alignment. This was already taken care of, however, in the Unicode system in the IDOC_CONVERT_TO_EDI_DD40_U function with the method call CALL METHOD CONT_NLS->STRUC_TO_CONT ... while writing to the (IDoc) container. Now we're back in the MDMP system, which you can see from the query for IF CL_ABAP_CHAR_UTILITIES=>CHARSIZE = 1 ..., so that the following statements for Container Alignment will not be enhanced here (only in the reverse transfer direction). The transfer of the enhanced data to the standard IDoc takes place within a loop with the statement MOVE-CORRESPONDING LS_IDOC_DATA_REC_ 40_U TO LS_IDOC_DATA_REC_40 (see Listing 3.8). Afterwards, we find ourselves back in the standard ALE inbound processing.

```
*"------------------------------------
FUNCTION IDOC_CONVERT_TO_EDI_DD40.
*"------------------------------------
*"*"Local Interface
*"   TABLES
*"       IDOC_CONTROL_REC_40 STRUCTURE   EDI_DC40
*"       IDOC_DATA_REC_40_U STRUCTURE   EDI_DD40_U
*"       IDOC_DATA_REC_40 STRUCTURE   EDI_DD40
*"------------------------------------------------------------
DATA LS_IDOC_DATA_REC_40    TYPE EDI_DD40.
DATA LS_IDOC_DATA_REC_40_U TYPE EDI_DD40_U.
DATA LV_CALLER_RFC_DEST     TYPE RFCDISPLAY-RFCDEST.
DATA LT_LANGU_CODEPAGE      TYPE NLS_LANGU_CP_TAB.
DATA LS_LANGU_CODEPAGE      TYPE NLS_LANGU_CP_LINE.
DATA LV_IS_MULTIBYTE        TYPE BOOLEAN.
DATA LV_IS_UNICODE_SYSTEM   TYPE BOOLEAN.
CLASS CL_NLS_CODEPAGE_PROPERTIES DEFINITION LOAD.
DATA CONT_NLS TYPE REF TO CL_NLS_STRUC_CONTAINER_SNAME.
CLASS CL_ABAP_CHAR_UTILITIES DEFINITION LOAD.

* Check if this is a Unicode system
IF CL_ABAP_CHAR_UTILITIES=>CHARSIZE = 1.
  LV_IS_UNICODE_SYSTEM = ' '.
ELSE.
  LV_IS_UNICODE_SYSTEM = 'X'.
ENDIF.
IF NOT LV_IS_UNICODE_SYSTEM IS INITIAL.
*   Take RFC destination of the caller from the
```

```
*   IDOC control structure
    READ TABLE IDOC_CONTROL_REC_40 INDEX 1.
    LV_CALLER_RFC_DEST = IDOC_CONTROL_REC_40-SNDPRN.
*   Get language - codepage assignment of the sending
*   system
    CALL FUNCTION 'NLS_GET_LANGU_CP_TAB'
      EXPORTING
        DESTINATION           = LV_CALLER_RFC_DEST
      TABLES
        CP_TAB                = LT_LANGU_CODEPAGE
      EXCEPTIONS
        SYSTEM_FAILURE        = 1
        COMMUNICATION_FAILURE = 2
        UNKNOWN_ERROR         = 3
        OTHERS                = 4.
    IF SY-SUBRC <> 0.
*       <own error handling>
    ENDIF.
ENDIF.
CLEAR IDOC_DATA_REC_40[].
LOOP AT IDOC_DATA_REC_40_U INTO LS_IDOC_DATA_REC_40_U.
  CLEAR LS_IDOC_DATA_REC_40.
  IF NOT LV_IS_UNICODE_SYSTEM IS INITIAL.
*     Process only textrelevant segments
    IF NOT LS_IDOC_DATA_REC_40_U-SLANGU IS INITIAL.
*       Get codepage from language
        READ TABLE LT_LANGU_CODEPAGE INTO
        LS_LANGU_CODEPAGE WITH KEY LANGU =
        LS_IDOC_DATA_REC_40_U-SLANGU.
*       Check, if it is a multibyte codepage
      CALL METHOD CL_NLS_CODEPAGE_PROPERTIES=>IS_MULTIBYTE
          EXPORTING
            CODEPAGE = LS_LANGU_CODEPAGE-CODEPAGE
          RECEIVING
            VALUE    = LV_IS_MULTIBYTE.
*       Container alignment is only for multibyte
*       codepages necessary
        IF NOT LV_IS_MULTIBYTE IS INITIAL.
          DATA LV_IDOC_FORMAT LIKE EDI_DC-TABNAM.
          DATA LV_SEGNAM LIKE EDI_DD40-SEGNAM.
          LV_IDOC_FORMAT = 'EDI_DC40'.
          LV_SEGNAM = LS_IDOC_DATA_REC_40_U-SEGNAM.
*         Convert external name of segment to internal
*         name of segment
          CALL FUNCTION 'SEGMENT_INTERNAL_NAME_GET'
```

```
        EXPORTING
          SEGNAM                = LV_SEGNAM
          IDOC_FORMAT           = LV_IDOC_FORMAT
        IMPORTING
          SEGTYP                = LV_SEGNAM
        EXCEPTIONS
          SEGNAM_UNUSABLE       = 1
          CONVERSION_NOT_AVAILABLE = 2
          UNKNOWN_FORMAT        = 3
          OTHERS                = 4.
      IF NOT SY-SUBRC IS INITIAL.
*         <own error handling>
      ENDIF.
      LS_IDOC_DATA_REC_40_U-SEGNAM = LV_SEGNAM.
*       Do the container alignment
CONT_NLS =
  CL_NLS_STRUC_CONTAINER_SNAME=>CREATE_FOR_FIXED_CODEPAGE(
  CODEPAGE = LS_LANGU_CODEPAGE-CODEPAGE
  STRUC_NAME = LV_SEGNAM ).
      CONT_NLS->CONT_TO_STRUC(
        EXPORTING LANGU = ' '
        CHANGING  CONT  = LS_IDOC_DATA_REC_40_U-SDATA ).
      FREE CONT_NLS.
      ENDIF.
    ENDIF.
  ENDIF.
*   Fill standard IDOC segment structure
  MOVE-CORRESPONDING LS_IDOC_DATA_REC_40_U
                  TO LS_IDOC_DATA_REC_40.
  APPEND LS_IDOC_DATA_REC_40 TO IDOC_DATA_REC_40.
ENDLOOP.
```

Listing 3.8 Filling the Standard IDocs from the Enhanced IDocs

From this detailed description of the prototype, it can easily be seen that the effort of custom development and adaptations is not insignificant. Even for one specific ALE message type MATMAS, multiple ALE-specific components must be adapted and extended.

Summary of the ALE prototype

For other ALE message types, each would have to have a function written to transfer the texts and language keys from the segments into the enhanced language-dependent IDoc transfer structure, as was done in the IDOC_CONVERT_TO_EDI_DD40_U (outbound) and IDOC_CONVERT_TO_EDI_DD40 (inbound) functions for the message type MATMAS.

In summary, for the development of your own solution with an ALE Unicode/MDMP scenario, we make the following recommendations:

▸ It should always be checked first whether a simplification of the ALE communication scenarios is possible by reduction to multiple single code page transfer, so that the development effort and all consequences of a modification would only be minimal.

▸ Because this is a combined solution involving custom programming, user exits, and enhancements of SAP standard programs, maintenance of such a solution will generally be difficult because of the continual correction for support packages and future upgrades, and should not be underestimated.

▸ The solution depends on the ALE message type. For each message type considered for multilingual transfer, you must precisely analyze how the language-dependent rows of the enhanced IDoc structure EDI_DD40_U will be filled correctly with the texts of the multilingual business data from the original tables. For MATMAS this case is rather simple because of the language-dependent table MAKT with the material texts and the assigned IDoc segments E1MAKTM, E1MTXHM, and E1MTXL. For other multilingual ALE message types, like the frequently used CREMAS for customer master data, matters look a lot more complicated, since the assignment between the tables of multilingual names and addresses and IDoc segments is more complicated.

▸ An attempt should be made to use standard ALE user exits as often as possible.

▸ As already described for the prototype for MATMAS, in a custom solution it should be attempted to restrict the modifications to the collective transfer of IDocs.

General Scenarios: Communication Between Components of the SAP Business Suite and SAP R/3

Unicode/MDMP solution for the SAP Business Suite Because the MDMP solution is basically only suitable for an R/3 system, there are even more challenges regarding data transfer from Unicode to non-Unicode for global multilingual use of the components of SAP Business Suite. Except for a few special exceptions (older releases), MDMP is not supported in SAP Business Suite, with the exception of SAP R/3. Components such as SAP CRM, SAP SRM, or SAP NetWeaver BI systems are only operated as either single code page or Unicode systems.

Because such a system is usually coupled with an R/3 system, which is often also the master system, other SAP components such as BI or CRM have been converted to Unicode before SAP R/3 or have been installed as Unicode when they were introduced. The databases of the business suite components are usually much smaller in comparison with SAP R/3, so that the downtime of a Unicode conversion is lower.

Because most global R/3 systems are configured with MDMP, the result is necessarily a Unicode/MDMP communication scenario. Analogous to the ALE scenario previously described, during the transfer with RFC there must also be language-dependent transfer structures with linguistically correctly filled texts available so that a parallel conversion from or to Unicode can be performed. Because the different components of the SAP Business Suite use different interfaces and middleware technologies to connect to SAP R/3, the solutions for the Unicode/MDMP scenario look different, but they all have the same goal, namely, to make the transfer structures language dependent.

Large global R/3 systems not yet in Unicode

Before you get into a possibly very complex solution requiring a lot of effort, you should first investigate whether simplification is possible by reduction to the Unicode/single code page scenario: The application texts for a country or a certain organizational unit are only in one language or code page, so that the transfer of a corresponding data object is actually not multilingual.

Reduction to multiple Unicode/ single code page transfer

For instance, orders in a global Unicode CRM system for China are only entered in Chinese (and maybe English), so that a transfer of such an order to an R/3 system (MDMP) is actually a case of "Unicode (Chinese)/single code page (Chinese)." There is no need for parallel conversions of Unicode into multiple code pages. In this case, it suffices to ensure that the RFC connection code page is Chinese, and the conversion will take place automatically.

This can be achieved using the standard configuration tools and the selection of the right logon language in the Unicode system (in this case, Chinese). Whether this simplification is possible depends on a few factors, which in turn largely depend on the concrete applications and data objects used by the global enterprise. While the simplification for country-specific orders is realistic, it is probably not realistic for something like the transfer of products. A product is usually used globally with multilingual product descriptions, so that the data exchange between a Unicode and an MDMP system necessitates parallel RFC conversions.

In the following sections, we will take a closer look at the solution for the scenario SAP CRM (Unicode) with SAP R/3 (MDMP) and SAP NetWeaver BI (Unicode) with SAP R/3 (MDMP). Because of the commonalities in the middleware between SAP CRM and SAP SRM, several solution aspects for SAP CRM can also be used in the scenario SAP SRM (Unicode) with SAP R/3 (MDMP). These can be found with additional detail in SAP Note 745030 and references, and also in SRM-specific documentation.

Scenario: SAP CRM/SRM (Unicode) and SP R/3 (MDMP)

The following requires at least releases SAP CRM 4.0/SAP SRM 4.0 (Unicode) or later, and SAP R/3 4.6C (MDMP) or later. If the R/3 release is lower, please contact SAP to investigate whether such a scenario can be supported. The connection between SAP R/3 and SAP CRM and SAP SRM[15] takes place through a special CRM/SRM middleware, which transfers business data in BDocs using qRFC technology. BDocs can be grouped into the types *customizing data, master data*, and *application data*.

Similar to transfer with IDocs, during the RFC transfer an internal structure BAPIMTCS is used. This structure is filled by the transfer applications with data, including the texts. For multilingual texts with multiple code pages, we must ensure that this structure is language-dependent and filled with the linguistically correct texts. Besides a language key in BAPIMTCS, therefore, the send and receiver application are needed for the correct processing of the texts, just as in the ALE scenario. The special middleware functions in R/3 are contained in the plug-in (PI) components, which must already have been installed.

A complete overview of all existing solutions or solution approaches for ABAP-based components can be found in SAP Collective Note 745030, with corresponding references and attachments with additional documentation.

---

15 For the IDocs also used in SAP SRM, the scenario ALE Unicode/MDMP can be consulted.

For the communication scenario, the latest support packages and kernel patches for SAP CRM, SAP SRM, and PI have made some significant improvements, so that the systems involved must first be brought to a new maintenance level. Besides the existing language key in BAPIMTCS (see Figure 3.53), the following data objects are now supported for Unicode/MDMP transfer. These require little or no enhancement, provided that the texts in these data objects are maintained by the applications with existing language keys and always in the correct language:

Language key in BAPIMTCS

▶ Almost all customizing objects

▶ Business partners

▶ Products

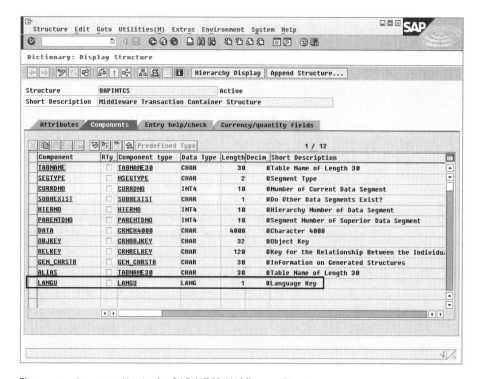

Figure 3.53 Language Key in the BAPIMTCS Middleware Structure

All other data objects and some customizing objects with tables without language keys can only be transmitted using custom development and enhancements.

Luckily, the middleware components for SAP CRM and SAP SRM offer this without modification of the SAP standard with user exits and BAdIs alone. The basic process of such an extension project is as follows:

▶ First, all components involved must be brought to the latest maintenance level. In particular, on the R/3 side, the SAP plug-in component PI 2004 should be installed with the latest available support package.

▶ Then the data objects and resulting BDocs should be determined which contain texts with different code pages and which are exchanged between SAP CRM and SAP R/3. It should also be clarified whether the transfer of texts with mixed code pages takes place bidirectionally or only in one direction.

▶ The BAPIMTCS transfer structure already has a language key LANGU in higher maintenance levels of SAP CRM and the R/3 plug-in, so that no action is required.

▶ Depending on the direction of transfer, different user exits and BAdIs are used:

▷ **Case 1: SAP R/3 sending to SAP CRM**
Here, the general user exit CRM0_200 in the R/3 plug-in is activated and extended with corresponding logic. Before the RFC call, all transfer data runs through this exit, in which the necessary adaptations can be made. Because generally several data objects and BDocs must be prepared for transfer, we recommend that you work with a wrapper function, which acts as a dispatcher to call the individual functions for the specific data objects. Detailed information can be found in SAP Note 691585 with attachments and references.

▷ **Case 2: SAP CRM sending to SAP R/3**
Here, several user exits and BAdIs must be used, depending on the data object and BDoc, user exit SMOUTIL2 for business partners and CRM_DATAEXCHG_BADI for orders (sales) and other objects. You can find the documentation for this in SAP Notes 691585 and 797815, along with attachments and references.

▶ After selecting suitable user exits or BAdIs, the corresponding logic is programmed, which ensures that (with some exceptions) the BAPIMTCS transfer structure is always filled with the right language keys and texts before the RFC call. It should be noted that BAPIMTCS includes a so-called long container field, which is filled with multiple fields of different data types.

If texts of the Asian languages JA, KO, ZH, and ZF are transmitted, the different lengths of a character in Unicode and MDMP system (Double-Byte languages) must be taken into account, so that under some circumstances additional programming effort will be necessary in the area of Container Alignment.

For additional illustration, here is a small example. During an initial download of customizing data from an MDMP system to a Unicode system (SAP R/3 to SAP CRM) it is determined that multilingual addresses with different code pages are transferred incorrectly from tables BNKA and PAYM. An analysis of these two tables shows that they have no language key, but they do have fields for text. Although the initial download is initiated from the CRM system, the actual transfer takes place from SAP R/3 to SAP CRM. As a result, Case 1 is a good approach, with a user exit that in this case would derive a language from the country of the address and then assign it to the BAPI-MTCS transfer structure (see Figure 3.54).

Container fields

Example of a customizing initial download

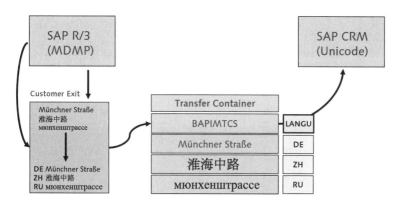

Figure 3.54 Data Transfer from SAP R/3 (MDMP) to SAP CRM Unicode

First, user exit CRM0_200 is activated and a wrapper function Z_MDMP_OBJECT_WRAPPER created. The download data objects for tables BNKA and PAYM are DNL_CUST_BNKA and DNL_CUST_PAYM, which can be seen from the CRM middleware configuration.

Data transfer from SAP R/3 (MDMP) to SAP CRM (Unicode)

Z_MDMP_OBJECT_WRAPPER includes a CASE statement which determines the current download object being transferred from SAP R/3 to SAP CRM using the IMPORT variable I_OBJ_NAME and then branches to a specific function Z_MDMP_DNL_CUST_BNKA for table BNKA or Z_MDMP_DNL_CUST_PAYM for table PAYM (see Listing 3.9).

```
FUNCTION Z_MDMP_OBJECT_WRAPPER.
*"----------------------------------------------------------
*"*"Local interface:
*"  IMPORTING
*"     VALUE(I_OBJ_CLASS) LIKE BAPICRMOBJ-OBJCLASS
*"     VALUE(I_OBJ_NAME) LIKE BAPICRMOBJ-OBJ_NAME
*"     VALUE(I_BAPICRMDH2) LIKE BAPICRMDH2
*"     STRUCTURE BAPICRMDH2 OPTIONAL
*"     VALUE(I_KEYWORD_IN) LIKE CRM_PARA-KEYWORD_IN
*"     VALUE(I_CRMRFCPAR) LIKE CRMRFCPAR STRUCTURE CRMRFCPAR
*"     OPTIONAL
*"  EXPORTING
*"     VALUE(E_DO_NOT_SEND) LIKE CRM_PARA-XFELD
*"  TABLES
*"     T_INT_TABLES STRUCTURE BAPIMTCS
*"     T_BAPISTRUCT STRUCTURE BAPIMTCS
*"     T_MESSAGES STRUCTURE BAPICRMMSG
*"     T_KEY_INFO STRUCTURE BAPICRMKEY
*"     T_OTHER_INFO STRUCTURE BAPIEXTC
*"     T_BAPIIDLIST STRUCTURE BAPIIDLIST
*"  CHANGING
*"     VALUE(C_BAPICRMDH2) LIKE BAPICRMDH2
*"     STRUCTURE BAPICRMDH2
*"     VALUE(C_RFCDEST) LIKE CRMRFCPAR STRUCTURE CRMRFCPAR
*"     VALUE(C_OBJNAME) LIKE BAPICRMOBJ-OBJ_NAME
*"----------------------------------------------------------
  case i_obj_name.
  when 'DNL_CUST_BNKA'. "No language key in BNKA
* Specifc function for table BNKA
  CALL FUNCTION 'Z_MDMP_DNL_CUST_BNKA'
  EXPORTING
  I_OBJ_CLASS = i_obj_class
  I_OBJ_NAME = i_obj_name
  I_BAPICRMDH2 = i_bapicrmdh2
  I_KEYWORD_IN = i_keyword_in
  I_CRMRFCPAR = i_crmrfcpar
  IMPORTING
  E_DO_NOT_SEND = e_do_not_send
  TABLES
  T_INT_TABLES = t_int_tables
```

```
  T_BAPISTRUCT = t_bapistruct
  T_MESSAGES = t_messages
  T_KEY_INFO = t_key_info
  T_OTHER_INFO = t_other_info
  T_BAPIIDLIST = t_bapiidlist
  CHANGING
  C_BAPICRMDH2 = c_bapicrmdh2
  C_RFCDEST = c_rfcdest
  C_OBJNAME = c_objname.
  when 'DNL_CUST_PAYM'. "No language key in BNKA
* "Specifc function for table PAYM
  CALL FUNCTION 'Z_MDMP_DNL_CUST_PAYM'
  ...
  when... " more cases
  when others.
  endcase.
ENDFUNCTION.
```

Listing 3.9 Example of a Wrapper Function for User Exit CRM0_200

The actual processing takes place in the specific functions, which we will show Z_MDMP_DNL_CUST_BNKA here. The problem is to copy the bank addresses in the local language without a language key in table BNKA correctly into the transfer structure BAPIMTCS (here, as variable BAPIMTCS). BNKA includes a country field BNKA-BANKS, from which the language of the bank address can be derived by accessing the general SAP table for countries, T005. The language key T005-SPRAS found is then assigned to the transfer structure language key LS_BAPIMTCS-LANGU.

Determining the language in the user exit

Thus, for instance, the Russian bank addresses would be placed together with the correct language key RU in the BAPIMTCS transfer structure, and will be converted correctly into Unicode (see Listing 3.10).

```
FUNCTION Z_MDMP_DNL_CUST_BNKA.
*"----------------------------------------------------------
*"*"Local interface:
*"  IMPORTING
*"     VALUE(I_OBJ_CLASS) LIKE BAPICRMOBJ-OBJCLASS
*"     VALUE(I_OBJ_NAME) LIKE BAPICRMOBJ-OBJ_NAME
*"     VALUE(I_BAPICRMDH2) LIKE BAPICRMDH2 STRUCTURE BAPICRMDH2
*"     OPTIONAL
*"     VALUE(I_KEYWORD_IN) LIKE CRM_PARA-KEYWORD_IN
*"     VALUE(I_CRMRFCPAR) LIKE CRMRFCPAR STRUCTURE CRMRFCPAR OPTIONAL
*"  EXPORTING
```

```
*" VALUE(E_DO_NOT_SEND) LIKE CRM_PARA-XFELD
*" TABLES
*" T_INT_TABLES STRUCTURE BAPIMTCS
*" T_BAPISTRUCT STRUCTURE BAPIMTCS
*" T_MESSAGES STRUCTURE BAPICRMMSG
*" T_KEY_INFO STRUCTURE BAPICRMKEY
*" T_OTHER_INFO STRUCTURE BAPIEXTC
*" T_BAPIIDLIST STRUCTURE BAPIIDLIST
*" CHANGING
*" VALUE(C_BAPICRMDH2) LIKE BAPICRMDH2 STRUCTURE BAPICRMDH2
*" VALUE(C_RFCDEST) LIKE CRMRFCPAR STRUCTURE CRMRFCPAR
*" VALUE(C_OBJNAME) LIKE BAPICRMOBJ-OBJ_NAME
*"---------------------------------------------------------
 data: ls_bapimtcs type bapimtcs value is initial.
 data: ls_bnka type bnka value is initial.
 data: lt_t005 type table of t005.
 data: ls_t005 type t005.
 select * from t005 into table lt_t005.
 loop at t_bapistruct into ls_bapimtcs where segtype = 'DA'.
 case ls_bapimtcs-tabname.
 when 'BNKA'.
 move_x ls_bapimtcs-data ls_bnka.
 read table lt_t005 into ls_t005
 with key land1 = ls_bnka-banks.
 ls_bapimtcs-langu = ls_t005-spras.
 modify t_bapistruct from ls_bapimtcs.
 endcase.
 endloop.
ENDFUNCTION.
```

Listing 3.10 User Exit Function for the Language of Bank Addresses in BNKA

Scenario: SAP NetWeaver BI (Unicode) and SAP R/3 (MDMP)

Data transfer from SAP R/3 to SAP NetWeaver BI in one direction

Similarly to the connection of SAP CRM (Unicode) and SAP R/3 (MDMP), there is often a need to connect SAP NetWeaver BI (Unicode) with SAP R/3 (MDMP). Happily, the data transfer runs only in one direction—from SAP R/3 to SAP NetWeaver BI—so that in this scenario only one case must be considered.

First, we again should attempted to reduce the matter to single code page; i.e., to investigate whether it is possible to operate SAP NetWeaver BI in only a single code page, perhaps for a transition period. If so, rules apply that are analogous to those for the previously presented scenarios, so that no invalid texts or languages can make it from SAP R/3 into SAP NetWeaver BI.

If SAP NetWeaver BI must run under Unicode, a simplified solution variant is the reduction of the extraction to multiple transfers with one code page apiece. This is supported by the infrastructure of SAP NetWeaver BI, in that one extraction job is configured for each code page. However, certain prerequisites are necessary for this, which will be described a bit later.

Multiple extraction jobs

If SAP NetWeaver BI is operated under Unicode and if simplification is impossible (which includes multiple extraction jobs), then a similar procedure must be followed as you saw in the second scenario. During the transfer, all text data must be available with language keys in the transfer structures, so that RFC, which is also used in the connection to SAP NetWeaver BI, can be converted in parallel.

General solution

The transfer of data from SAP R/3 to SAP NetWeaver BI is done using extractors which enable a targeted and configurable selection of the data to be transmitted. This concept benefits this communication scenario, since it makes it possible to define your own structures and equip them with language keys. To connect SAP R/3 with SAP NetWeaver BI, an SAP plug-in is also required, which should be at the latest possible maintenance level, at least release PI 2004.1.

Data sources (extractor structures) that already contain language keys are not a problem. With the important provision that the assignments between language keys and texts are correct (especially that under language key EN only Western European languages exist in the rows), no other significant actions are required.

Language-dependent data sources

An example of a language-dependent data source is the material texts 0MATERIAL_TEXT: Transaction RSA6 shows the field SPRAS for this data source, which must be marked in the field **Selection** (see Figure 3.55). A double-click on **SPRAS** shows the data type LANG, and another click on **SPRAS** shows that the text language flag is set, so that this is a valid language key. This means that with no further effort, multilingual materials texts can be transferred from SAP R/3 (MDMP) to SAP NetWeaver BI (Unicode) with correct conversion.

It is significantly more difficult if the data sources have no language keys, as for example with customer names in data source 0CUSTOMER_TEXT. Transaction RSA6 only shows the two fields KUNNR for the customer number and TXTMD; that is, there is no language key. If the customer names are transferred from SAP R/3 to

Multilingual data sources without language keys

SAP NetWeaver BI without adaptation, only the texts in the RFC connection code page will be transmitted correctly. Figure 3.56 shows this with an example of customer names with three code pages.

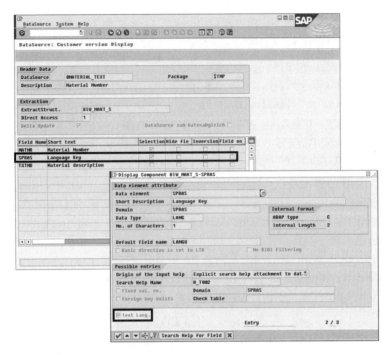

Figure 3.55 Language-Dependent Data Source 0MATERIAL_TEXT

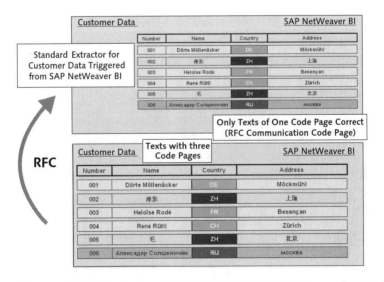

Figure 3.56 Data Transfer from SAP R/3 (MDMP) to SAP NetWeaver BI (Unicode)

To solve this problem there are two possible approaches:

- ▶ **Reduction to multiple extractor jobs with one per code page**
  As mentioned earlier, under certain circumstances a solution can be found without extension of the data sources with a language key and user exists, and this should be attempted first. This approach assumes that one extractor job per code page is possible if the language-independent data source has a field from which a single code page can be unambiguously determined, for instance a country or a company code.

  Multiple extractor jobs with Unicode/single code page conversion

  The extraction is started from SAP NetWeaver BI in a background job; that is, the Unicode system calls a non-Unicode system and determines an RFC communication code page from the RFC rules for Unicode/non-Unicode, whereby the step language of the background job is relevant. The extractor job initiates the RFC call with subsequent transfer, whereby all extracted texts are converted from the single (RFC) code page into Unicode. If multiple extractor jobs are configured, one per code page in the data source, the problem is solved.

  This is a reduction to a Unicode single code page case with multiple transfers. But this method has some disadvantages:

  - ▷ It is not always possible to separate each data source unambiguously into one dedicated job per code page.

    Disadvantages of multiple transfers

  - ▷ Particularly for large amounts of data to be extracted, this procedure can degrade performance during the transfers, because multiple jobs must either run in parallel or place a higher load on the system. In the case of sequential execution, the time window for extraction, often a narrow one, may under some circumstances be insufficient.

- ▶ **Enhancement of the data source together with user-exit programming**
  To convert all texts correctly, the concept of language-dependent data sources helps. Because these have language keys, the transfer functions correctly with no further action. Language-independent data sources must be extended with a language key, together with logic which fills the rows correctly with the texts and assigns the correct language keys.

  Extension of the data source with language key and user exit

However, this requires programming effort again, for which SAP NetWeaver BI provides a user exit. The significant steps, described in detail in the documentation, are:

▸ Determination of the relevant data sources in SAP R/3 that have no language keys and contain texts from multiple code pages. A utility program is given in the documentation cited which can be of great use in this step.

▸ Enhancement of every relevant data source with a language key field, which must be of type LANG (as of SAP Web AS 6.10) and for which the text language flag must be set. This is done in Transaction RSA6 with the function **Enhance Extractor Structure**, which is technically an extension with an append structure. The new language key field must be actively selected in the data source.

Creating a user exit
with Transaction
CMOD

▸ Creating a user exit with Transaction CMOD; RSAP0001 is selected for an enhancement to SAP NetWeaver BI. Here, the focus is on the two exit functions EXIT_SAPLRSAP_002 for enhancements to master data and texts, and EXIT_SAPLRSAP_001 for enhancements to transaction data.

▸ In the case of EXIT_SAPLRSAP_002, programming of the ABAP Include ZXRSAU02 with the necessary custom logic to fulfill the requirement above. Similarly to the Unicode/MDMP scenario with SAP CRM and SAP R/3, it makes sense here to first create a wrapper utility function. This acts as a dispatcher to branch to individual functions for each special data source, thus enabling a modular design for multiple data sources. An example program for a user exit to extend the data source 0CUSTOMER_TEXT is described in the documentation cited.

▸ After activation of the user exit with Transaction CMOD, transfer of the multilingual texts from SAP R/3 (MDMP) to SAP NetWeaver BI with parallel RFC conversion. Here, it is not necessary to change the transfer structure in SAP NetWeaver BI.

You should carefully consider which solution approach is the best in the concrete case, considering all advantages and disadvantages. Detailed documentation can be found in the SAP Collective Note 745030 and the corresponding references, as well as the included document *How to Connect SAP NetWeaver BI Unicode with an MDMP Source System*.

Additional Communication Scenarios

There are, of course, a whole range of additional scenarios in which a Unicode component of SAP Business Suite is to be integrated with an MDMP system based on SAP R/3. As you can easily see from the scenarios described for ALE, SAP CRM, or SAP NetWeaver BI, it requires a lot of effort to enable correct multilingual data transfer. It is no different for other components, and often even more difficult.

It is especially important that there is no suitable solution approach for the scenario "Java-based SAP application communicating with SAP R/3 (MDMP)." The main reason is the integration between the Java and the ABAP application through SAP Java Connector or variants. Unfortunately, the parallel conversion feature of RFC cannot be used, since this applies only to a connection between two ABAP applications. And not all single code pages, particularly the complex Asian ones, are round-trip capable. That is, if texts are converted incorrectly from/to Unicode (from or to Java) and back (from or to ABAP), Asian texts in particular can be lost.

Integration through the SAP Java Connector

The only usable option would be to configure multiple logical connections between the Java Unicode application and the ABAP application. This would involve multiple JCos and break the data transfer down into multiple individual transfers for each code page, and each JCo could then convert one single code page from/to Unicode. We can't devote more space to this at this point, and instead refer to you the information in SAP Collective Note 745030.

For additional clarity, we will describe the procedure of conversion in a connection between a Java application and an ABAP application (with SAP R/3 as the back end) using the SAP Java Connector. The data flows as follows (see Figure 3.57), and the conversion is only correct for one code page per connection:

▶ **Data flow from Java (Unicode) to SAP R/3 (back end)**

   ▷ Conversion from Java Unicode UTF-16 into local ISO single code page (1)

   ▷ Conversion from ISO single code page to the SAP code page according to the RFC logon language of the JCo in SAP R/3 (2)

▶ **Data flow from SAP R/3 (back end) to the Java application**

  ▶ Conversion of the current SAP single code page (determined by the logon language) to the local ISO single code page (3)

  ▶ Conversion of the ISO code page to Unicode UTF-16 (4)

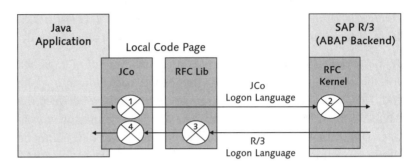

Figure 3.57 Communication of Java Unicode with ABAP Non-Unicode

For other components of the SAP Business Suite based on ABAP that must communicate with SAP R/3, similar approaches apply, much like those already described for SAP ALE, SAP CRM, and SAP NetWeaver BI. For this reason, it should always be the goal to make RFC communication structures language-dependent, if they are not already. You can find more information in the SAP Collective Note 745030 and references.

Summary

In general, the Unicode/MDMP communication scenarios shown and mentioned are very complex, and a solution is possible only with a great deal of effort. For data exchange between ABAP-based components, the solution approach is always to make the transfer structure defined for RFC language-dependent, if it is not already so. This is usually achieved with a data dictionary extension of the underlying transfer structure with a language key, together with a user exit or BAdI implementing the logic needed to fill this structure correctly at runtime with texts, and assign a language key.

For communication between Java and MDMP applications under SAP R/3, there is no generally usable solution, because the parallel RFC conversion feature is not available for the SAP Java Connector usually used.

3.6   Expansion into New Countries with Unicode

Many global enterprises, when discussing Unicode, often think of it as a purely technical procedure, something like an OS/DB platform migration, and one which is also quite cost-intensive at that. One of the first questions from, management is how it adds value for the company when Unicode is used.

Unicode isn't just a technical necessity for a large global system; it also opens entire new perspectives that can support market strategies and global activities for the company. Unicode simplifies the expansion into new countries with new languages. SAP may offer a lot of country versions and translations, and is extending that offering every day, but global companies increasingly want new markets in "new" countries, which they want to implement in their global SAP system, but for which SAP at the current time and release doesn't yet have country versions or translations.

Unicode as door opener for new markets

To operate in a new country, it is often necessary for legal reasons to use the local national language in the IT systems, so the question arises as to how that can be done in an existing SAP system. From a legal standpoint, the translation of the user interface plays less of a role here than internal business data, such as names and addresses of business partners, or text elements in legally required reports, or business documents which must be provided to the national authorities. But it is not only the legal aspect that are worth mentioning here, but also the fact that using a local language leads to better acceptance and therefore more growth.

Even if a new language with a character set from a code page already configured is to be introduced in a non-Unicode system, this can quickly lead to problems without Unicode. In a non-Unicode system, the number of different language keys is very limited. For instance, a single code page installation of SAP ERP 2004 allows a total of 40 different language keys, including Z1 as a custom language key. You can easily see this in your non-Unicode system by looking at the number of entries in table T002 with Transaction SE16. New language keys for dialects, for instance for Canadian French or Brazilian Portuguese, shall be introduced in order to support terminology which often varies for each country, and thereby to help achieve better language quality and end-user acceptance. But in a non-Unicode system, you will

Only up to 40 languages possible in non-Unicode systems

quickly reach the technical limits. Additional language keys may even be necessary on an industry-specific basis, for instance with respect to different industrial solutions which use their own terms for many standard terms. For instance, in the consumer products sector, instead of the term "material," the word "item" is often used.

ISO 639-2-compli-ant language keys in SAP Unicode Unicode allows the much larger number of several hundred language keys in an SAP Unicode system, which can be created as needed. These include new dialects such as Canadian French, for which SAP requires a separate language key for completeness.

SAP defines two-character new language keys according to the ISO 639-2 standard. A new language key is based on an internal, unused Asian character. An overview of important languages with their associated countries and SAP language keys can be found in Appendix B. A complete list of all available language keys and additional details can be found in SAP Note 73606 and references.

3.6.1 Technical Configuration of a New Language in SAP Unicode

Prerequisites for a new language As you know, Unicode defines every character of an arbitrary language, so that you may well think that the introduction of a new language would be very easy. That's not quite the case. To be able to work properly with a new language, the following basic prerequisites must be fulfilled:

▸ The front-end must support the new language for input and display, along with some other functions. That means a keyboard layout and a suitable *Input Method Editor (IME)* method must exist, especially to allow entry of complex characters including composed characters (*Character Rendering*) or even—as for Arabic—a switch between writing directions. Before the language can be introduced into an SAP Unicode system, it must therefore be possible to set up this language on the front end (for instance a PC with Microsoft Windows XP) and enter, display, and also print texts.

> **Example**
>
> If the new language Kazakh is to be introduced, the front-end software, for instance Microsoft Windows XP Office 2003, must be capable of creating and printing a document in that language. If the SAP GUI is used as the SAP front end, several special configuration steps must be performed.

▶ Because you will generally also need to print in the new language, suitable printers which support the new language must be available, along with a printer driver. A Unicode printer fulfills this requirement, but it is somewhat more expensive and not always available, so simpler printers and printing methods should also be considered. If the front end is capable of printing in the new language, for instance, Microsoft Windows XP in Kazakh, a simpler method is possible without a special Unicode printer.

▶ If data exchange is planned with texts in this new language in the data packets, all partner systems should ideally also be running Unicode, and the new language key must also be available or defined in the partner system. If this is not the case, you must investigate on an individual basis whether the new language uses a supported non-Unicode SAP single code page.

The introduction of a new language into an SAP Unicode system can therefore be categorized into different levels of difficulty, depending on the language and character set properties. For instance, a dialect such as Canadian French is very easy to set up, while an Asian language with several thousand characters or a language from the Arabic group with a different writing direction is much more difficult to implement.

Introducing a new language

Table 3.15 shows a possible categorization according to three levels of effort: low, medium, and difficult.

Effort categories for new languages

Category	Description	Examples	Effort
1	Character set of the new language is already supported in SAP	▶ Dialects (e.g., Canadian French) ▶ Catalan (Latin) ▶ Bahasa (Latin) ▶ Macedonian (Greek)	low
2	Character set of the new language has alphabetic behavior and a limited number of characters	▶ Kazakh ▶ Azerbaijani	medium

Table 3.15 Effort Categories for New Languages in SAP Unicode Systems

Category	Description	Examples	Effort
3	Character set of the new language has a complex character set with many characters, composed characters, and/or different writing direction	▸ Vietnamese ▸ Hindi ▸ Farsi	high
Reference: Unicode character sets 4.1			

Table 3.15 Effort Categories for New Languages in SAP Unicode Systems (cont.)

To introduce a new language in an SAP system, the following significant steps are necessary:

▸ General analysis of the new language according to linguistic and general usage criteria in the SAP Unicode system

▸ Analysis of the character set of the new language and other characteristics, for instance the writing direction, whether each character is defined in Unicode, or whether only individual character elements must be composed for display or for printing

▸ Discussion with native speakers or translators as well as end users about the new language

▸ Concentration on the use of business data in the new language

▸ Determination of a translation strategy for the new language, in particular, clarification of whether it will suffice to maintain only selected business data in the new language or whether the translation of the user interface into the new language will be necessary

▸ Analysis of the front end to determine if the new language can be supported in at least the following points:

  ▸ The front-end software must support the new language and should be installable or configurable for this purpose. For Microsoft Windows XP, for example, the new language should be available under **Settings • Control Panel • Regional and Language Options • Languages • Details** and also be installed.

  ▸ A suitable keyboard layout and input method must be available on the front end for the new language and, if necessary, installed.

  ▸ A suitable test is the entry and printing of a document in the new language on the front end.

- Analysis of the level of use of the new language in applications according to the following criteria:

  - Which (customer) data must be available in the new language?

  - Must forms be created and printed in the new language? If so, you should note that *SAPscript* forms are generally unsuitable for languages of categories 2 or 3 from Table 3.15, but you should rather use *SAP Smart Forms* or *Adobe Document Services*.

  SAPscript, SAP Smart Forms, and Adobe Document Services (ADS)

- Analysis of the printer environment:

  - What printer models support the new language?

  - What suitable print drivers and fonts are there?

  - Should a Unicode printer be used?

Ultimately, a study of the introduction of the new language must be performed to handle the points listed above.

3.6.2 Case Study: Introduction of Vietnamese in an SAP Unicode System

A concrete case study will illustrate the introduction of the new language, Vietnamese (with a high category), based on the different implementation steps. The following business process is assumed.

Implementing the Vietnamese language

> **Scenario**
>
> A large enterprise with a global SAP Unicode system, because of the growing market opportunities, wants to expand into Vietnam. Because of the legal requirements in the *Vietnamese Accounting Standard* (VAS), it needs various types of business data in Vietnamese. At the time, SAP offers no country version for Vietnam and no Vietnamese translation in SAP ERP 2005. There are local software products, such as Microsoft Windows and a translation program, but they are of limited use for the company, and also provide no simple integration with the global SAP system. Special printing systems allowing the local translation of a form (for instance in English) from the SAP system into Vietnamese, but they are not suitable, and they can only print and cannot allow interactive use of the new language. Thus Vietnamese is to be set up in an SAP Unicode system.

The first step is an analysis of the language and the character set in order to determine a level of difficulty. In Figure 3.58, you can see an excerpt of the Vietnamese character set. It is immediately obvious that these are easy-to-read Latin characters, but the difficulty and

Analysis of the language and the character set

complexity lies in the many combinations with top and bottom diacritical marks. More detailed research at *http://www.unicode.org* and information from native speakers reveals that Vietnamese is a technically very complicated language. It is similar to Thai in that it uses combined characters of different length, as well as double and mixed upper and lower diacritical marks. Thus the language is in Category 3 in Table 3.15.

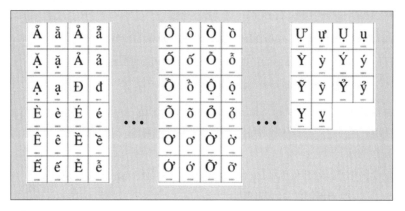

Figure 3.58 Excerpt from the Character Set for Vietnamese

Translation strategy

As a translation strategy, in this case only the business data and some reports are needed in the local language. Translation of the user interface is not needed, and the language supplementation method can be used from English after the technical setup of the logon language Vietnamese. If a translation of the user interface (or parts thereof) should be required, the standard translation tool Transaction SE63 can be used at any time to perform the translation.

The next step is to configure the front end, in this case Microsoft Windows XP, for Vietnamese. First, you need to check whether Windows XP technically supports the Vietnamese language. This is the case for Windows XP Professional SP1 or higher. You can also quickly determine this for other languages by following these instructions analogously for the new language. If this is not found in the selection lists, you must ask Microsoft whether there is any add-on package for the new language. Without language support it is not possible to use the new language actively, because there will be no suitable input method and no fonts.

To install Vietnamese on the PC, after calling **Start • Settings • Control Panel** open the icon **Regional and Language Options** and select **Vietnamese** from the selection list, as shown in Figure 3.59. Finally, the **Languages** and **Details** tabs will show you the input languages for the configuration of the input method and keyboard layout. Using the **Add** button, select **Vietnamese** from the following selection list, and Windows XP will take care of the rest. Now you have the fonts necessary and an input method for Vietnamese, as shown in Figure 3.60.

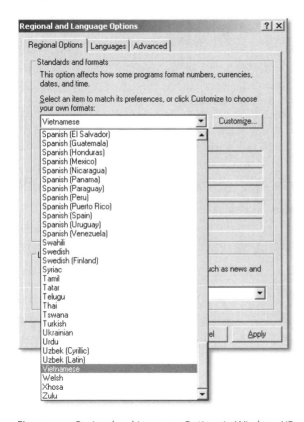

Figure 3.59 Regional and Language Options in Windows XP

As the next important step, the new language key for Vietnamese must be created in the SAP Unicode system. Transaction I18N or the familiar program RSCPINST and function **Extend Language List** are used for this task. In the selection list of all available language keys and languages (**F4** key), select **Vietnamese** with language key **VI** (see Figure 3.61), so that **VI** is accepted (see Figure 3.62) and installed with the **F8** (**Execute**) key.

XP setup for Vietnamese

Figure 3.60 Language Support for Vietnamese in Windows XP

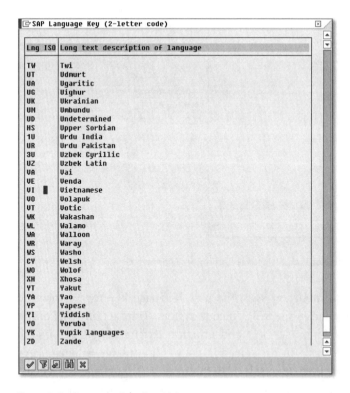

Figure 3.61 Language Selection List

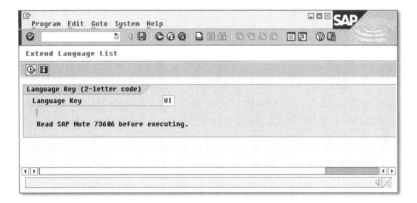

Figure 3.62 Selection and Installation of Language Key VI

Vietnamese is now technically configured, as shown in Figure 3.63.

New language key VI in the SAP Unicode system

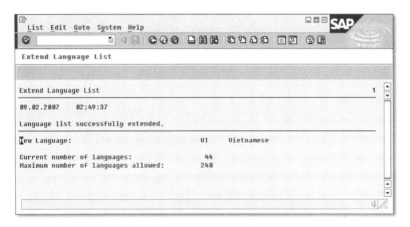

Figure 3.63 New Language Key VI in the SAP Unicode System

The SAP system generates an internal language key as an unused Asian character 뱝. If VI is to be used as a logon language, it must be added to the instance profile's internal language vector in parameter `zcsa/installed_languages`. This is best done using Transaction RZ10 for profile changes, because of the problem of input for the internal Asian language key. The new language vector then looks like this:

Unused Asian character for internal language key

```
zcsa/installed_languages = BDEFIMNPRS 뱝
```

Language import
and supplementa-
tion with SMLT
After the language key for Vietnamese is configured (it still has to be added to the used language list with RSCPINST) and the language is allowed as logon language, a language package with the SAP translation for Vietnamese must be imported and/or a supplementation with English or another complete replacement language performed.[16] This is necessary to be able to execute all ABAP-based applications in the logon language VI. Details on the translation, language import, and supplementation can be found in Chapter 5.

Since the translation for Vietnamese is not available (as of March 2007), in this case study we will have to be content with the complete supplementation from English and perform our own translations. To do this, in the language management transaction SMLT, after the classification of VI and determination of the supplementing language English, the full supplementation of VI by English is selected. Other complete supplementing languages are also possible in a Unicode system. This procedure is also described in detail in Chapter 5.

SAP GUI settings
for Vietnamese
After the correct settings are configured in the SAP GUI—the I18N option and the fonts must be selected which support Vietnamese— the translation and subsequent work with Vietnamese can be started.

Manual transla-
tion of customizing
texts
Finally, in this case study a few customizing texts will be translated from English into Vietnamese. This can either be done using Transaction SE63 or directly in the customizing view SM30 through the menu entry **Goto • Translation** (see Figure 3.64 and Figure 3.65).

Printing in
Vietnamese
To be able to print in Vietnamese from the SAP Unicode system, there are different possibilities, for which we refer you to Section 3.2.5. Here is a short overview:

▶ **Use of a Unicode printer**
A Unicode printer has a Unicode font that supports all characters, including Vietnamese. By default under SAP ERP 2005/SAP ECC 6.0, SAP supports Unicode printers by Lexmark and Hewlett-Packard with device types LEXUTF8 and HPUTF8.

---

16 If a translation system is used for this new language, for which the SAP translation environment is set up, no supplementation may be done.

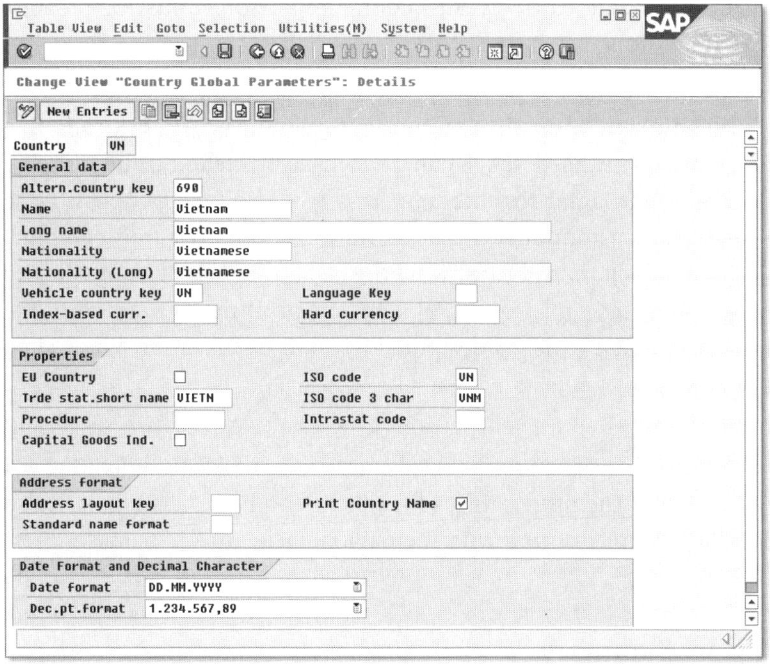

Figure 3.64 Customizing View for Configuration of Countries

Cou	Language	Name	Long name	Nationality	Nationality (Long)	
VN	English	Vietnam	Vietnam	Vietnamese	Vietnamese	
	Vietnamese	Việt	Tiếng Việt			

Figure 3.65 Translation of Country Texts into Vietnamese

▶ **Use of cascading fonts technology**[17]
A Unicode font on the Unicode printer is universal, but it has the disadvantage that it is very large. Normally, printing is only needed for one language or a few languages, so that the large Unicode font is largely unused. On the other hand, a simple font isn't sufficient if documents with languages in multiple character sets are to be printed. The classical fonts such as Arial, Courier New, or Times New Roman don't cover the entire Unicode standard. Thus

---

17 You can find more information in SAP Note 812821 in the appendix *Cascading Font Configuration Guide*, and in SAP Note 906031.

it is desirable to be able to configure custom fonts for printing which support printing of the desired character sets.

For this purpose, SAP provides the *Cascading Font Generator*, which makes it possible to configure arbitrary SAP font combinations; for instance, the Japanese font **DB Mincho** can be assigned to the font **Times New Roman**. This tool also makes it possible to generate custom device types with the configured font combinations, which then always select the right font. It is even possible to use the tried and true `SAPWIN-saplpd` printing method with cascading fonts, which is described in more detail in the Notes cited above.

The printing of ABAP lists and SAP Smart Forms is supported, and the printing of SAPscript forms as well (see SAP Note 812821 for details). If the prerequisites for this method are satisfied, it is also available for printing with the new language of Vietnamese.

3.7 Summary

At the conclusion of this very long chapter, let's summarize all the discussed aspects of Unicode in SAP systems.

▶ The introduction of Unicode in all SAP products means that all languages can be technically perfectly supported with all character sets and over arbitrary system boundaries, without the previous complicated limitations and risks. Thus for global enterprises it is significantly simpler and more cost-effective to introduce new countries and languages into a global SAP system. Unicode is a globally recognized IT standard and SAP's strategic language platform. All SAP products as of SAP Web AS 6.20 are available in Unicode, and in the future only SAP Unicode products will be delivered.

▶ SAP Unicode systems use the UTF-16 format on the application server with Big Endian or Little Endian encoding depending on the CPU. The database uses the UTF-8 or UTF-16 (or similar) format depending on the manufacturer. For communication with the SAP GUI and server-based file processing, the platform-independent UTF-8 format is used.

▸ To convert SAP non-Unicode systems to Unicode, SAP provides corresponding tools to enable an efficient conversion. The Unicode conversion of an SAP system is based on the system copy or platform migration. During the export of the database, all text data is converted from single code page into the Unicode format. At the same time, a new, empty Unicode system is installed, into which the exported data is imported. This procedure takes place during the downtime and must be runtime optimized, for which SAP provides suitable optimization tools.

▸ If SAP systems with an MDMP or blended code-page configuration must be converted to Unicode, special preparation steps are necessary with Transaction SPUMG. Because many texts cannot be unambiguously assigned to a language or code page, after several database scans a vocabulary is created containing the unknown words, which must be assigned a language either automatically or manually by translators. Incorrectly converted words must be corrected in the new Unicode system using Transaction SUMG. MDMP and blended code pages will no longer be supported as of SAP NetWeaver 2004s and SAP ERP 2005.

▸ In order to bring SAP systems with non-Unicode-capable releases to Unicode as efficiently as possible, there are combined upgrade and Unicode conversion procedures available. An R/3 system with release level 4.6C (MDMP) can be upgraded and converted to Unicode with the CU & UC combined procedure after vocabulary preparation in the starting release with Transaction SPUM4.

For older systems, the TU & UC combined procedure can be used. This works with a copy of the production system and enables the upgrade and immediately subsequent Unicode conversion.

▸ In order to develop efficiently in Unicode and follow general progress in IT, the ABAP programming language has been extended and in part changed as of SAP Web AS 6.10/6.20, whereby the quality of programs can also be significantly improved.

The new syntax is identical for Unicode and non-Unicode systems, so that the same ABAP program can run in both types of system. One of the most important changes is that character processing is now strictly separated from byte processing. An Asian character is handled identically to a Latin one. ABAP custom development must therefore be adapted to the new ABAP syntax during a Unicode-conversion project.

The integrated tool UCCHECK is available for that purpose, which allows the adaptations to be performed in the non-Unicode system, so that after the Unicode conversion, the custom developments are immediately executable.

▶ Communication between Unicode systems (SAP and non-SAP) is ideal and possible with no limitations, given that every character of every language is unambiguously defined. In reality, however, Unicode systems must usually communicate with non-Unicode systems within a heterogenous system landscape, including SAP and non-SAP systems.

If a Unicode system exchanges language and text data with a non-Unicode system, they must be converted between Unicode and the single code page belonging to the text language. In RFC connections, this is performed automatically using the SAP RFC processor, which converts all transmitted text data in both directly after determination of the communication code page of the non-Unicode partner system. If texts are transferred from the Unicode to the single code page system, only texts with languages valid for the single code page system are selected.

For file processing from an SAP Unicode system, there is conversion functionality analogous to that of RFC: Single code page files are converted from/to Unicode in the SAP Unicode system during reading and writing.

▶ If an SAP Unicode system communicates with an MDMP system, this is a very complicated case, for which a solution can often require high or very high effort. In the case of transmission of data in language-dependent structres, RFC is capable of performing parallel conversions of multiple code pages from and to Unicode, which contributes to a significant simplification of this scenario.

For a language dependency to exist, the underlying transfer structure or table must include an active language key. If this is not the case and if no simplification is possible via reduction to Unicode-single code page communication, additional development, user exits, or even modifications to the SAP standard code are necessary to achieve that language dependency.

▶ Unicode helps a global company expand into new countries in that new and previously untranslated languages can be configured in a few steps. An SAP Unicode system includes several hundred language keys (non-Unicode systems only 40), so that even different country-specific or regional dialects of the same basic language are possible.

In order to implement a new language, it must be supported on the front end and a suitable printer, which must first be set up. Then the language is configured in the SAP Unicode system using Transaction I18N and a few additional steps.

All SAP applications are available based on Unicode. In this chapter, you will learn how you can optimally plan and execute a new installation or the conversion of an existing system.

4 Guidelines for Unicode Projects

Today, all SAP applications are available in Unicode-based versions, and new software products from SAP such as the SAP NetWeaver Exchange Infrastructure (SAP XI) or the SAP NetWeaver Portal are now *only* delivered as Unicode versions. The support for obsolete solutions for the combination of languages and code pages—such as MDMP in SAP R/3—is being terminated step by step, so that SAP ERP 2005 no longer supports MDMP. As of 2007, all new installations of applications based on SAP NetWeaver will only be possible under Unicode.

4.1 New Installation

The new installation of a Unicode-based system is basically no different from that of a non-Unicode installation. However, the following should be taken into consideration in the implementation project:

New installation has not changed

▶ As mentioned in Chapter 3, a Unicode system has somewhat higher hardware requirements; these must be taken into account.

▶ If there are interfaces to non-Unicode systems, the configuration must be undertaken with care, in order to eliminate such risks as data loss because of incorrect conversion.

▶ The same applies for uploads or downloads of files which come to the system over the network (by means of FTP, for example).

▶ If third-party software will be integrated, you must carefully check that it will function smoothly with the SAP Unicode installation. A request to the appropriate SAP software partner will usually suffice.

> ▶ When creating custom developments, you should proceed in compliance with Unicode, as described in the *SAP Unicode Enabling Cookbook* (see Appendix C) and in Section 3.4.

Tip
SAP Globalization Services offers different services and workshops that explore individual Unicode aspects in detail according to customer requirements, either before or during a project. The *SAP Unicode Workshop* is the ideal introduction for all Unicode projects. You can find a list of all services at SAP Service Marketplace (*http://service.sap.com/globalization*) in the **Service Offerings** area.

4.2 Unicode Conversion

4.2.1 Typical Steps in a Conversion Project for an Environment with Three Systems

You can see a rough overview of the conversion of *one* SAP system in Figure 4.1, which shows the typical phases of a conversion. The plan for a conversion is always the same: **Preparation** takes on a very important role, followed by the **conversion** itself, and then the phase of **postprocessing**.

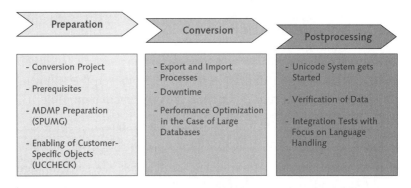

Figure 4.1 Overview of the Steps Necessary for the Conversion of an SAP System

In the following sections, we will describe in more detail how a Unicode conversion project for a three-system environment might be structured. In the *evaluation phase*, we work out the consequences Unicode will have for the existing system environment and which Unicode strategy is to be followed. The actual preparation phase for a particular system environment follows. Then, a sandbox conversion is carried out as the first test environment. The sandbox conversion may need to be repeated several times. In parallel with this, the *development system* (DEV) or the *consolidation system* (QAS) can already be converted. After all the tests in QAS and in the sandbox system have been completed successfully, the conversion of the *production system* (PRD) follows.

The steps presented here must be adapted to the actual customer situation. This list also makes no claim to completeness.

Project Evaluation Phase

Before any Unicode conversion project, we must clarify what Unicode means in the specific situation of the client. In general, cost and effort are the focus. However, we also should consider what efforts will be caused and what consequences will result if Unicode is *not* introduced. It is often necessary to have a "business case" to justify extensive investments in new technology.

At the end of this phase, the general Unicode strategy of the company regarding SAP technology should be clear. However, the strategy may still need to be adapted as conditions change, so its validity must be verified at regular intervals.

The following points describe possible factors to be taken into account in this step:

▶ **Unicode conversion process and consequences**
In this phase, it is important to understand the principle of Unicode conversion. What steps and effort are necessary, and where must the customer make adaptations?

> What has to be done during a Unicode conversion?

▶ **Acquiring relevant customer-specific information**
To be able to produce a reasonable Unicode strategy, the information on Unicode available from SAP must be complemented with the customer's own data. The following list includes the most important points:

> Information acquisition

  ▷ Overview of the system landscape (systems, releases, support packages, front-end software, and so on)

  ▷ Database sizes (in GB), the 50 largest tables, and the hardware configuration of all relevant systems

> ▸ Requirements pertaining to tolerable downtime for individual systems

> ▸ Code page setup of all systems (Unicode, MDMP, single code page, blended code page)

> ▸ Description of the interfaces between the systems and to non-SAP systems ("rough interface catalog")

> ▸ Existing add-on solutions (SAP and non-SAP)

> ▸ Number and type of existing custom developments

> ▸ Existing rollout plans in other countries for the different systems

> ▸ Planned system mergers

> ▸ Possible conversion strategies

Attention to these points generally results in the conversion sequence for the existing systems. For the systems to be converted, the first option at this point is to discuss the procedures for conversion strategies (for instance, the creation of a sandbox system) and also ways to minimize downtime (see Chapter 3).

Conversion strategies

▸ **Evaluation of the consequences should Unicode conversion be postponed**
Customers should consider carefully what the postponement of Unicode means from short-term and long-term perspectives. SAP Note 79991 regarding the SAP support for non-Unicode should be considered carefully in this context (see Table 2.7 in Chapter 2).

▸ **Experience of other customers**
An exchange of experiences with other customers at the start of the project and also over the course of the project promotes better understanding of possible problems and workarounds.

▸ **First "rough" estimate of effort**
A first approximate estimate of effort should consider the points of hardware requirements, resource requirements, and project duration.

▸ **Business case and creation of initial project plan**
The analysis above allows a preliminary project plan to be created. This plan generally doesn't include any exact details of the conversion.

Project Preparation Phase

In the preparation phase of the project, we begin the system-specific preparations for the coming Unicode conversion. Conditions and limitations must be checked and patches may need to be installed. The necessary hardware must be procured. All available documents on Unicode conversion should also be studied. It is recommended to create a detailed project plan for the coming sandbox conversion. The following points should be taken into consideration:

▶ **Detailed prerequisites and restrictions**
  If products from other manufacturers are used in the SAP environ-   Preparatory steps
  ment, we recommend that the Unicode capability of these solu-
  tions should be certified by the manufacturers. In general, you
  can't assume that an SAP certification also means Unicode capability.

  For relatively "old" patch levels in SAP solutions, there is a high
  probability that an update will be necessary. For extensive
  changes (SAP GUI for Windows, for example), the tests should
  first be performed with the current patch level before a global rollout is started.

▶ **Interface catalog with language dependencies**
  A list of all interfaces and their language dependencies (e. g., "are
  tests with special characters transmitted?") helps identify critical
  areas.

▶ **Hardware procurement**
  For larger systems, a sandbox conversion is absolutely recommended. The temporary hardware needed for this must be provided. If the hardware is to be updated during the production conversion, this must be planned in advance.

▶ **Options for performance optimization**
  To prepare a sandbox conversion, we should have examined what
  means are available for runtime optimization and what will make
  sense for the initial conversion. It may well be that certain methods are not yet fully available. In that case, additional steps may be
  necessary.

▶ **Determination of the strategy for handling ABAP objects
  (UCCHECK)**
  In this example, we will assume that the ABAP objects are already
  adapted in advance (see the subsequent bullet point on ABAP).

▶ **Use of all possible archiving options to reduce database size**
By reducing the size of the database, it is possible to improve several aspects of the conversion. These include the export and import times for the production conversion. The runtime of Transaction SPUMG will be shorter if there is less data to scan.

▶ **Necessary documentation and SAP Notes**
All necessary guidelines and associated SAP Notes should be downloaded. During the course of the project, we recommend that you check regularly whether there are changes to the SAP Notes or in the conversion guidelines.

▶ **Enabling of ABAP objects (Unicode enabling)**
The handling of ABAP objects is fully possible only as of Basis Release 6.10 using Transaction UCCHECK. If the release is 6.10 or higher, the objects can be adapted in advance. The objects are then ideally executable either under under Unicode or in a non-Unicode environment. Since the result is a certain independence from the Unicode conversion, the UCCHECK processing is performed as a separate task. For new developments (creation of new ABAP objects) the Unicode flag is set by default as of SAP Web AS 6.10, so that in this case Unicode capability is largely assured. Existing objects without the Unicode flag that must be adapted during ongoing maintenance should also be made Unicode-capable now, because these objects then must only be tested once.

Structure and Conversion of the Sandbox System

"Proof of concept"

Once the prerequisites for the sandbox conversion have been fulfilled, you can carry out the first test conversion. Care should be taken that even during the first attempt the known performance optimizations are used during export and import. The following list provides an overview of the steps:

Steps for sandbox
conversion

▶ **Structure of the sandbox system as a copy of PRD**
In the ideal case, the hardware of the sandbox system already corresponds roughly to the hardware of the PRD system for this initial test. In that case, the results of the scan times and the export/import times can be accurately used in estimating the behavior of the production system.

In practice, however, there is usually no comparable hardware available, so that at first the process of conversion itself is being tested with no real focus on the runtimes. For large systems, however, this can result in very long runtimes, so that the entire test takes a very long time.

▶ **Preparatory steps for Unicode conversion**
The main area for preparation for Unicode conversion of an MDMP system is Transaction SPUMG. Sufficient time must be budgeted for the scans which build the system vocabulary, for processing of the vocabulary, and also for the reprocessing scans. The runtimes of the scans for large systems run in the range from a few days to several weeks. The scan without language codes generally requires the longest time, but the reprocessing scan can also require a large percentage of the project time.

Time also is needed for assignment of the vocabulary entries. Because the system vocabulary maintained in the sandbox system forms the basis for the later conversion of all existing systems, this process should be executed immediately at the outset with all necessary care.

▶ **Export and import**
This area includes the tests relevant to runtime optimization. If Transaction SPUMG has already been sufficiently well tested, it is not necessary to execute this transaction repeatedly as a preparation scan. This would take—in the worst case—several weeks each time. Alternatively, a backup after completion of the SPUMG work can be used as a starting system.

▶ **Execution of post-conversion tasks**
Transaction SUMG covers the most important reprocessing steps. This transaction can be used to estimate the effort for manual repair. Repair hints may already be generated here.

▶ **Test phase**
After the Unicode conversion is complete, tests of the applications follow. For instance, a part of the custom ABAP objects can be tested. If possible, interface tests should also be performed at this point. Normally, however, this is only fully possible in the QAS, because in the sandbox system the interfaces must first be set up.

However, it is always the case that all tests that can already be performed in the sandbox system should be performed there. The earlier a problem is discovered, the more time you will have to correct it.

▶ **Analysis and results of the sandbox conversion**
The sandbox conversion provides results for the R3load runtime optimization, the procedure, and the scan runtime for Transactions SPUMG and SUMG, as well as for initial Unicode testing after the conversion phase. Based on these results, you now must decide whether additional sandbox conversion runs are needed and when the next systems in the landscape should be converted. There follows a corresponding refinement and adaptation of the project plan to the continuing procedure.

▶ **Repetition of the sandbox conversion (depending on the results of the previous conversion)**
The sandbox conversion should be repeated until the requirements for downtime are met. In parallel with this, the conversion of the QAS or the DEV system can be started.

Converting the Development or the Quality Assurance System

The conversion of the DEV or the QAS system is performed analogously to conversion the sandbox system. Under some circumstances, it may be possible to accept longer downtimes here than with the production system.

Meaningful interface and integration tests are generally only possible on the quality assurance system. A parallel preliminary test of Transaction SPUMG on the PRD system at this point will ensure that the scan duration of this transaction is not underestimated.

Converting the Production System

Factors influencing the effort of a Unicode conversion
Based on the experience with the sandbox system as well as the DEV and QAS systems, the conversion of the production system can now proceed. It is important that the conversion is performed under exactly the same conditions as those pertaining to the test system. For instance, the patch level of the kernel (particularly the R3load version) should be identical to that of the other systems.

The first day or the first week after the conversion generally requires particular attention, since there may be problems in some areas. You should take this into consideration in your planning.

4.2.2 Determining Factors of a Conversion Project

At the outset of a Unicode project, there is a typical series of questions, which will be clarified in this section. The following list shows initial possible reasons for a Unicode conversion:

Possible reasons for a Unicode conversion

▶ The organization desires an upgrade of the existing MDMP system to SAP ERP 2005 (see SAP Note 79991).

▶ English should be possible as the central logon language for all countries or languages.

▶ The data exchange between MDMP and Unicode causes problems.

▶ Java technologies (such as ESS/MSS on SAP ERP 2004) should be used in the MDMP environment.

▶ Rollout is needed in other countries that are not covered by the existing non-Unicode solution in the system.

▶ The organization needs to consolidate systems with different code-page configurations.

▶ The organization anticipates rollout in countries whose characters are not supported except in Unicode (for example, Arabic or Vietnamese).

▶ Support of dialects (such as Canadian French) is needed.

▶ The organization needs to display certain characters (e. g., the € character) that are not supported except in Unicode.

▶ Internet connection (e. g., a Web store) is needed.

▶ Strong Java integration of the system is needed.

The project duration for a Unicode conversion, like that for an upgrade, is determined by many factors. The main areas are shown in Table 4.1. In addition, the duration depends on the number of resources available and their state of knowledge.

Duration of a conversion project

Factors / Effort	Easy	Medium	Difficult
Language technology used	Single code page	Asian code page	MDMP
SAP solution used	SAP Web AS (standalone)	SAP ERP or SAP R/3 Enterprise	SAP CRM with Mobile Sales

Table 4.1 Effort Involved in a Unicode Conversion

Effort \ Factors	Easy	Medium	Difficult
Database size	Database < 300 GB	Database between 300 GB and 1,500 GB	Database > 1,500 GB
Downtime accepted	Downtime > 4 days	Downtime from 2 to 4 days	Downtime < 2 days
Hardware properties	Very fast hardware	Medium hardware	Slow hardware
ABAP objects enabling	Small number of objects	Medium number of objects	Large number of objects
Conversion method	Standard	Split of large tables	IMIG/CU & UC
SAP interfaces	Unicode systems	Single code page systems	MDMP systems
Non-SAP interfaces	Unicode systems	Single code page Latin-1	Asian code page

Table 4.1 Effort Involved in a Unicode Conversion (cont.)

As a minimum value for the conversion of a three-system landscape, you can assume about four weeks of project runtime. On average, these projects take about three to four months. For very large MDMP systems with very many custom ABAP objects or interfaces to other MDMP systems, the runtime can even be more than a year.

Costs of a Unicode conversion

A cost estimate, too, depends on the factors listed in Table 4.1. Moreover, in this area the additional hardware requirements must be taken into account. Expenses for testing and for the adaptation of custom reports may under some circumstances represent a large part of the overall budget.

Specialists needed

A Unicode project also requires expertise in the area of ABAP enabling as well as in the interface area. Specialists in the programming environment and employees with SAP NetWeaver knowledge will be needed. Transaction SPUMG is generally executed by SAP NetWeaver experts. For the preparation of the system vocabulary, however, people will also be needed who know each language. The export and import procedures and optimization are comparable to an upgrade and also require technical knowledge. Testing is generally the responsibility of the application.

Figure 4.2 shows two possible scenarios for a Unicode conversion: On the left is a conversion with a sandbox, and on the right you see a scenario without a sandbox, where the QAS is converted before the development system.

Conversion variants in a three-system landscape

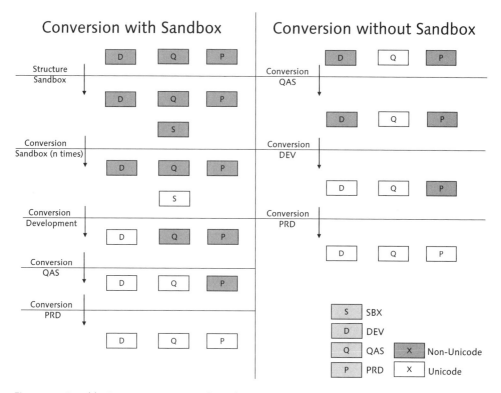

Figure 4.2 Possible Conversion Scenarios for a Three-System Landscape

The conversion using a sandbox is the procedure recommended by SAP for a Unicode conversion. However, this still doesn't answer the question of when a sandbox conversion is absolutely necessary. In the following cases, a sandbox conversion is difficult to avoid:

Sandbox conversion

▶ **Critical requirements for downtime or conversion of very large systems**

Conversion runtimes can only be meaningfully tested on sandbox systems with comparable hardware parameters. Extrapolation of runtimes from very weak servers to production environments is extremely uncertain. As a result, the probability of surprises during the production conversion increases if sufficient testing does not take place under comparable conditions.

▶ **MDMP conversion**
In the case of an MDMP conversion, SAP strongly recommends a test conversion of a copy of the production system. This is the only way to completely test the conversion.

▶ **Combined upgrade and conversion solutions**
The basic prerequisite for more complex solutions like CU & UC (see Section 3.3) is the construction of separate test systems. In the case of TU & UC, a twin system must be built anyway.

▶ **QAS conversion before DEV conversion**
It is worth considering whether the QAS should be converted before the development system. A "proper" test of the interfaces is often only possible on the QAS. Problems with interfaces, however, should be identified quickly, given that correction may be difficult under some circumstances. In principle, the same thing applies for a meaningful integration test.

▶ **Conversion with "Maintenance landscape"**
Analogous to upgrades, there is a scenario of non-Unicode maintenance systems (DEV and QAS) which will support the non-Unicode production system during the Unicode conversion. This ensures that a critical problem that occurs differently in a non-Unicode environment than with Unicode can be corrected quickly.

4.2.3 Comparison with Upgrade Projects and OS/DB Migration

On the topic of upgrades, there is a great deal of documentation, and most customers already have been through at least one upgrade project. Some customers also have experience in the area of OS/DB migration. With this type of background, the following comparison of a Unicode conversion with an upgrade and OS/DB migration can be quite helpful:

Functional changes in a Unicode conversion and an upgrade

▶ **Functionality**
During an upgrade, applications may change thoroughly, so that existing custom development may need to be adapted. In a Unicode conversion or OS/DB migration, the application end of the system changes only minimally.

▶ **System Downtime**

The dependency of downtime for the conversion of the production system on the database size is significantly larger for a Unicode conversion. In an upgrade, this dependency is generally compensated for by hardware, which tends to be better on a larger system. This trend can also be seen in Unicode conversions, but corresponding efforts must be made to optimize performance.

Comparison of downtime between a Unicode conversion and an upgrade

The downtime in a Unicode conversion is comparable to the downtime in an OS/DB migration. However, the CPU requirements for a Unicode conversion are significantly higher, because the compressed cluster tables, for instance, must be subjected to many computationally intensive operations (the data is decompressed, converted, and then recompressed).

▶ **Comparison with UCCHECK and SPUMG Enabling**

The adaptations in the area of custom development (through Transactions SPAU or SPDD) can best be compared to the UCCHECK enabling; however Transaction UCCHECK shows directly where objects must be changed. Moreover, the objects can be adapted in the non-Unicode system, even before Unicode conversion. This generally doesn't apply for an upgrade. For an MDMP system, Transaction SPUMG corresponds to no particular step in an upgrade. A scan of the entire database and the associated maintenance of the results are not necessary for an upgrade.

Unicode enabling needed

Adaptations in the interfaces for a Unicode conversion, particularly for an MDMP system, require particular attention (see Chapter 3). In the case of an OS/DB migration, adaptations must be made to custom ABAP objects which contain database-specific commands (e. g., Native SQL).

▶ **Release Limitations**

In an upgrade, the release of the SAP system changes after the process is finished. Generally, an upgrade is possible in the source system for most of the releases still supported.

Release limitations for a Unicode conversion

A Unicode conversion, on the other hand, is executed by default on a single release. There are limitations, both on the Unicode side (R/3 releases up to 4.6C don't support Unicode) and on the non-Unicode side (MDMP or blended code pages are no longer supported as of SAP ERP 2005).

In an OS/DB migration, there are only a very few release limitations. Generally, a migration can be performed on any supported release. Just as for a Unicode conversion, the release does not change during a migration.

When is a development freeze necessary?

▶ **Development Freeze During the Project**

In an upgrade, transportation between the different releases is not supported. That means that a development freeze during the upgrade project can hardly be avoided.

In the case of a Unicode conversion, it is quite possible to perform a transport between Unicode and non-Unicode releases (with limitations where MDMP is concerned). That means that a development freeze may not be absolutely necessary. SAP's recommendation, however, is to minimize the number of projects as far as possible during the Unicode conversion, as there may very well be differences between Unicode and non-Unicode systems (for instance, where interfaces are concerned).

How often must a Unicode conversion be performed?

▶ **Frequency**

A Unicode conversion must be performed exactly once per system. After that, no more projects are necessary. An upgrade, on the other hand, must generally be performed on a regular basis. An OS/DB migration lies somewhere in between. For most customers it is a rather unusual task and is not repeated often for each system.

What needs to be considered in terms of user training?

▶ **End User Training**

For an upgrade, end users must often be trained, since the functionality may have changed.

For a Unicode conversion, there are only a very few areas where the users even notice that there has been a technical change. Examples are the Word editor for SAPscript editing and uploads and downloads, where a target code page may need to be given under some circumstances. If the Unicode conversion is combined with an upgrade, however, there must be corresponding training for the end users.

4.2.4 Converting Complex Landscapes

Besides an ERP application, many customers use a number of other SAP applications. These are generally connected, and the question immediately arises as to the order in which the different systems should be converted.

In what order should SAP systems in complex landscapes be converted?

It is generally impossible to convert all systems in one weekend, because there would be an extremely great effort associated with that. But the risk that the entire conversion fails on one weekend is also very high for such a "big bang" conversion." If you assume that five closely connected production systems are to be converted in a single weekend, then no system can be allowed to have a significant program that cannot be corrected immediately, because otherwise *all* the systems will need to be reset.

Based on the following criteria, a customer-specific evaluation should be made as to the optimum order:

Criteria for conversion of complex landscapes

▶ **Unicode capability of the different SAP applications (releases)**
The prerequisite for Unicode conversion is the Unicode capability of the release. For instance, if a system is running on SAP R/3 4.6C, the conversion can only take place after an upgrade.

▶ **Requirements pertaining to languages and countries in the different systems**
Systems that must handle data from multiple "old code pages" should be higher-priority candidates for Unicode conversion. Systems without corresponding requirements (purely single code-page systems) can be converted at a later date.

▶ **Minimization of interfaces between MDMP and Unicode systems**
The interface problems described in Section 3.5 between Unicode and MDMP systems leads to the very important criterion that the number of MDMP systems in the system environment should be kept as low as possible.

▶ **Upgrade planning for MDMP systems based on SAP NetWeaver 2004s**
As of SAP NetWeaver 2004s, MDMP is no longer supported (see SAP Note 79991). Thus, for upgrade planning for corresponding solutions, Unicode conversion should be planned as well.

▶ **Consolidation plans**
For planned consolidations, particularly when different code pages are in use, a conversion to Unicode is a good alternative.

▶ **Database sizes of different systems and quickly growing databases**
The effort of a Unicode conversion depends strongly on the size of the database. If there are systems in the environment that have a high rate of growth, then you should consider converting that system earlier rather than later.

▶ **Planned projects and regular actions**
Unicode conversion should ideally happen in a "project-sparse" time. Ideally, existing projects should be postponed until after the conversion. But critical projects like annual reporting must also be taken into account. Unicode conversion shortly before annual reporting is generally problematic.

4.3 Release Changes and Unicode Conversion

How can an upgrade and Unicode conversion be combined?

Upgrades (release change) and Unicode conversions are both projects in the course of which a great deal of application testing is necessary. Although these are two logically independent steps (see Figure 3.3 in Chapter 3) there is still the question of how well the two tasks can be combined.

In Section 3.3, appropriate combined procedures were already described. These are particularly interesting in relation to an upgrade from a non-Unicode-capable release with MDMP to SAP ERP 2005, because in that target release MDMP is no longer supported (see SAP Note 79991).

In summary, these are the possibilities for integration tasks into an upgrade:

Greatest possible logical separation of upgrade and Unicode conversion

▶ **Separate projects**
The upgrade is executed completely separately from Unicode conversion.

▶ **Consideration of ABAP objects during the upgrade**
The enabling of ABAP objects to the stricter Unicode syntax rules is considered during the upgrade. Separate integration tests for the changes to ABAP objects in non-Unicode are not necessary.

▶ **Upgrade and Unicode conversion in one project, but on separate weekends**

It is possible to perform the conversion and the upgrade in one project, but to select a different weekend for the conversion of the production system. Assuming that the upgrade is performed before the conversion, this means that tests must be performed both in the non-Unicode and the Unicode systems, as in this case the non-Unicode system will be going live on the new release.

Advantages and disadvantages of the combination of upgrade and Unicode conversion into one project

The advantages of this approach would be that a sandbox system could be used both for the upgrade and for the conversion, and that tests may be performed twice, but otherwise would still be performed shortly after one another in an identical procedure.

▶ **Upgrade and Unicode conversion on the same weekend**

The main criterion for the decision whether the conversion and the upgrade can be performed on one weekend is the runtime of both procedures. If a Unicode conversion already results in 30 to 40 hours of downtime despite the use of all possible optimization methods, a combined procedure with all the necessary preparation and postprocessing within 48 hours will be possible only in very occasional cases. As a result, either a longer downtime must be accepted, or the alternatives described in the previous points must be selected.

A combined solution also means a significant increase in the complexity of the project. The procedure for an upgrade alone is well documented in great detail, and there is also documentation of separate Unicode conversion. The integration of the two projects requires detailed planning for which there is currently very little background information available. An example might be the handling of ABAP objects during an upgrade, with conversion starting from release SAP R/3 4.6C.

▶ **Combined Upgrade & Unicode Conversion**

This CU & UC method was primarily developed for MDMP customers who have SAP R/3 4.6C as their source release and are working towards a technical upgrade to SAP ERP 2005. In SAP Note 928729, the releases supported and their limitations are described in more detail.

Combination of the upgrade from SAP R/3 4.6 C with a Unicode conversion

A significant component of this technology is the use of Transaction SPUM4, which represents an equivalent to Transaction

SPUMG under SAP R/3 4.6C (see Section 3.3.2). This is necessary because the principle behind Transactions SPUMG and SPUM4 is that the transaction will be performed online during production operation. Because the runtimes of Transaction SPUMG for MDMP customers will run at least for a matter of days, the performance of SPUMG in the target release is impossible during the downtime. Thus SPUMG was implemented in SAP R/3 4.6C as SPUM4, so that online performance would be possible under this release.

In contrast, Unicode enabling (Transaction UCCHECK, for instance) is not possible under SAP R/3 4.6C. This preparation step must be performed on a sandbox system on a Unicode-capable release (on non-Unicode or Unicode). The results can then be transported into the production system after the upgrade is complete.

Figure 4.3 shows a schematic diagram of one possible procedure for a CU & UC. In the sandbox system (SBX), the Unicode enabling must first be done, and the results can then be used in the PRD system after the upgrade is complete. The upgrade and Unicode conversion in the sandbox system can alternatively be performed separately in the initial step so that the UCCHECK activity can proceed on the non-Unicode system.

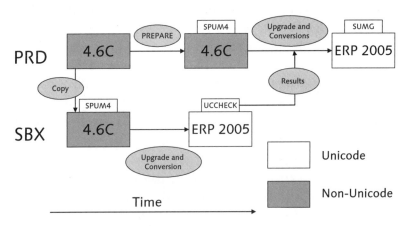

Figure 4.3 Sample Procedure for CU & UC

▶ **Twin Upgrade & Unicode Conversion**

CU & UC cannot be performed for source system releases prior to SAP R/3 4.6C. In order to provide a solution for these customers, the method TU & UC has been developed. In this procedure, a parallel twin system is constructed as a copy of the production system, and an upgrade is performed without Unicode conversion (see Figure 4.4)

Combination of upgrade and conversion for R/3 systems with Release < 4.6C

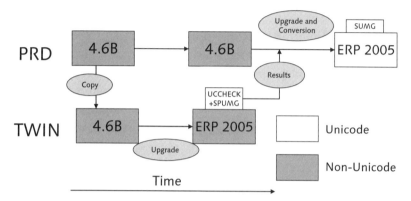

Figure 4.4 Sample Procedure for TU & UC

Transaction SPUMG can now be run on the copy. The results are then transferred to the production system for a production upgrade before the Unicode conversion and used there. Here, there is a delta (table entries that have entered PRD after the construction of the twin system), which becomes larger the older the system copy of the production system. As a result, you must take into account the fact that the tasks after conversion (SUMG) will take more time.

In SAP Note 959698, the releases supported and the limitations of TU & UC are described in more detail.

4.4   System Consolidation

For the purpose of simplifying the system landscape, there are efforts on the part of many customers to reduce the number of existing systems. One option is to integrate systems with similar applications but which have been constructed for other countries into one

Simplification of the system landscape

existing system. Here there is an opportunity to use a Unicode system as a basis.

In general, the systems to be migrated are non-Unicode systems, and conversion of the data during the migration would be desirable and usually possible. MDMP systems are again an exception in this respect, as the conversion is not as simple as for a single code page system. The SPUMG logic can currently not be used for a data migration.

Client migration server

SAP System Landscape Optimization has plans for tools which will make it possible to migrate from SAP R/3 4.6C (non-Unicode) to SAP ERP 2005 (Unicode). So here, three steps—an upgrade, a Unicode conversion, and a system consolidation—will be combined into one. The technology used will be called the *Client Migration Server*, or CMIS. For more complete and up-to-date information, you can consult the SAP Service Marketplace (*http://service.sap.com/slo*).

4.5 Summary

The focus of this chapter has been the planning for Unicode conversion in a complex system landscape. A new installation is relatively simple, because it hardly differs from the installation of a non-Unicode system. In the conversion of a three-system landscape, on the other hand, there are already many different options for the implementation of Unicode.

An estimate of the effort of the Unicode project is not possible without exact knowledge of a variety of factors. Here, database size, the possible use of MDMP, the number of custom programs, and the type and number of interfaces all play significant parts. A comparison of Unicode conversion with an upgrade project made it clear that, depending on the conditions, the Unicode conversion may easily take as much time as a release upgrade. A combined upgrade and conversion procedure is available for customers, but the complexity of such a project should not be underestimated.

Unicode provides the technical basis and infrastructure needed to process all characters in all languages correctly. However, to work with multilingual applications it is necessary to translate not only the user interface but the text of various business data, custom developments, and adaptations into the required languages.

5 Languages and Translation

In a global enterprise, the choices of which countries to expand into are usually made at high levels of management. The key criteria are the market opportunities and the associated business aspects. If a decision is made, the IT department must then implement these new countries in the IT system to meet the expectation that every language in a new country will be supported in the IT system.

Even if no translation of the user interface is available—SAP offers more than 30 supported languages—in most cases languages must be supported for legal reasons, for instance for reporting or in order to process the addresses of business partners in the local language.

Reasons for the use of different languages

Global companies often need certain text elements, business data, and documents in more than one language. For instance, the development of custom programs or customizing is performed in a primary language, also called the original or master language. For these text objects then to be usable in the different countries, they must be translated into the corresponding country languages. English is often used as the original language, but master data and certain business data must often be available in more than one language. This typically includes addresses of business partners or material descriptions, which may—for example—need to be maintained in Russian and in English. Thus, for an international customer, it is important to have a consistent concept and a suitable strategy for the *translation of internal business data*.

Unicode provides the only universal, technically workable, and cost-effective solution, because all the characters in all languages are unique, so that all the technical prerequisites are fulfilled for the introduction of the language. With a Unicode system, one is always ready from a technical standpoint to introduce any new language into a single global system. First, the new language must be technically configured (see Section 3.6), and then the translation tools and worklists for the new language can be created. The essential basis is thus provided for the implementation of the translation of the desired data and applications.

5.1 Language and Translation Management

SAP language package and your own translations

A global solution must support the user interface, business data, and legally required documents in multiple languages, and the translation into the different languages may start from different sources. Thus the business data, that is the customizing, master, and transaction data, is entered by the users in the local language, while the translation of the user interface and some documents are available in the SAP language package for more than 30 available languages (SAP ERP 2005).

To translate custom development, documents, and forms, as well as other objects, into all the languages used, intelligent translation tools are necessary. SAP provides these for customers, and they are a standard part of every SAP system. Thus the customer is capable of determining an optimum translation strategy and implementing it as efficiently as possible.

Unicode does not solve the translation issue

However, there is often a misconception that the introduction of Unicode will solve all language problems. Unicode is a technical platform that allows the technically perfect use of any combination of languages in a system, but it doesn't absolve you of the need to translate texts in an application into each language. For instance, if customizing texts are created in English, they must first be explicitly translated into Russian before a Russian user can edit them in Russian. There are indeed tools today for machine translation, but they are useful only in very limited circumstances, if at all. We will not spend any more time discussing them.

5.1.1 Translation Objects

If you examine the different objects and data in a global system for linguistic relevance, the following groups can be identified as requiring translation:

Objects relevant for translation

- ▶ **Development objects**
  This group particularly includes the objects in the user interface, menus, input forms, field descriptions, but also the textual elements in reports, custom-defined functions, transactions, and more.

- ▶ **Business documents for printing**
  These especially include the legally required forms that must be printed or electronically transmitted to governmental offices and business partners.

- ▶ **Customizing and configuration data**
  Global customizing texts which must be available throughout the enterprise in all countries in the local language must be translated.

- ▶ **Master data**
  Master data to be translated includes, among other things:

  - ▶ **Names and addresses of business partners**
    Generally (and this is recommended) these are first entered for global access in an international version (usually in English) and the local version in the home country of the partner (usually in the local language).

  - ▶ **Material and product data**
    Because a global enterprise offers identical products in many countries, the product descriptions must be translated into all the languages of these countries.

- ▶ **Selected transaction data**
  For transaction data such as texts on invoices or delivery notes, management of the local language of the relevant country can often suffice. If the texts are to be globally available, however, as they are for enterprisewide reporting or for a shared service center in a different country, this data—like addresses—must at least be available in English and the local language.

5.1.2 Language Installation

Language import and supplementation

The SAP system supports a number of translated languages. The language with which a dialog user works is determined at logon by a selection on the logon screen, by a system default, or by a default setting in the user master record.

For logon in the desired language to be possible, it must first be loaded into the SAP system via language import. After the new installation of an SAP system, initially only the languages German (DE) and English (EN) are installed. More languages can be loaded using Transaction SMLT.

When selecting a language (except for German, English, and Japanese), note that it is only partially translated. The language elements not translated must be provided by a so-called *supplementation language*. This supplementation language must itself be a fully translated language. This can also be configured recursively.

Language-dependent objects

There are a number of different language-dependent objects. Depending on the language, these are more or less completely translated. The incomplete part is completed by the supplementation language; this applies to delivered objects.

Figure 5.1 shows a selected example of a dynpro from user data maintenance; the language-dependent and translation-relevant objects will be explained based on this example. The elements marked by arrows originate in the ABAP Repository (user interface, ABAP Dictionary, Screen Painter), customizing, and master data. There is an important difference for translation planning between static objects in the ABAP Repository and the dynamically changing customizing and master data. While static objects need only be translated ones (or only when they are changed), an ongoing translation process is generally necessary for dynamic objects.

If new language-dependent texts are entered by the customer, and if no language key can be selected, then the entry applies only for the language version corresponding to the logon language. That means that these texts are not changed for other languages. This can lead to inconsistent data: For instance, a user working under a different logon language may not even see the text.

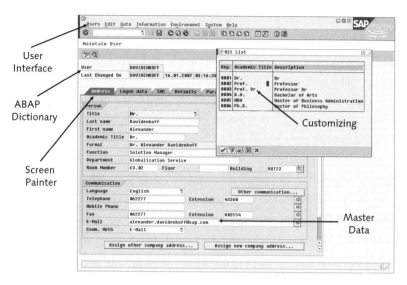

Figure 5.1 Language-Dependent Objects

So there may be an error message along the lines of "Please enter all required fields" for objects that have long since been entered. Individual objects, however, may behave differently:

▸ The text is displayed in an alternative language.

▸ Nothing is displayed.

▸ The user receives a warning or an error message.

▸ The transaction can no longer be executed.

5.2 Customer-Specific Translations

5.2.1 Translation Strategies

While technical language support is essential in the global system, the company must determine its own optimum translation strategy. For instance, an enterprise with English as its primary company language in the country subsidiaries and as its communication language with business partners may need to translate less than an enterprise with primarily local languages in the countries. However, this should not lead to another common misconception: that one can get by only with English everywhere in the world. Local languages are legally required in most countries, so that this alone is already reason

Translation strategies for global customers

enough to configure the language technically and to have to translate the corresponding objects, even if only a few.

But even without the legal aspects, in practice it is simply impossible or not very well accepted in many countries to force English use on all employees and business partners. In Japan, for instance, no business can generally be completed without Japanese, and in Russia the English language is rare in many companies even at a very good general level of education.

Which translation strategy and volume are most suitable and necessary for a global enterprise depend on many factors. In the following section, we'll list the most common ways in which global company languages differ according to use and degree.

From "English only" to "no English at all"

The extent to which individual languages must be loaded into the SAP system and how far these need to be completely translated, however, depends not only on business conditions, but also on political and cultural ones. The acceptance of the user is an important aspect of this. A global enterprise is often forced to use an enterprise-wide language everywhere in the world, usually English, so that often not all texts must be available in local languages. This has led to the language practices described below, which describe the degree of translation in a global system:

▸ **Language and translation "English only"**
In this case, the SAP system supports only English as a logon language and for printing. All reports are generated in English and all communication takes place in English. Here, the problem of language-dependent objects is eliminated, and there are no costs for translation.

The question here is not just whether the user has problems with the English language, but also whether English-language reports, such as annual reports, can even be accepted from a purely legal standpoint. So this is a valid solution only for a small number of countries: those which presumably use English as their official language anyway.

▸ **Language and translation "mostly English"**
Here, it is assumed that the users are fluent in English. They log on in English, and the menus and so forth are also in English.

Reports, however, are generated in the local language, and language-dependent objects are translated upon request.

This requires a certain effort for translation and a little customizing (e. g. for units of measurement). The master data is available in the local language and communication also takes place in the local language.

▶ **Language and translation "some English"**
This solution can be seen as the ideal recommendation for global systems with many countries and different languages. The master language of the system is English, but the users need no deeper knowledge of English. They log on in their local languages and can therefore also use the language-dependent objects like menus, input forms, and so on. Communication and all legally relevant reports take place in the local language, and non-translated texts are displayed in the supplementation language, English.

Depending on the degree of translation of each language, there may be no translations available in some areas. Upon request, additional texts can be translated, but in many internal areas this is unnecessary. There is a periodic language supplementation for newly generated texts, and the standard tools are used for this task. Manual translations remain manageable.

▶ **Language and translation "no English"**
In this case, the users have no English fluency at all, or English is not accepted for political or cultural reasons. Here, the corresponding country language must be loaded and all texts not delivered in translated form must also be manually translated. English is not possible as a supplementation language. That means ongoing translation activity in a multilingual system.

Even if the system is operated in only one language, this effort is still necessary, since every SAP support package and every release upgrade will introduce into the SAP system new language-dependent texts that may still need translation.

5.2.2   SAP Translation Tools

SAP provides different translation tools and procedures for the objects listed above. A distinction is made between low, medium, and high translation volumes. For small volumes, the texts can still

Translation tools for ABAP systems

be translated and proofed manually. A high volume such as the complete translation of your own larger custom development requires the full SAP translation environment that generates so-called *worklists*, which show the translators exactly what they need to translate. Statistical reports show how much has already been translated, and a proposal pool contains all the terms translated. These are generated during the initial translation and can then be used uniformly for all later translations by other translators; so one speaks rather of *semiautomatic translation*.

In Table 5.1, a summary is shown of the major functions and properties of the translation tools which are of interest especially for large translation plans. You can find more details in the online documentation in the SAP Help Portal (*http://help.sap.com*) under the components **Documentation and translation tools (BC-DOC).**[1]

Function/property	Description
Possible uses	You can use the SAP translation tools to translate most of the texts created in the SAP system.
Integration	The translation tools are completely integrated into the text editing and documentation tools in the SAP system.
Transaction SE63	You can use Transaction SE63 to access the translation tools. In the initial screen of this transaction, you can also call up individual objects for translation.
Statistics	The statistics function can be used to check translation effort and progress. You can display statistics according to different criteria, for instance for a particular translator or for all packages in the system.
Worklist	You should translate the objects using a worklist. With worklists, you can quickly find and translate translation-relevant objects.
Proposal pool	The proposal pool is a database in which translations of short texts are stored. This allows short texts to be translated more efficiently and more uniformly.

Table 5.1 Functions of SAP Translation Tools

---

1 We are limiting ourselves here to the translation of ABAP-based applications. Information on translation tools and processes for Java applications, such as the SAP NetWeaver Portal (texts from iViews, roles, attributes, PAR files (*Resource bundles*), etc.), can be found in the documentation, or by contacting SAP if necessary.

Function/property	Description
Short text editor	In the short text editor, you have different functions for the translation of short text objects.
Long text editor	In the long text editor, you have different functions for the translation of long text objects.
Translation of online repository texts (OTR texts)	Online repository texts are translated in their own transaction with their own editor.

Table 5.1 Functions of SAP Translation Tools (cont.)

5.2.3 SAP Translation Workbench

The Translation Workbench is the central tool for the translation of language-dependent texts, which supports translation with a proposal pool. The Translation Workbench can be used to continue the translation of partially translated languages, to translate new languages for which no SAP translation is available (see Section 3.6), or to undertake arbitrary custom translations.

Translation environment for custom translations

It is called through Transaction SE63. Here, you will find appropriate editors for different language-dependent texts. You can translate texts using a worklist (usually at high volume) using a proposal pool which automatically stores the translations, or using direct translation of the text objects (generally for low to medium volume).

Figure 5.2 shows the components of the translation tools. The translation volume is determined by the **Worklist**, which is specified at the start of the translation project and can be updated. The actual translation takes place in the **Translation Editor** in Transaction SE63. If a term to be translated has already been translated, the translator is initially presented with this translated term from the **Proposal Pool**, which can then be accepted or retranslated. Every newly translated term is stored in the proposal pool, so that over the course of the project more and more terms can be used uniformly. The progress and degree of completion of the translation are determined using special **Statistics**.

Completed translations and changes are stored in special **Transport Requests** for further transport, which are then transported by the *SAP Transport Management System* (TMS).

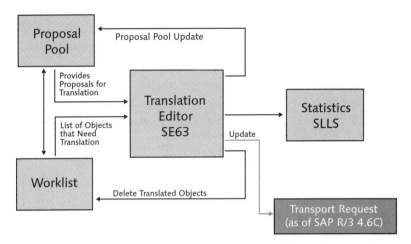

Figure 5.2 Components of the Translation Workbench

5.2.4 Language Transport

Language export and transport of custom translations

While the SAP language packages are delivered entirely on a CD/DVD and can be imported directly into each SAP system, custom language transports and language packages must be created for customer-specific translations. Translations are transported within the system landscape in a way similar to custom developments and customizing. That is, they use a standard system group, from the development or translation system through the text/quality assurance system into the production system.

Translation transports

For the transport of custom translations, the following options are available:

▶ **Link of the translation environment to the Transport Management System (as of R/3 Release 4.6C)**
From the Translation Workbench in Transaction SE63, changes and transport requests are created directly from the translation. They can then be transported by TMS and the transport tools tp and R3trans into the receiving systems. Here, only the text elements in the translated language are transported.

▶ **Creation of custom transport requests with the translations for underlying transport objects**
Integration with the SAP TMS also enables the manual creation of transport requests, which only contain text elements. To do this,

in the object list of a transport request, the program ID is selected in orders and tasks as a component of object type LANG, which selects the language-dependent part of the corresponding object. For instance, the object entry LANG PROG RFUMSV00 transports all translations of the text elements of sales tax report RFUMSV00, but not the ABAP program and associated dynpros themselves. The configuration of TMS can be used to control the languages allowed for transport.

▶ **Creation of a customer-specific language package**

To create your own language package, which can be imported into another SAP system using Transaction SMLT like a SAP language package, you can use Transaction SMLT_EX. It includes a wizard that helps you with the selection of the objects necessary for a language export. This takes place in the following steps:

Transaction SMLT_EX for language export

> ▸ **Selection of the export language**
> You can export one or more languages at the same time. Here, it should be noted that an SAP Unicode system, in contrast with non-Unicode systems (where there are problems with code-page combinations) is not subject to any limitations.

> ▸ **Selection of the object type**
> ABAP Repository objects like programs, transactions, dynpros, customizing objects, objects with special treatment, and so on.

> ▸ **Selection range**
> Here, you can limit the selection range. You can export the language inventory of multiple software components or the language-dependent part of transport requests or parts lists.

> ▸ **Job and task control**
> Here is where you can specify the starting time and server, as well as influence the number of transport requests generated.

A customized language package built in this manner provides advantages, particularly at high translation volumes. It supports the quality of your own translation and its completeness, in that the complete language package is imported into a different system for testing, which can be performed more than once. If the translations are complete and of sufficient quality, the package is imported into the production system.

Translated languages that are either delivered by SAP on CD/DVD or are customer translations can be loaded into an SAP system using Transaction SMLT.

During an import or a language supplementation, the SAP system blocks language management activities for the language affected. The system denies all additional activities that should be performed regarding a locked language. Other languages are not affected by this procedure, so that parallel actions operating on different languages may be performed.

SAP provides support packages to correct errors that occur in SAP transactions. SAP support packages can contain language-dependent data such as message texts, ABAP text pool entries, or dynpro texts. After the import of an SAP support package using Transaction SPAM, the translated texts for these objects are at the latest level in all languages existing in the system.

Problems may occur if another language is to be imported from the language CD on a system where SAP support packages already have been loaded. Because the language CD was created before the appearance of the first SAP support package, and the objects of the SAP support packages are only provided with translations to the languages already imported, a subsequent import of a language can bring the objects contained in the SAP support packages into an undefined state, as far as translation is concerned. Texts can either be obsolete and therefore wrong, or they may be missing entirely (see also SAP Note 352941). Since SAP Basis 4.6C, you can load the language data contained in the SAP support packages at a later date in order to achieve a consistent language state.

Language import takes place with Transaction SMLT. An essential prerequisite of the language import is the technical support of the languages in the system. For instance, in a single code page system, only the languages that match that code page can be imported. In a Unicode system, where all languages and character sets are possible, a new non-SAP standard language must previously be configured, as described in Section 3.6.

Figure 5.3 shows Transaction SMLT for language management. The displayed languages, German and English, are always available in every SAP system and are not imported, but they are still displayed.

Before the language import, a new language is first classified (**Language · Classify**). After the files with the language package for the language to be imported are stored on the file system of the server, the language is imported using **Language · Import package**. After the import, the language is supplemented with **Language · Supplement language** with the previously defined supplementation language, so that it then represents a 100% language.

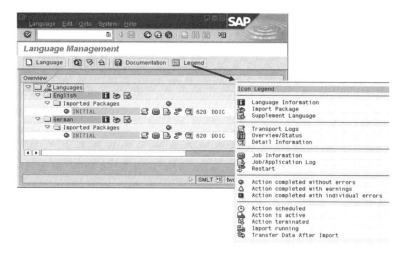

Figure 5.3 Language Import Using Transaction SMLT

Several languages may be imported in parallel. Depending on the capability of your SAP system, the simultaneous import of several languages may place a higher load on the system than the sequential importing of the languages. After the importing of the languages, you must still import the language data contained in the support packages. To do this, select the language affected in Transaction SMLT and select **Language · Special Actions · Import Support Packages**.

Language importing with Transaction SMLT is described in detail in the individual installation guidelines, which can be found on the installation CDs/DVDs or at the link *http://service.sap.com/instguides*.

5.2.5 Language-Dependent Customizing

Special procedure for language-dependent customizing

In a language import with supplementation of the translation gaps, language-dependent objects in the SAP language package are loaded and supplemented. For language-dependent and client-dependent customizing texts, the importing and the supplementation are somewhat more complicated, so we will describe those in greater detail. These texts may not have been translated into all languages and must therefore be supplemented in with a replacement language. You shouldn't forget that most customizing texts are client-dependent.

Figure 5.4 shows an example customizing object from marketing for the maintenance of sales organizations, whose data is stored in several tables. Here, TVKO (general data for sales organizations) and TVKOT (text with description) form a so-called *customizing view*. The table TVKOT is language-dependent and therefore relevant for translation. If a user logs onto the system in a logon language—e. g., EN—and then sees and edits the texts in TVKOT with the same language key as the logon language, an entry in TVKOT in a different language is not visible. The user thus doesn't notice that these are language-dependent texts being edited.

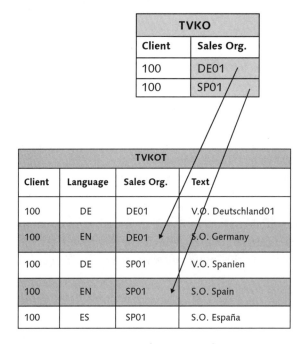

Figure 5.4 Language-Dependent Texts in Customizing

Customizing data is data which are only generated when the customer does so in the context of customizing. This customizing data of a customer client account is not overwritten during language import or an upgrade. The import of data always takes place in Client 000.

The reason is that customizing places the responsibility for the customizing data into the hands of the customer, and afterwards it may not be overwritten by data from SAP. This applies without limitations and it applies equally to translations.

However, where translation is concerned it is sometimes desirable for the customer to refresh the sample data and pre-settings with the current translation from SAP. The clients should always be copied out of Client 000 first, after it is supplied with all the languages needed. To update a translation language for customizing on an existing customer client, you have two options:

SAP customizing translations

- ▶ Use of tools
- ▶ Manual translation

To close the existing translation gaps in a language, language supplementation should always be started after a language import. The supplementation actions are client-dependent, and language supplementation is performed for the client in which you are logged on. If you use several clients, then you must explicitly perform language supplementation in every production client.

Supplementing customizing using Transaction SMLT

You can access texts stored in client-independent database tables from all clients at the same time. The pre-setting is selected in such a way that client-independent tables are supplemented when you are logged on in Client 000.

For the definition of the supplementation logic, the following rules apply:

Definition of the supplementation logic

- ▶ Languages with translation level 1 (complete languages) cannot be supplemented. If this is necessary anyway, please consult SAP Note 111750.
- ▶ You should specify a supplementation language for every language in the system (except for languages with translation level 1). In a Unicode system, in contrast to a non-Unicode system (code-page

problems), this language can be selected arbitrarily, as long as it is complete.

▶ You can only supplement texts from a language with translation level 1, or from a language which has already been supplemented from a language of translation level 1.

Special tool for supplementing customizing translations When supplementing customizing texts using Transaction SMLT after selection of the language, the following options can be selected via **Language · Special actions · Supplementation (Basic)** (see Figure 5.5):

▶ **Combined with RSREFILL** (default option)
Three steps are performed in one operation: the retraction of a supplementation performed in the past, RSREFILL, and the supplementation. The RSREFILL step copies texts out of the customizing tables in Client 000 into the current client. A reference language is required as further information, because only for texts which are the same in both clients in the reference language is the translation copied out of Client 000 into the logon client. Comparison with a reference language is used so that only semantically meaningful text lines are copied and the translation remains consistent. We select the reference language to be the language in which the customizing was performed in the target client. The reference language must be different from the target language. This mode can only be used in clients other than 000.

▶ **Combined with Client Maintenance**
Three steps are performed in one operation here, as well: the retraction of a supplementation, client administration, and the supplementation. Client administration differs from RSREFILL in the following respect. There is no comparison with a reference language, so that more text lines in the target language are copied from Client 000 into the current client. That introduces the risk that semantically incorrect text lines will be copied and the translation will be inconsistent. This mode can only be used in clients other than 000.

▶ **Supplement Only**
Here, missing texts (those not translated) in the language are completed with the corresponding lines from the supplementation language.

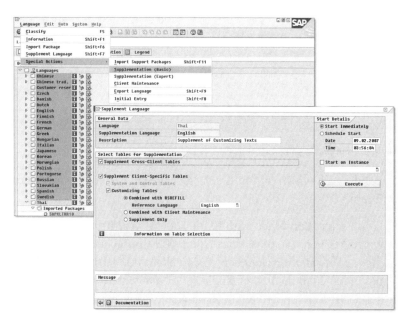

Figure 5.5 Supplementing the Customizing Translations from Client 000

At this point, it should be noted that when implementing a new country whose country version is supported in the SAP system (see **Country Information** at *http://service.sap.com/globalization*), country customizing is included as a template in Client 000. After the import of the language package for the country, its translation is also available in Client 000. During the implementation of the country version, the supplementation method can be used to import the translated country-customizing template into the working clients.

Customizing translations from SAP Country Versions

In the following example, customizing texts should be supplemented (see Table 5.2). The language-dependent text for the translation of the term "company code" for the new language 1G (German Austria)—a language key that is only available in a SAP Unicode system—is missing in Client 100 and should now be supplemented. The supplementation language is DE, and the reference language is EN.

Example of supplementing customizing texts

Client	Language	Text
000	EN	Company code
000	DE	Buchungskreis

Table 5.2 Supplementing Customizing Texts

Client	Language	Text
000	1G	Bucki
100	EN	comp. code
100	DE	Buchungskreis
100	1G	(empty)

Table 5.2 Supplementing Customizing Texts (cont.)

Depending on which option is selected, the supplementation works differently.

▸ If you select **Combined with RSREFILL**, the text from the new language 1G is not copied from client 000 into client 100, because the text of reference language EN in client 000 (company code) is not identical to the text of language EN in client 100 (comp. code). So the text of supplementation language DE is copied from client 100. The result: **Buchungskreis**.

▸ If you select **Combined with Client Maintenance** there is no comparison with a reference language, and the text of language 1G is copied from client 000. Result: **Bucki**.

▸ If you select **Supplement Only**, the text from the fill-in language DE is simply copied from client 100. Result: **Buchungskreis**.

Figure 5.6 shows option **Supplement Only** in graphical form with another example: The texts from the sales organizations are stored in table TVKOT which are edited during customizing in the sales area through Transaction SPRO, whereby the language key belonging to the logon language is automatically pulled into table TVKOT during the customizing activity. In this example, if a user with logon language EN edited the text entry "S.O. Germany," a Spanish user with logon language ES (Spanish) cannot see it, as it is still empty. If no Spanish translation is possible or desired, a supplement from the supplementation language EN into the logon language ES copies the existing text "S.O. Germany" from table TVKOT with language key EN into the line with ES, so that the Spanish user then also sees "S.O. Germany."

TVKOT			
Client	**Language**	**Sales Org.**	**Text**
100	DE	DE01	V.O. Deutschland
100	EN	DE01	S.O. Germany
100	ES	DE01	S.O. Germany
100	DE	SP01	V.O. Spanien
100	EN	SP01	S.O. Spain
100	ES	SP01	S.O. España

Figure 5.6 Language Supplementation During Customizing

The link of the translation environment to the Transport Management System makes it possible to create translated customizing texts in a special system, mark them in transport requests, and then distribute them specifically around the system landscape. You translate the rest of the customizing texts with Transaction SE63—marking the translation activity in transport requests—and finally distribute the orders in the system landscape using the Transport Management System (Transaction STMS).

Manual translation of customizing

5.2.6 Address Versions

Names and addresses of business partners must often be available in more than one language. This is particularly necessary when information about business partners must be available globally and for all users around the world, which can only be achieved using a company-wide global language or font (usually English). A new business partner in China is initially created in Chinese, which most of the colleagues in the other countries cannot read or understand. Thus, the name and the address must also be available in (usually) English, so that the company can do global business with this partner. This leads to the general necessity to translate master data from customers, suppliers, partners, and so on, within master-data maintenance (MDM). However, it is often sufficient to use the translated names and addresses only for the printing of business documents, a practice that

Address versions with translation of master data

is connected with additional functionality and logic in the printing program. Since the address format is also usually different in the different countries, we don't call this pure translation, but use the term *address versions* instead.

International address versions (versions for short) are a property of Business Address Services to enable the printing of addresses in the different country-dependent fonts. In this context, "different fonts" are not simply country-specific details within character sets (like umlauts in German or accents in French), but rather fonts consisting of their own character sets.

When printing addresses (see also Section 3.2.5), it must be noted that the font of the addresses to be printed is often not determined by the current logon language or by the logon language at the time of creation of the address. Rather, the international address versions offer the option of printing one and the same address in different fonts depending on certain parameters. For instance, a Japanese address should be printed in Kanji (Japanese characters) if the country of the sender is also Japan, but in international characters if the sending country is not Japan (see SAP Note 316331).

The default version of an address can in principle be entered in any allowed or existing fonts. In the interests of uniform reporting, however, it makes sense to enter all default versions of addresses in one installation in the same font. For a global system, English or the global character set is recommended.

In all applications using Business Address Services, address versions are available which can be configured. Figure 5.7 shows the architecture of address versions based on an example. A customer with customer number 1234, whose data is stored as a default version in table KNA1, the standard address in Germany, will receive two address versions for Russia and Japan. Central address management creates three entries for this in the central table ADRC: The first has an empty field NATION containing the standard address and thus the value from KNA1, a second has NATION=R with the Russian version, and a third has NATION=J with the Japanese version. The connection to the identical customer with CustNr = 1234 takes place through the field ADDRNUMBER, which contains the same value 1000 in both tables ADRC and KNA1. So a business partner can have multiple address versions, making this a 1: n relation.

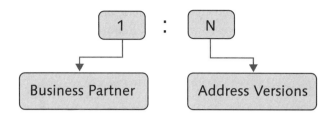

KNA1 (Customer data)		
CustNo	AddrNumber	Data fields
1234	1000	xxxx

ADRC (Central Address Management)		
AddrNumber	Nation	Data fields
1000		Standard Address
1000	R	Russian Address
1000	K	Kanji Adress

Figure 5.7 Address Versions

Because address versions must semantically match the default version and only represent a possibility for entry of one address in different fonts, we must ensure that the entries for the address in the default version and associated address versions are consistent. For this reason, numeric fields in the address (e. g., house number, postal code, and telephone numbers) from the default version are offered as suggested values in the additional versions. Changes to these fields are written back into the default version of the address. Only text fields can be different from one another in the different versions.

5.3 Summary

For multilingual operation of a global system, there must be suitable translations available for the languages in use as well as the technical support of languages. SAP offers the translation of SAP products in the form of language packages, which are imported and supplemented after the technical setup of the language (the supplementation is not needed for Japanese).

An SAP system contains numerous language-dependent objects that are relevant for translation, and can be broken down into static development objects and dynamic, changing data objects. For the customer, the latter are of particular importance, because during ongoing operations the customer's own customizing, master, and transaction data, along with forms and other objects, must be consistently translated.

SAP provides translation tools so that customers can undertake their own translations efficiently and, if possible, in great volume. The important thing is a consistent translation strategy for all languages. The connection of translation into the SAP transport system enables efficient language transport. Special steps are necessary especially to manage language-dependent customizing in the different language consistently. Important master data is translated using the concept of address versions.

To satisfy the requirements of a truly global IT solution, software must manage global and local processes at one and the same time. For this reason, every large company has the challenge of supporting different languages. In this book, we have explained to you how SAP supports Unicode as a technologically progressive basis for all software products.

6 Summary

Unicode makes it possible to assign nearly any character in any language in the world its own unique number, independent of system, program, and language. The Unicode code page offers you the option of defining more than a million characters, so that besides languages you can also use historical fonts, symbols, arrows, and the like.

Thanks to Unicode's formulation of the optimum technical prerequisites for language support, expansion in new countries is simplified, and would often be impossible without this technology. Intelligent translation tools provided by SAP simplify translation into different languages as needed.

To be able to realize these advantages, it is necessary to convert existing systems. When migrating from non-Unicode to Unicode, one speaks of "Unicode conversion," and and when switching operating systems or database platforms, SAP uses the term "OS/DB migration." The different procedures for converting to Unicode have been explained in detail in this book.

In ABAP programming, too, there are some details regarding Unicode that were covered in Section 3.4 of Chapter 3. Furthermore, Section 3.3, on communication via interfaces, covered another important topic which must be considered for all data transfers between Unicode and non-Unicode systems.

Because all SAP applications are now available based on Unicode, Chapter 4—which covers Unicode projects—is important to study, in particular Sections 4.1 and 4.2. It gives you a practical path for new installation or conversion of an existing system, thus simplifying your work in planning and executing Unicode projects.

We'd like to make two basic points in summary:

Future-proofing with Unicode

▶ The widespread availability of Unicode and the future-readiness of this global standard provide all the prerequisites for problem-free support of the world's languages.

Smooth conversion to Unicode

▶ A smooth conversion to Unicode, implemented and supported by a variety of SAP tools, is now possible for any application.

"When the world wants to talk, it speaks Unicode." Join the conversation!

Appendix

A   Code Page Tables

This appendix presents the most important non-Unicode code pages in tabular form.

The Microsoft and ISO code pages are generally mapped into the Single-Byte code pages (see Figures A.1 through A.15). The ISO code page is used by the SAP system, while the Microsoft code page is used for Windows in the SAP GUI.

For four Asian code pages, the direct listing of the characters is not possible, given that the number of characters is too great (see Figures A.16 through A.19). As an alternative, the tables show the hex-code range in which the corresponding characters appear. These are all Double-Byte code pages: The first byte of these code pages is shown on the y axis, while the second byte is represented by the x axis.

If you have problems with specific characters during a Unicode conversion of an MDMP system, you can use these tables to check where the problems may be arising. A "fool the system" situation (see Chapter 2) may be implemented using the Microsoft code pages. This makes the tables an important aid in many Unicode conversions, and they should be a part of the standard repertoire of any Unicode consultant.

In addition to using the code page tables shown here, it can also be useful to use the page at *http://www.eki.ee/letter* to check which special characters are used in a given language.

A0	A1 ¡	A2 ¢	A3 £	A4 ¤	A5 ¥	A6 ¦	A7 §	A8 ¨	A9 ©	AA ª	AB «	AC ¬	AD -	AE ®	AF ¯
B0 °	B1 ±	B2 ²	B3 ³	B4 ´	B5 µ	B6 ¶	B7 ·	B8 ¸	B9 ¹	BA º	BB »	BC ¼	BD ½	BE ¾	BF ¿
C0 À	C1 Á	C2 Â	C3 Ã	C4 Ä	C5 Å	C6 Æ	C7 Ç	C8 È	C9 É	CA Ê	CB Ë	CC Ì	CD Í	CE Î	CF Ï
D0 Ð	D1 Ñ	D2 Ò	D3 Ó	D4 Ô	D5 Õ	D6 Ö	D7 ×	D8 Ø	D9 Ù	DA Ú	DB Û	DC Ü	DD Ý	DE Þ	DF ß
E0 à	E1 á	E2 â	E3 ã	E4 ä	E5 å	E6 æ	E7 ç	E8 è	E9 é	EA ê	EB ë	EC ì	ED í	EE î	EF ï
F0 ð	F1 ñ	F2 ò	F3 ó	F4 ô	F5 õ	F6 ö	F7 ÷	F8 ø	F9 ù	FA ú	FB û	FC ü	FD ý	FE þ	FF ÿ

Figure A.1 Code Page ISO 8859-1 (Western Europe)

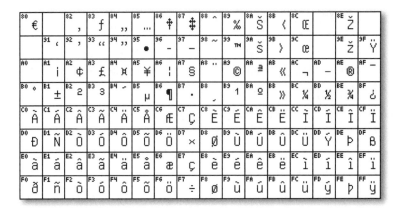

Figure A.2 Code Page Microsoft 1252 (Western Europe)

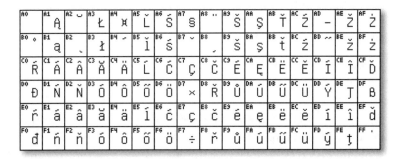

Figure A.3 Code Page ISO 8859-2 (Eastern Europe)

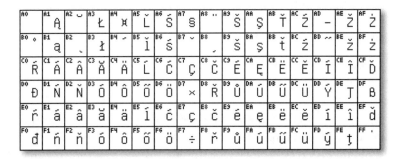

Figure A.4 Code Page Microsoft 1250 (Eastern Europe)

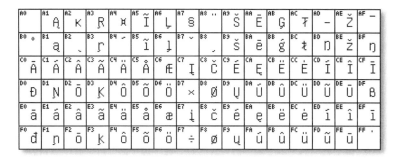

Figure A.5 Code Page ISO 8859-4 (Baltic Countries)

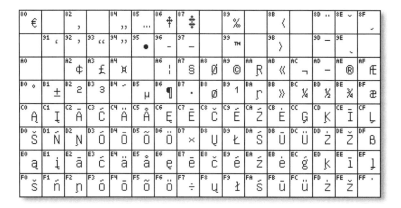

Figure A.6 Code Page Microsoft 1257 (Baltic Countries)

Figure A.7 Code Page ISO 8859-5 (Cyrillic)

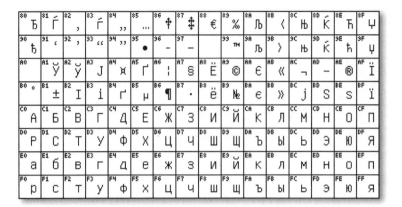

Figure A.8 Code Page Microsoft 1251 (Cyrillic)

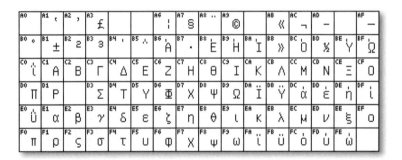

Figure A.9 Code Page ISO 8859-7 (Greek)

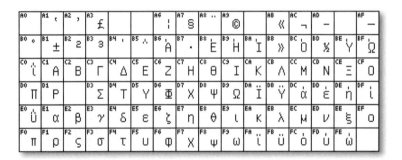

Figure A.10 Code Page Microsoft 1253 (Greek)

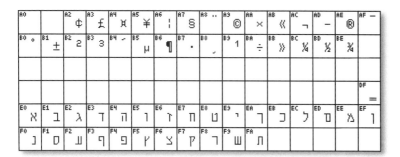

Figure A.11 Code Page ISO 8859-8 and Microsoft 1255 (Hebrew)

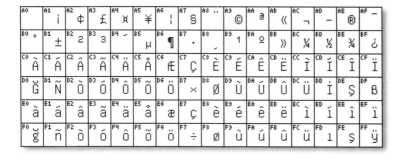

Figure A.12 Code Page ISO 8859-9 (Turkish)

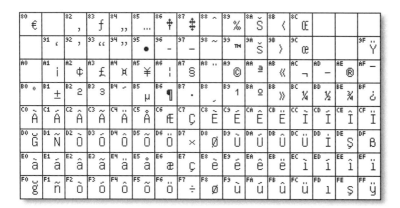

Figure A.13 Code Page Microsoft 1254 (Turkish)

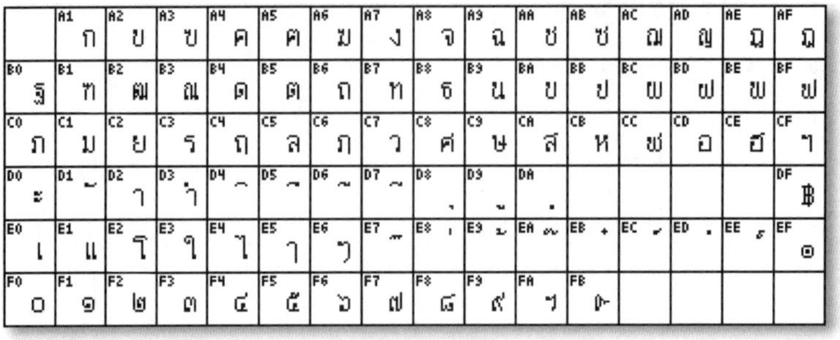

Figure A.14 Code Page ISO Latin-11 (Thai)

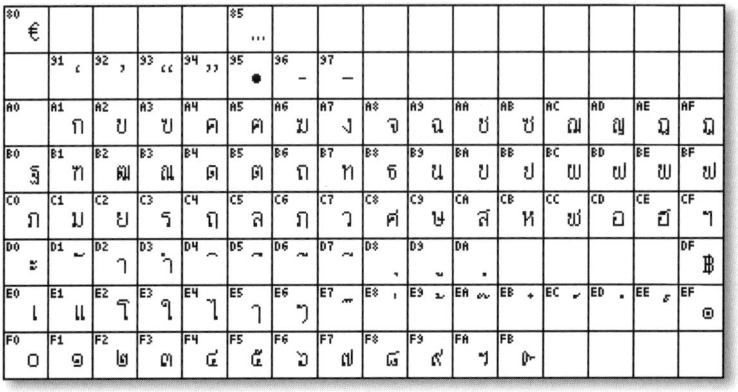

Figure A.15 Code Page Microsoft 874 (Thai)

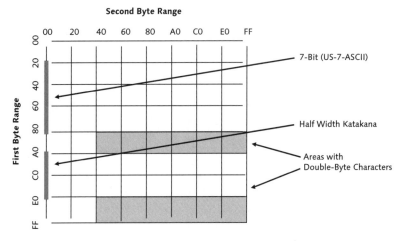

Figure A.16 Code Page Japanese/JISX208-1996

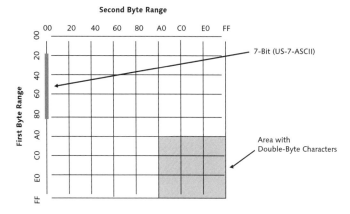

Figure A.17 Code Page Korean/KSC5601-1992

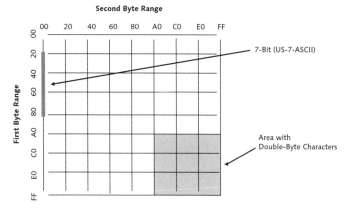

Figure A.18 Code Page Mandarin Chinese (Simplified)/GB2312-80

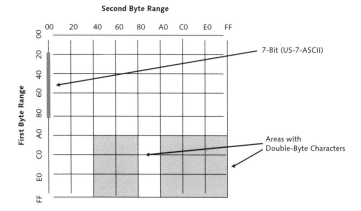

Figure A.19 Code Page Chinese (Traditional)/Big Five

B   Languages in an SAP Unicode System

Table B.1 shows a selective list of languages for which language keys are defined in an SAP Unicode system (as of August 2006). The complete and latest version, with additional details, can be found in SAP Note 73606.

Information on the SAP translation of a language can be found at *http://service.sap.com/globalization*.

Legend
▶ **Language** Language, language designation: languages in bold are also available on non-Unicode systems (*Default Set*)
▶ **Description** Brief description of the languages and dialects
▶ **Countries** Countries with this language
▶ **Script** Character set of the language; if blank, it is ambiguous or unknown
▶ **SAP** SAP language code in the Unicode system; language codes in bold denote the SAP Default Set

Language	Description	Countries	Script	SAP
Afrikaans	Afrikaans	South Africa, Botswana, Malawi, Namibia, Zambia	Latin	**AF**
Albanian	Albanian	Albania, Kosovo, Serbia and Montenegro	Latin	SQ
Arabic	Arabic	Comoros Islands, Djibouti, Mali, Mauritania, Niger, Nigeria, Palestinian West Bank and Gaza, Saudi-Arabia, Somalia, Sudan	Arabic	AR
Arabic	Arabic Algeria	Algeria	Arabic	1A

Table B.1 Selective List of Possible Languages in an SAP Unicode System

Language	Description	Countries	Script	SAP
Arabic	Arabic Bahrain	Bahrain	Arabic	2A
Arabic	Arabic Egypt	Egypt	Arabic	3A
Arabic	Arabic Iraq	Iraq	Arabic	4A
Arabic	Arabic Jordan	Jordan	Arabic	5A
Arabic	Arabic Kuwait	Kuwait	Arabic	6A
Arabic	Arabic Lebanon	Lebanon	Arabic	7A
Arabic	Arabic Libya	Libya	Arabic	8A
Arabic	Arabic Morocco	Morocco	Arabic	9A
Arabic	Arabic Oman	Oman	Arabic	0A
Arabic	Arabic Qatar	Qatar	Arabic	1B
Arabic	Arabic Syria	Syria	Arabic	2B
Arabic	Arabic Tunisia	Tunisia	Arabic	3B
Arabic	Arabic U.A. Emirates	UAE	Arabic	4B
Arabic	Arabic Yemen	Yemen	Arabic	5B
Armenian	Armenian	Armenia, Iran, Turkey	Armenian	HY
Avaric, Avaro, Dagestani	Avaric	Azerbaijan, Kazakhstan, Russia, Turkey	Cyrillic	AV
Azerbaijani	Azerbaijani Cyrillic	Azerbaijan, Armenia	Cyrillic	5R
Azerbaijani	Azerbaijani Latin	Azerbaijan, Armenia	Latin	AZ
Bangla, Bengali	Bengali Bangladesh	Bangladesh, Nepal, Singapore	Bengal	BN
Bangla, Bengali	Bengali India	India	Bengal	6B
Basque	Basque	France, Spain	Latin	EU
Belorussian	Belarussian	Belarus, Lithuania, Poland, Ukraine	Cyrillic	BE
Bihari	Bihari	Bangladesh, India	Devanagari	BH
Bosnian	Bosnian	Bosnia-Herzegovina, Albania	Latin	BS

Table B.1 Selective List of Possible Languages in an SAP Unicode System (cont.)

Language	Description	Countries	Script	SAP
Breton	Breton	France	Latin	BR
Bulgarian	Bulgarian	Bulgaria, Greece, Moldova, Turkey	Cyrillic	**BG**
Burmese	Burmese	Myanmar, Bangladesh	Latin	MY
Catalan	Catalan	Spain, Andorra	Latin	**CA**
Chinese (simplified)	Chinese China	People's Republic of China	Hans	**ZH**
Chinese (simplified)	Chinese Singapore	Singapore	Han	3C
Chinese (traditional)	Chinese Taiwan	Taiwan, Brunei, Indonesia, Malaysia, Mongolia, Thailand, Tibet, Vietnam	Hant	**ZF**
Chinese (traditional)	Chinese Taiwan	Taiwan	Han	4C
Chinese (traditional)	Chinese Hongkong SAR	Hongkong SAR	Han	1C
Chuang, Zhuang	Zhuang	People's Republic of China	Latin	ZA
Chuvash	Chuvash	Russia	Cyrillic	CV
Cornish	Cornish	United Kingdom	Latin	KW
Corsican	Corsican	France, Italy	Latin	CO
Croatian	Croatian	Croatia, Albania, Bosnia-Herzegowina	Latin	**HR**
Czech	Czech	Czech Republic	Latin	**CS**
Danish	Danish	Denmark, Faroe Islands, Greenland, Germany	Latin	**DA**
Dutch	Dutch Netherlands	Netherlands, France, Netherlands Antilles	Latin	**NL**
Dutch	Dutch Belgium	Belgium	Latin	1D
Dzongkha	Dzongkha Bhutan	Bhutan	Tibetan	2D
Dzongkha	Dzongkha Nepal	Nepal	Tibetan	DZ
English	English United Kingdom	United Kingdom	Latin	6N

Table B.1 Selective List of Possible Languages in an SAP Unicode System (cont.)

Language	Description	Countries	Script	SAP
English	English United States	USA, American Samoa, Botswana, Brunei, Cameroon, Eritrea, Ethiopia, Fiji, Ghana, Guam, Israel, Lesotho, Malawi, Malta, Marshall Islands, Namibia, Nauru, Nigeria, Pakistan, Papua New Guinea, Puerto Rico, Swaziland, Tanzania, Tonga, Uganda, Vanuatu, Western Samoa, Zambia	Latin	**EN**
English	English Australia	Australia	Latin	1E
English	English Canada	Canada	Latin	3E
English	English India	India	Latin	6E
English	English Ireland	Ireland	Latin	8E
English	English Malaysia	Malaysia (peninsula)	Latin	0E
English	English New Zealand	New Zealand	Latin	1N
English	English Philippines	Philippines	Latin	2N
English	English South Africa	South Africa	Latin	4N
English	English Zimbabwe	Zimbabwe	Latin	7N
Esperanto	Esperanto	Several countries	Latin	EO
Estonian	Estonian	Estonia	Latin	**ET**
Finnish	Finnish	Finland, Norway, Russia, Sweden	Latin	**FI**
French	French France	France, Algeria, Andorra, Benin, Burkina Faso, Burundi, Central African Republic, Chad, Comoros Islands, Congo, Djibouti, French Polynesia, Gabon, Guinea, Lebanon, Madagascar, Mauretania, Mauritius, New Caledonia, Niger, Rwanda, Togo, Tunisia, Vanuatu	Latin	**FR**

Table B.1 Selective List of Possible Languages in an SAP Unicode System (cont.)

Language	Description	Countries	Script	SAP
French	French Belgium	Belgium	Latin	1F
French	French Cameroon	Cameroon	Latin	2F
French	French Canada	Canada	Latin	3F
French	French Congo DRC	Congo DRC	Latin	4F
French	French Cote d'Ivoire	Côte d'Ivoire	Latin	5F
French	French Haiti	Haiti	Latin	6F
French	French Luxem-bourg	Luxembourg	Latin	7F
French	French Mali	Mali	Latin	8F
French	French Monaco	Monaco	Latin	9F
French	French Morocco	Morocco	Latin	1H
French	French Senegal	Senegal	Latin	3H
French	French Switzer-land	Switzerland	Latin	4H
Frisian	Frisian	Germany, Netherlands	Latin	FY
Gaelic	Gaelic	United Kingdom	Latin	GD
Gallegan, Galicien	Gallegan	Spain	Latin	GL
Georgian	Georgian	Iran, Georgia, Turkey	Mkhedruli	KA
German	German Germany	Germany, Belgium, Czech Republic, Denmark, Italy	Latin	**DE**
German	German Austria	Austria	Latin	1G
German	German Liechten-stein	Liechtenstein	Latin	2G
German	German Luxem-bourg	Luxembourg	Latin	3G
German	German Switzer-land	Switzerland	Latin	4G
Greek	Greek	Albania, Cyprus, Egypt, Greece	Greek	**EL**

Table B.1 Selective List of Possible Languages in an SAP Unicode System (cont.)

Language	Description	Countries	Script	SAP
Greenlandic; Kalaallisut	Greenlandic	Denmark, Greenland	Latin	KL
Guaraní	Guarani	Argentinia, Bolivia, Brazil, Paraguay	Latin	GN
Gujarati	Gujarati	India, Pakistan, Tanzania, Uganda	Gujarati	GU
Haitian; Haitian Creole	Haitian	Dominican Republic, Haiti	Latin	HT
Hausa	Hausa	Benin, Niger, Nigeria	Latin	HA
Hawaiian	Hawaiian	USA (Hawaii)	Latin	HW
Hebrew	Hebrew	Israel	Hebrew	**HE**
Hindi	Hindi	India, Nepal	Devanagari	HI
Hungarian	Hungarian	Hungary, Russia, Serbia and Montenegro, Slovakia, Ukraine	Latin	**HU**
Icelandic	Icelandic	Iceland	Latin	**IS**
Indonesian	Indonesian	Indonesia	Latin	**ID**
Interlingua	Interlingua	Several countries	Latin	IA
Interlingue	Interlingue	Several countries	Latin	IE
Irish Gaelic	Irish	Ireland	Latin	GA
Irish (Middle)	Irish, Middle		Latin	IM
Italian	Italian Italy	Italy, Croatia, San Marino, Slovenia, Vatican State	Latin	**IT**
Italian	Italian Switzerland	Switzerland	Latin	1I
Japanese	Japanese	Japan	Hiragana, Han (Kanji), Katakana, SJIS	**JA**
Javanese (Bali, Java)	Javanese	Indonesia, Malaysia (Sabah)	Latin, Hanacaraka	JV
Kannada	Kannada	India	Kannada	KN

Table B.1 Selective List of Possible Languages in an SAP Unicode System (cont.)

Language	Description	Countries	Script	SAP
Kashmiri	Kashmiri	India, Pakistan	Devana-gari	KS
Kazakh	Kazakh	Kazakhstan, China, Mongolia	Cyrillic	KK
Khmer	Khmer	Cambodia, Vietnam	Khmer	KM
Kirghiz	Kirghiz	Kyrgyzstan, China, Turkey	Cyrillic	KY
Kongo	Kongo	Democratic Republic of Congo, Angola	Latin	KG
Korean	Korean South	South Korea, China, Japan	Hangul, Han	**KO**
Korean	Korean North	North Korea	Hangul, Han	2K
Kurdish, Kurdi	Kurdish	Armenia, Azerbaijan, Iran, Iraq	Cyrillic	KU
Lao	Lao	Laos	Lao	LO
Latin	Latin	Vatican State	Latin	LA
Latvian	Latvian	Latvia	Latin	**LV**
Luxembour-gish	Luxembourgish	Luxembourg, Belgium	Latin	LB
Limburgan; Limburgish	Limburgish	Belgium	Latin	LI
Lingala	Lingala	Democratic Republic of Congo, Congo	Latin	LN
Lithuanian	Lithuanian	Lithuania	Latin	**LT**
Macedonian	Macedonian	Macedonia, Albania, Greece	Cyrillic	MK
Malay	Malay Malaysia	Malaysia, Indonesia, Singapore	Latin	**MS**
Malay	Malay Brunei Darussalam	Brunei	Latin	1M
Malayalam	Malayalam	India	Malay-alam	ML
Maltese	Maltese	Malta	Latin	MT

Table B.1 Selective List of Possible Languages in an SAP Unicode System (cont.)

Language	Description	Countries	Script	SAP
Manchu	Manchu	China	Hangul, Han	MQ
Maori	Maori	New Zealand	Latin	MI
Miscellaneous	Miscellaneous			M8
Moldavian	Moldavian	Moldova	Cyrillic	MO
Mongolian	Mongolian	Mongolia, China	Cyrillic	MN
Multiple	Multiple languages			M0
Neapolitan	Neapolitan			N1
Nepali	Nepali Nepal	Nepal, Bhutan	Devanagari	NE
Nepali	Nepali India	India	Devanagari	9N
Norwegian	Norwegian	Norway	Latin	**NO**
Norwegian, Bokmål	Norwegian, Bokmål	Norway	Latin	NB
Norwegian; Nynorsk	Norwegian; Nynorsk	Norway	Latin	NN
Punjabi	Punjabi India	India	Gurmukhi	PA
Punjabi	Punjabi Pakistan	Pakistan	Arabic	3P
Pushto	Pushto	Afghanistan, Pakistan, UAE	Arabic	PS
Persian, Farsi	Farsi	Iran, Afghanistan, Iraq, Oman, Pakistan, Qatar, Tajikistan, UAE	Arabic	FA
Phillipine	Phillipine			P1
Polish	Polish	Poland		**PL**
Portuguese	Portuguese Portugal	Portugal, Angola, Cape Verde Islands, Guinea-Bissau, Mozambique, Democratic Republic of São Tomé and Príncipe	Latin	1P
Portuguese	Portuguese Brazil	Brazil	Latin	**PT**

Table B.1 Selective List of Possible Languages in an SAP Unicode System (cont.)

Language	Description	Countries	Script	SAP
Provençal; Occitan	Occitan	France, Italy, Monaco	Latin	OC
Quechua	Quechua	Argentinia, Bolivia, Chile (Northern), Colombia (Southern), Ecuador, Peru	Latin	QU
Rajasthani	Rajasthani			RJ
Raeto-Romance	Rhaeto-Romance	Switzerland	Latin	RM
Reserved	Reserved for customer	(Customized language)		**Z1**
Romance	Romance			RE
Romanian, Moldovan	Romanian Moldova	Moldova	Latin	7R
Romanian	Romanian Romania	Romania, Ukraine	Latin	**RO**
Rundi	Rundi	Burundi	Latin	RN
Russian	Russian Russia	Russia, China, Mongolia	Cyrillic	**RU**
Russian	Russian Moldova	Moldova	Cyrillic	8R
Saami (Inari), Lapp	Inari Sami	Finland	Latin	IY
Saami (Skolt), Russian Lapp	Skolt Sami	Finland, Russia	Latin	XM
Saami (Southern); Lapp	Southern Sami	Sweden, Norway	Latin	X1
Saami (Northern), Lapp	Northern Sami	Finland, Norway, Sweden	Latin	SE
Samoan	Samoan	American Samoa, Western Samoa	Latin	SM
Sango	Sango	Central African Republic	Latin	SG
Sanskrit	Sanskrit	India	Sinhala, Devanagari	SA

Table B.1 Selective List of Possible Languages in an SAP Unicode System (cont.)

Language	Description	Countries	Script	SAP
Sardinian, Sardu	Sardinian	Italy	Latin	SC
Scots	Scots			S6
Serbian	Serbian (Cyrillic)	Serbia and Montenegro, Albania, Bosnia-Herzegowina	Cyrillic	**SR**
Serbian	Serbian	Serbia and Montenegro, Albania, Bosnia-Herzegowina	Latin	**SH**
Sichuan Yi	Sichuan Yi	China	Yi	II
Sicilian	Sicilian	Italia (Sicily)		XC
Sign	Sign languages			XG
Sindhi	Sindhi India	India	Gurmukhi	SD
Sindhi	Sindhi Pakistan	Pakistan	Gurmukhi	4D
Sinhalese	Sinhalese	Sri Lanka	Sinhalese	SI
Slavic	Slavic			SO
Slovak	Slovak	Slovakia	Latin	**SK**
Slovenian	Slovenian	Slovenia, Austria	Latin	**SL**
Somali	Somali	Somalia, Djibouti, Ethiopia, Kenya	Latin	SO
Sotho, Northern	Sotho, Northern			N6
Sotho, Southern	Sotho, Southern	Lesotho, South Africa	Latin	ST
Spanish	Spanish Spain	Spain, Andorra, Cuba, USA (New Mexico)	Latin	**ES**
Spanish	Spanish Argentina	Argentina	Latin	1S
Spanish	Spanish Bolivia	Bolivia	Latin	2S
Spanish	Spanish Chile	Chile	Latin	3S
Spanish	Spanish Columbia	Colombia	Latin	0S
Spanish	Spanish Costa Rica	Costa Rica	Latin	4S

Table B.1 Selective List of Possible Languages in an SAP Unicode System (cont.)

Language	Description	Countries	Script	SAP
Spanish	Spanish Dominican Republic	Dominican Republic	Latin	5S
Spanish	Spanish Ecuador	Ecuador	Latin	6S
Spanish	Spanish El Salvador	El Salvador	Latin	7S
Spanish	Spanish Guatemala	Guatemala	Latin	8S
Spanish	Spanish Honduras	Honduras	Latin	9S
Spanish	Spanish Mexico	Mexico	Latin	1X
Spanish	Spanish Nicaragua	Nicaragua	Latin	2X
Spanish	Spanish Panama	Panama	Latin	3X
Spanish	Spanish Paraguay	Paraguay	Latin	4X
Spanish	Spanish Peru	Peru	Latin	5X
Spanish	Spanish Puerto Rico	Puerto Rico	Latin	6X
Spanish	Spanish Uruguay	Uruguay	Latin	7X
Spanish	Spanish Venezuela	Venezuela	Latin	8X
Sukuma	Sukuma			XK
Sundanese	Sundanese	Indonesia (Java; Bali)	Latin	SU
Susu	Susu	Guinea	Latin; Arabic	XU
Swahili	Swahili	Kenya, Tanzania	Latin	SW
Swati	Swati	South Africa, Swaziland	Latin	SS
Swedish	Swedish	Sweden, Finland	Latin	**SV**
Syriac	Syriac			SY
Tagalog, Filipino	Tagalog	Philippines	Latin	TL
Tahitian	Tahitian	French Polynesia		TY
Tajiki, Tadzhik	Tajik	Tajikistan	Cyrillic	TG

Table B.1 Selective List of Possible Languages in an SAP Unicode System (cont.)

Language	Description	Countries	Script	SAP
Tamil	Tamil	India, Malaysia (peninsula), Mauritius, Singapore	Tamil	TA
Tatar	Tatar	Russia, China, Turkey	Cyrillic	TT
Telugu	Telugu	India	Telugu	TE
Thai	Thai	Thailand	Thai	**TH**
Tibetan	Tibetan	Tibet, Bhutan, China, India	Tibetan	BO
Sino-Tibetan	Sino-Tibetan			SF
Tonga	Tonga	Tonga	Latin	TO
Tsonga	Tsonga	Mozambique, South Africa	Latin	TS
Tswana	Tswana	Botswana, Namibia	Latin	TN
Turkish	Turkish	Turkey, Bulgaria, Cyprus, Greece, Macedonia, Uzbekistan	Latin	**TR**
Turkmen	Turkmen	Turkmenistan, Afghanistan, Iran	Latin	TK
Ukrainian	Ukrainian	Ukraine, Poland, Slovakia	Cyrillic	**UK**
Urdu	Urdu Pakistan	Pakistan, Mauritius	Arabic extended	UR
Urdu	Urdu India	India	Arabic	1U
Uzbek	Uzbek Cyrillic	Uzbekistan	Cyrillic	3U
Uzbek	Uzbek Latin	Uzbekistan	Latin	UZ
Venda	Venda	South Africa, Zimbabwe	Latin	VE
Vietnamese	Vietnamese	Vietnam, China	Latin; Chu Nom	VI
Walloon	Walloon	Belgium	Latin	WA
Welsh	Welsh	United Kingdom	Latin	CY
Yiddish	Yiddish	Israel	Hebrew	YI
Yoruba	Yoruba	Benin, Nigeria	Latin	YO
Zulu	Zulu	Malawi, South Africa, Swaziland	Latin	ZU

Table B.1 Selective List of Possible Languages in an SAP Unicode System (cont.)

C   Literature References and Other Support

C.1   Literature

▶ Bengel, Günther: *Verteilte Systeme*. Vieweg, 3rd edition, 2004.

▶ Blumenthal, Andreas; Keller, Horst: *ABAP–Fortgeschrittene Techniken und Tools*. SAP PRESS 2005.

▶ Comer, Douglas E.: *Computer Networks and Internets*. Addison-Wesley, 4th edition 2003.

▶ Fox, Jason: *Consider These 3 Questions When Deciding to Upgrade to mySAP ERP. www.sapinsider.com*, October–December 2005 issue.

▶ Fritz, Franz-Joseph: *Take Note! Custom Applications and Standard SAP Solutions: What's the Difference When It Comes to Lifecycle Management? www.sapinsider.com*, January–March 2005 issue

▶ Fritz, Franz-Josef: *Take Note! Unicode: Overhead or Necessity? www.sapinsider.com*, April–June 2006 issue.

▶ Harold, Elliotte R.: *Java Network Programming*. O'Reilly, 2nd edition, 2000.

▶ Heuvelmans, Wouter; Krouwels, Albert; Meijs, Ben; Sommen, Ron: *Enhancing the Quality of ABAP Development*. SAP PRESS 2004.

▶ Janssen, Susanne: *Performance & Data Management Corner: Targeted Methods and Tools for Right-Sizing Your Hardware Landscape. www.sapinsider.com*, January–March 2006 issue.

▶ Keller, Horst: *The Official ABAP Reference*. SAP PRESS, 2nd edition, 2005.

▶ Keller, Horst; Krüger, Sascha: *ABAP Objects*. SAP PRESS, 2nd edition, 2007.

▶ Korpela, Jukka: *Unicode Explained*. O'Reilly 2006.

▶ Mißbach, Michael; Gibbels, Peter; Karnstädt, Jürgen; Stelzel, Josef; Wagenblast, Thomas: *Adaptive Hardware Infrastructures for SAP*. SAP PRESS 2005.

▶ Ranum, Anders: *Open Integration—Tips & Tricks: SAP Infrastructure 3.0—Enterprise Ready! www.sapinsider.com*, April–June 2004 issue.

▶ SAP AG: *Requirements for ABAP Programs in Unicode Systems* ("SAP Unicode Enabling Cookbook"). Version 2003.

▶ SAP AG: *SAP NetWeaver and Globalization*. SAP AG Whitepaper. Version 2.0, 2005, SAP material No. 50057742.

▶ Vanstechelman, Bert; Mergaerts, Mark: *The OS/DB Migration Project Guide*. SAP PRESS Essentials 2005.

▶ Wong, Clinton: *HTTP Pocket Reference*. O'Reilly 2000.

C.2   Links

Globalization

▶ Country-specific information:
http://service.sap.com/localization

▶ Global solutions without boundaries:
*http://www.sap.com/solutions/business-suite/erp/pdf/BWP_SB_
Global_Solutions_Without_Boundaries.pdf*

▶ SAP Globalization Services:
http://service.sap.com/globalization

Unicode

▶ General SAP information:
http://service.sap.com/unicode

▶ Unicode-specific introductions:
http://service.sap.com/unicode@ sap

▶ Unicode Consortium:
http://www.unicode.org

SAP Support for Unicode Projects

▶ Consulting:
http://service.sap.com/consulting

▶ Calculation of hardware requirements for SAP applications:
http://service.sap.com/sizing

- GoingLive check:
  http://service.sap.com/goinglivecheck
- GoingLive functional upgrade check:
  http://service.sap.com/goinglive-fu
- Notes on system copies:
  http://service.sap.com/systemcopy
- Installation and upgrade information:
  http://service.sap.com/instguides
- Creating customer messages with the wizard:
  http://service.sap.com/message
- OS/DB migration:
  http://service.sap.com/migrationkey
- Partner information:
  http://service.sap.com/partners
- Portal to the SAP Support pages:
  http://service.sap.com/support
- Release information:
  http://service.sap.com/releasenotes
- SAP Notes:
  http://service.sap.com/notes
- System Landscape Optimization:
  http://service.sap.com/slo
- Upgrade services:
  http://service.sap.com/upgradeservices

C.3   SAP Notes

Number	Title
73606	Supported Languages and Code pages
79991	Multi-Language and Unicode support of SAP solutions
80727	Transporting non-Latin-1 texts
215015	Unicode UTF-8 printing with a Lexmark printer
316903	SAP GUI: How to use I18N mode

Table C.1 Important SAP Notes on Unicode

Number	Title
330267	Transports between Basis Releases 4.6* and 6.*
379940	Unicode-based SAP availability
508854	SAP GUI: How to use Unicode
540911	Unicode restrictions for R/3 Enterprise, ECC 5.0, ECC 6.0
543715	Projects for BW migrations and system copies
547444	RFC enhancement for Unicode/non-Unicode connections
548016	Conversion to Unicode
552464	What is Big Endian/Little Endian? What endian do I have?
585116	Translation after installation of WebAS SP25
638357	Transport between Unicode and non-Unicode systems
647495	RFC for Unicode/non-Unicode connections
673244	SAP GUI: Recent corrections for Unicode support
693168	Pilot projects for incremental migration (IMIG)
741821	Release limitations concerning SAP ERP 2004
742662	MS Word as Editor in SAPscript and Smart Forms
745030	MDMP-Unicode interfaces: Solution overview
747036	SAP ERP 2004 upgrade for R/3 MDMP customers
750219	Unicode UTF-8 printing with HP printers
784118	System copy Java tools
790099	R/3 Parameter settings for Unicode conversion
795267	System copy for "SAP Web AS Java" based systems
806554	FAQ: I/O-intensive database operations
812821	Cascading font settings
814707	Troubleshooting for RFC connections Unicode/non-Unicode
852235	Release restrictions for SAP ERP 2005
855772	Distribution Monitor
857081	Unicode conversion: downtime estimate
871541	Frequently used text patterns
895560	Support for languages only available in Unicode system

Table C.1 Important SAP Notes on Unicode (cont.)

Number	Title
896144	SAP ERP 2005 upgrade for R/3 or ERP MDMP customers
902083	Unicode Collection Note for CRM 4.0
920831	RFC with inactive text language
928729	Combined upgrade & Unicode conversion FAQ
932779	Unicode conversion—analysis of nametab problems
936441	Oracle settings for R3load-based system copy
952514	Pilot projects for table splitting

Table C.1 Important SAP Notes on Unicode (cont.)

C.4 Documents Needed for Unicode Conversions

There are primarily three documents needed for a Unicode conversion:

▶ **Release-dependent installation guidelines (application)**
The installation guidelines are used to build the Unicode system after the export is complete.

▶ **Release-dependent system copy guidelines (basis)**
The system copy is the technical starting point for the Unicode conversion. As a result, this guideline must be used.

▶ **Release- and support package-dependent Unicode conversion guidelines (Unicode Conversion Guide)**
The conversion guide is the main document for the Unicode conversion. From there, there are references to the other documents as needed. The corresponding SAP Note is 548016.

C.5 Typical Process of Testing a Unicode Conversion

▶ **Construction of a sandbox (copy of the production system)**

  ▷ Loading of all needed support packages, patches, etc.

  ▷ Procurement of the documentation needed

- **Preparation of the Unicode conversion**
  - General preparation
  - SPUMG transaction
  - Vocabulary construction
  - Vocabulary maintenance
  - Reprocessing phase
  - Special preparation (SAP CRM, SAP NetWeaver BI, etc.)
  - Execution of export
  - Execution of import
- **Activities after the Unicode conversion**
  - Post-processing (SUMG transaction)
  - Special follow-up steps (SAP CRM, SAP NetWeaver BI, etc.)
  - Creation of the backup
  - Testing and any needed editing of Unicode-capable ABAP programs
  - Testing and any needed editing of interfaces
  - Unit testing in the Unicode conversion test system
  - Evaluation of the results of Unicode conversion
  - Application testing
- **Final evaluation and judgment**
  - Analysis of the conversion logs to optimize the conversion
  - Update of the conversion procedure
  - Analysis of the SPUMG and SUMG procedures
- **Test management**
  - Preparation of test cases
  - Creation of the test plan

D   Glossary

ALE *Application Linking and Embedding* (earlier *Application Link Enabling*), SAP interface technology for asynchronous connection of systems

ANSI *American National Standards Institute* and Microsoft's name for Windows code pages

API *Application Programming Interface*

Application Server Computer that executes application programs

Asynchronous transmission Data transmission between systems that are not continually connected over time

Backup Saving of data

Bandwidth Transmission speed

Batch Bundling together of messages or records which are processed together

BDC *Batch Data Communication*, a synonym for batch input

BTF *Behind the firewall*

Bi-directional Writing system which can run either right to left or left to right

Big Endian Computer architecture which puts the most significant byte (MSB) first for numbers consisting of multiple bytes

Binary file Files with data which are not in a text format (e. g., hexadecimal entries)

Blended code page SAP's own code page, which allows the combination of languages from different code pages (e. g., Latin-1 languages and Japanese) in a single code page (with some limitations). Since the advent of Unicode, this is considered an obsolete Technology.

BOM *Byte Order Mark*

Byte Smallest storage unit addressable; 8 bits

Byte-Swapped Swapped order of a byte sequence

Case Some alphabets have the property that they contain letters in different forms (e. g., different in size). In Germany, for instance, upper case and lower case are possible.

CBL *Common Business Library*, an open XML specification for the exchange of business documents (industry-independent)

CGI *Common Gateway Interface*; data transmission interface

Character The smallest unit of a written language

Character Encoding Form Mapping of characters to numerical expressions

Character Encoding Scheme Character encoding with serialization; there are seven different ones under Unicode: UTF-8, UTF-16, UTF-16BE, UTF-16LE, UTF-32, UTF-32BE, and UTF-32LE

CJK Abbreviation for Chinese, Japanese, and Korean.

CJKV Abbreviation for Chinese, Japanese, Korean, and Vietnamese

Code page Encoding of a character set; e. g., the code page Latin-1 for Western European characters

CPU *Central Processing Unit*, the processor

Data Transformation For instance, between different storage formats

DBCS Double Byte Character Set

DMZ *De-Militarized Zone*: the neutral zone between the Intranet and the extranet

Double Byte Character Set Character sets in which characters are encoded with 2 bytes for each character, for instance for Chinese or Japanese

EBCDIC *Extended Binary Coded Decimal Interchange Code*; character sets (for mainframe computers) which encode characters with 8 bits. The first reserved positions (x00 through x3F) are control characters; the range from x41 to xFE are graphical characters. The English characters are divided, with capitals from xC1 to xC9, xD1 to xD9, and xE2 to xE9, and lowercase letters at x81 to x89, x91 to x99, and xA2 to xA9

eCATT Extension of the *Computer-Aided Test Tool*; can create test procedures from business processes.

EDIFACT *Electronic Data Interchange for Administration, Commerce, and Transport*: the standard format for the transmission of structured data in business data exchange

Encoding Form Short for → Character Encoding Form

Encoding Scheme Short for → Character Encoding Scheme

EUC *Extended (Enhanced) Unix Code*: method for the parallel use of single- and multibyte character tables

External vocabulary on table UMGPMDIT-based vocabulary for the transfer of assigned vocabulary entries to other SAP systems

Failover Process for fail-safe systems

Font Determines a style for the display of characters

FTP *File Transfer Protocol*: protocol for data transmission

German ASCII Variant of the American Standard Code for Information Interchange (ASCII) with German special characters added

Glyph Graphical representation of a character

GUI *Graphical User Interface*

Hangul The script of the Korean language

Hint Help for assignment words to language codes in the system vocabulary based on arbitrary attributes

HTML *Hypertext Markup Language*: text description language which combined unformatted text with formatting information. HTML is the language most used for websites.

I18N Acronym for internationalization; between the "I" and the "N" there are 18 letters

IDoc Standard SAP format for electronic data exchange between systems with special message formats (*IDoc types*)

INDX-type table Tables which have a transparent and a binary area, which must be handled specially in the SPUMG transaction

ISCII *Indian Script Code for Information Interchange*

ISO *International Organization for Standardization*

ITS *Internet Transaction Server*: interface between the Internet and SAP applications.

J2EE *Java-2-Platform Enterprise Edition*: development platform for (Web) applications in Java

JDBC *Java Database Connectivity*: programming interface for Java applications and databases.

JTA *Java Transaction Application Programming Interface*: programming interface for Java and transaction programs/monitors

Kanji Japanese name for Han characters; one of the two Japanese syllabaries

Katakana One of the two Japanese syllabaries; often used for the display of "difficult" kanji characters

Cryptography Technology of encryption

Latin-1 Character set for Western European languages

Latin-2 Character set for Eastern European languages

Latin-3 Character set for Southern European languages

Latin-4 Character set for Nordic/ Baltic languages

Little Endian Computer architecture which puts the least significant byte (LSB) first for numbers consisting of multiple bytes

Load balancing Process for distributing processing load over multiple computers or servers

LSB *Least Significant Byte*

Markup Command for structuring and/or formatting a document in a page description language

MBCS *Multi Byte Character Set*

MDMP *Multi Display Multi Processing*: process for using different code pages in one system. The logon language determines the code page used. Since the advent of Unicode, this is considered an obsolete technology.

Message Broker   Server for the distribution of messages between different applications

Message Queuing   Method for time-offset data transmission between applications

Middleware   Programs for data exchange between different applications; conversion rules may also be applied

MSB   *Most Significant Byte*

Multi Byte Character Set   Character set with a different number of bytes for the encoding of characters

NNTP   *Network News Transfer Protocol*: protocol for the exchange of news articles on Usenet

Octet   8 bits = 1 byte

ODBC   *Open Database Connectivity*: database (Web) interface

OS   *Operating system*

Patch   Program change for the correction of errors or extension of functionality

PCL   *Printer Communication Language*: printer protocol from Hewlett-Packard

PDF   *Portable Document Format*: format for text and graphics with precisely defined layout, from Adobe

Plain Text   Text which consists entirely of encoded characters and includes no formatting information at all

Portal   Web site used for access to the Internet, Intranet, or in general to a network. Consists of a group of links, content, and services adapted to the needs of a user or a group of users.

R3load   Tool on the kernel level for import and export during system installation, upgrade, and migration, as well as for the conversion of a system to Unicode

RAID   *Redundant Array of Independent Disks*; a cluster of multiple hard drives

RAM   *Random Access Memory*: working memory of the computer

RFC   *Remote Function Call*: SAP interface protocol which simplifies the programming of communication between systems

Rich Text   Text containing both encoded characters and formatting information (e. g., information about fonts or colors)

RMI   *Remote Method Invocation*: calling of methods or objects on different computers

Routing   Direction of data packets in the network

SBCS   *Single Byte Character Set*: character set using only one byte for the encoding of one character

Script   Defined set of letters and/or characters for the representation of a language. Example: Russian is written with a subset of the Cyrillic script.

SGML *Standard Generalized Markup Language*: the standard for markup languages for digital documents, standardized by the International Standardization Organization as ISO 8879

Sizing Definition of the hardware requirements for an SAP system; for instance the memory requirements, network bandwidth, and CPU power

Shift-JIS Encoding for Japanese characters, often used in PCs

SJIS Short for → Shift-JIS

SOA *Service-Oriented Architecture*: software architecture enabling the design, development, identification, and use of standardized services for the entire enterprise, whereby the reusability of services is a core idea

SPUMG Code page scanner; transaction for the preparation of an MDMP system for Unicode conversion

SQL *Structured Query Language*: language for database queries

Synchronous transmission Transmission of data between directly connected devices with immediate (not time-offset) response

SLO *System Landscape Optimization*: portfolio of services for process optimization, from individual applications to the harmonization of complete SAP environments

SUMG transaction Tool for the post-processing step after conversion of an MDMP system into Unicode

System vocabulary List of words which must be assigned a language code within the SPUMG transaction

TCP/IP *Transmission Control Protocol/Internet Protocol*: name of the network protocols TCP and IP

UCG *Unicode Conversion Guide*: top-ranking guideline for conversion of an SAP system to Unicode

UCS *Universal Character Set*: character set according to international standard ISO/IEC 10646

Unicode International standard in which every character in every script is assigned a uniform code

Unicode Encoding Form Format for the representation of Unicode characters; these include UTF-8, UTF-16, and UTF-32

Unicode Encoding Scheme Unicode character set

Unicode Transformation Format Another term for *Unicode Encoding Scheme*

US-7 ASCII range Corresponds to the concept 7-bit ASCII; English characters, symbols, and numbers included in every code page

UTF *Unicode Transformation Format*

UUEncode *Unix to Unix Encoding*: "packed" encoding of binary data as ASCII text

VoIP *Voice over IP*: transmission of voice in digital form via the Internet Protocol

W3C *World Wide Web Consortium, http://www.w3c.org*

WML *Wireless Markup Language*: page description language for websites which can be displayed on mobile terminals (like mobile phones)

WSDL *Web Service Description Language*: XML language for the description of Web services

XBRL *Extensible Business Reporting Language*: XML-based protocol for the transmission of financial documents over the Internet

XHTML *Extensible Hypertext Markup Language*, XML-compatible HTML

XML *Extensible Markup Language*; used for the transmission of structured data, using the Unicode character set as standard

E   The Authors

Nils Bürckel studied physics at the University of Oldenburg, Germany, and joined SAP AG in January 1999 in the technical-consulting department. By the time his trainee program ended, his focus was already on the area of globalization. He has provided technical support for many large customers while they were integrating new countries, giving him a great deal of relevant customer experience.

In 2002, he moved to SAP Globalization Services. That was just as Unicode was delivered for the first time by SAP. Nils was a member of the Unicode Task Force convened to support the introduction of Unicode. Unicode has become established, but the conversion of complex system environments is still full of challenges. For this reason, Nils leads consultant and customer training and workshops and helps customers with Unicode conversion projects. He also works in the back office for Unicode consultation within SAP.

After his studies in electrical engineering and completion of an engineering doctorate at the University of Karlsruhe, Germany, **Alexander Davidenkoff** joined SAP AG at the end of 1992. He started in R/3 basis support and technical consulting and soon concentrated on international topics such as language and code-page technologies in SAP products. He began collaboration with the national organizations in Eastern Europe and Russia, supported colleagues, customers, and partners in numerous activities and projects, and contributed significantly to the improvement of language support in SAP R/3. Since the late 1990s, he has been working closely with the countries in the Asia Pacific region.

In 1996, Alexander moved to International Development/Globalization Services at SAP, where he is responsible for project management of country versions, as well as globalization, localization, and translation issues. He now works in SAP Globalization Services as a solution manager for the Unicode rollout, global solutions, time zones, global integrated solutions using SAP NetWeaver, the architecture of complex system environments, and related topics. He also supports, advises, and trains numerous colleagues, clients, and partners in many countries.

 **Dr. Detlef Werner** earned his doctorate in 1989 from the University of Hamburg, Germany, as a chemist, where his work included computer-supported analytics. After an international career at medium-sized companies, Detlef joined SAP AG in 1998, working first on construction and conversion of the Internet Business Framework. Other work areas at SAP have included global partner management, the design of marketplaces for customers and partners, and support for customers on issues involving international implementation of business processes and related IT structures.

Detlef is currently working as a Solution Manager in SAP Globalization Services, where the introduction of Unicode in SAP has been a core topic for many years. Since 2003, he has taught at the International University of Bruchsal, Germany, as a Visiting Professor for international management and e-business.

Index

T

Developers guide for new techniques and technologies in SAP NetWeaver 2004s (ABAP 7.0)

New ABAP Editor, unit testing, Adobe Interactive Forms, Web Dynpro debugging, and more

Practical know-how straight from SAP's workshops and labs

approx. 330 pp., with CD, 69,95 Euro / US$ 69,95
ISBN 978-1-59229-139-7, June 2007

Next Generation ABAP Development

www.sap-press.com

R. Heilman, T. Jung

Next Generation ABAP Development

This book shows advanced ABAP programmers new concepts, technologies, techniques, and functions that have been introduced to ABAP ("Release 7.0") in the last few years. Based on a single real-world example that runs throughout the book—a university upgrading from SAP R/3 4.6C to SAP NetWeaver 2004s—you'll follow along with the university's lead ABAP developer as he develops a custom course booking system. This unique approach allows readers to view the entire process of design, development, and testing—right through the eyes of a developer. You'll quickly familiarize yourself with all of the new possibilities in ABAP while discovering a series of actual scenarios that could easily be encountered in a real-life project. In certain areas the authors also provide you with a glimpse towards upcoming ABAP releases, as well as references to former releases, as required.

Learn to design intuitive business applications with SAP Visual Composer for NetWeaver 2004s

Best practices for configuration settings and advice to master the development lifecycle

A comprehensive reference, providing you with complete A-to-Z details— directly from SAP

524 pp., 2007, 69,95 Euro / US$ 69,95
ISBN 978-1-59229-099-4

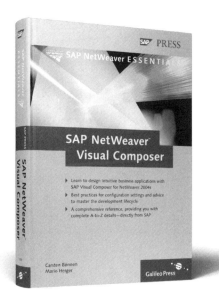

SAP NetWeaver Visual Composer

www.sap-press.com

C. Bönnen, M. Herger

SAP NetWeaver Visual Composer

Instead of conventional programming and implementation, SAP NetWeaver Visual Composer (VC) enables you to model your processes graphically via drag & drop—potentially without ever having to write a single line of code. This book not only shows you how, but also serves as a comprehensive reference, providing you with complete details on all aspects of VC. You learn the ins and outs of the VC architecture—including details on all components and concepts, as well as essential information on model-based development and on the preparation of different types of applications. Readers quickly broaden their knowledge by tapping into practical expert advice on the various aspects of the Development Lifecycle as well as on selected applications, which have been modeled with the VC and are currently delivered by SAP as standard applications.

Describes the complete SAP UI libraries and how to use them

Explains the process starting with design through development and test up to system configuration

Examines legal standards and how to be compliant

approx. 400 pp., 79,90 Euro / US$ 79,90
ISBN 978-1-59229-112-0, June 2007

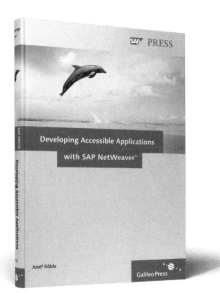

Developing Accessible Applications with SAP NetWeaver

www.sap-press.com

J. Köble

Developing Accessible Applications with SAP NetWeaver

This comprehensive reference book is a developer's complete guide to programming accessible applications using SAP NetWeaver technology. Readers get step-by-step guidance on the requirements and conceptual design and development using ABAP Workbench, NW Developer Studio, and Visual Composer. The authors provide you with a detailed presentation of all relevant design elements for Dynpro, WebDynpro (ABAP and Java), and Adobe Interactive Forms. In addition, you'll learn the ins and outs of testing applications, as well as configuration techniques for both front-end interfaces and back-end apps. With this unique approach, developers get a thorough introduction to all interface elements along with best practices for how to use them, and QA managers gain exclusive, expert insights on testing accessibility features.

Comprehensive guide to end-to-end process integration with SAP XI—from a developer's perspective

Practical exercises to master system configuration and development of mappings, adapters, and proxies

341 pp., 2007, 69,95 Euro / US$ 69,95
ISBN 978-1-59229-118-2

SAP Exchange Infrastructure for Developers

www.sap-press.com

V. Nicolescu, B. Funk, P. Niemeyer, M. Heile

SAP Exchange Infrastructure for Developers

This book provides both experienced and new SAP XI developers with a detailed overview of the functions and usage options of the SAP NetWeaver Exchange Infrastructure. The authors take you deep into the system with a series of practical exercises for the development and configuration of mappings, adapters, and proxies: RFC-to-File, File-to-IDoc, ABAP-Proxy-to-SOAP, and Business Process Management. Each exercise is rounded off by a description of relevant monitoring aspects and is combined in a comprehensive case study.

Examples of dynamic programming, componentization, integration of applications, navigation, and much more

Essential and practical knowledge about installation, configuration, and administration of the Web Dynpro runtime

497 pp., 2006, 69,95 Euro / US$
ISBN 1-59229-077-9

Maximizing
Web Dynpro for Java
www.sap-press.com

B. Ganz, J. Gürtler, T. Lakner

Maximizing Web Dynpro for Java

Standard examples of Web Dynpro applications can leave SAP developers with many questions and severe limitations. This book takes you to the next level with detailed examples that show you exactly what you need to know in order to leverage Web Dynpro applications. From the interaction with the Java Developer Infrastructure (JDI), to the use of Web Dynpro components, to the integration into the portal and the use of its services—this unique book delivers it all. In addition, readers get dozens of tips and tricks on fine-tuning Web Dynpro applications in terms of response time, security, and structure. Expert insights on the configuration and administration of the Web Dynpro runtime environment serve to round out this comprehensive book.

Second, completely new edition of the benchmark ABAP compendium

All-new chapters on Web Dynpro, Shared Objects, ABAP & XML, Regular Expressions, Dynamic Programming, and more!

1059 pp., 2. edition 2007, with DVD 5,
79,95 Euro / US$ 79,95
ISBN 978-1-59229-079-6

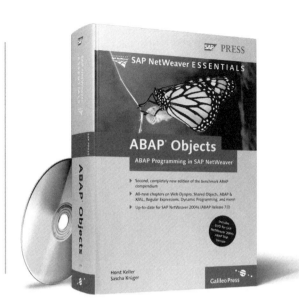

ABAP Objects

www.sap-press.com

H. Keller, S. Krüger

ABAP Objects

ABAP Programming in SAP NetWeaver

This completely new third edition of our best-selling ABAP book provides detailed coverage of ABAP programming with SAP NetWeaver. This outstanding compendium treats all concepts of modern ABAP up to release 7.0. New topics include ABAP and Unicode, Shared Objects, exception handling, Web Dynpro for ABAP, Object Services, and of course ABAP and XML. Bonus: All readers will receive the SAP NetWeaver 2004s ABAP Trial Version ("Mini-SAP") on DVD.

Basic principles, architecture, and configuration

Development of dynamic, reusable UI components

Volumes of sample code and screen captures for help you maximize key tools

360 pp., 2006, 69,95 Euro / US$
ISBN 1-59229-078-7

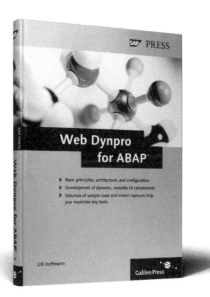

Web Dynpro for ABAP

www.sap-press.com

U. Hoffmann

Web Dynpro for ABAP

Serious developers must stay ahead of the curve by ensuring that they are up-to-date with all of the latest standards. This book illustrates the many benefits that can be realized with component-based UI development using Web Dynpro for ABAP. On the basis of specifically developed sample components, readers are introduced to the architecture of the runtime and development environment and receive highly-detailed descriptions of the different functions and tools that enable you to efficiently implement Web Dynpro technology on the basis of SAP NetWeaver 2004s. Numerous code listings, screen captures, and little-known tricks make this book your indispensable companion for the practical design of modern user interfaces.

**Improve your Design Process
with "Contextual Design"**

182 pp., 2006, 49,95 Euro / US$ 49,95
ISBN 978-1-59229-065-9

Designing
Composite Applications
www.sap-press.com

Jörg Beringer, Karen Holtzblatt

Designing Composite Applications

Driving user productivity and business innovation for
next generation business applications

This book helps any serious developer hit the ground
running by providing a highly detailed and
comprehensive introduction to modern application
design, using the SAP Enterprise Services
Architecture (ESA) toolset and the methodology of
"Contextual Design". Readers will benefit
immediately from exclusive insights on design
processes based on SAPs Business Process Platform
and learn valuable tricks and techniques that can
drastically improve user productivity. Anybody
involved in the process of enterprise application
design and usability/quality management stands to
benefit from this book.

Interested in reading more?

Please visit our Web site for all
new book releases from SAP PRESS.

www.sap-press.com